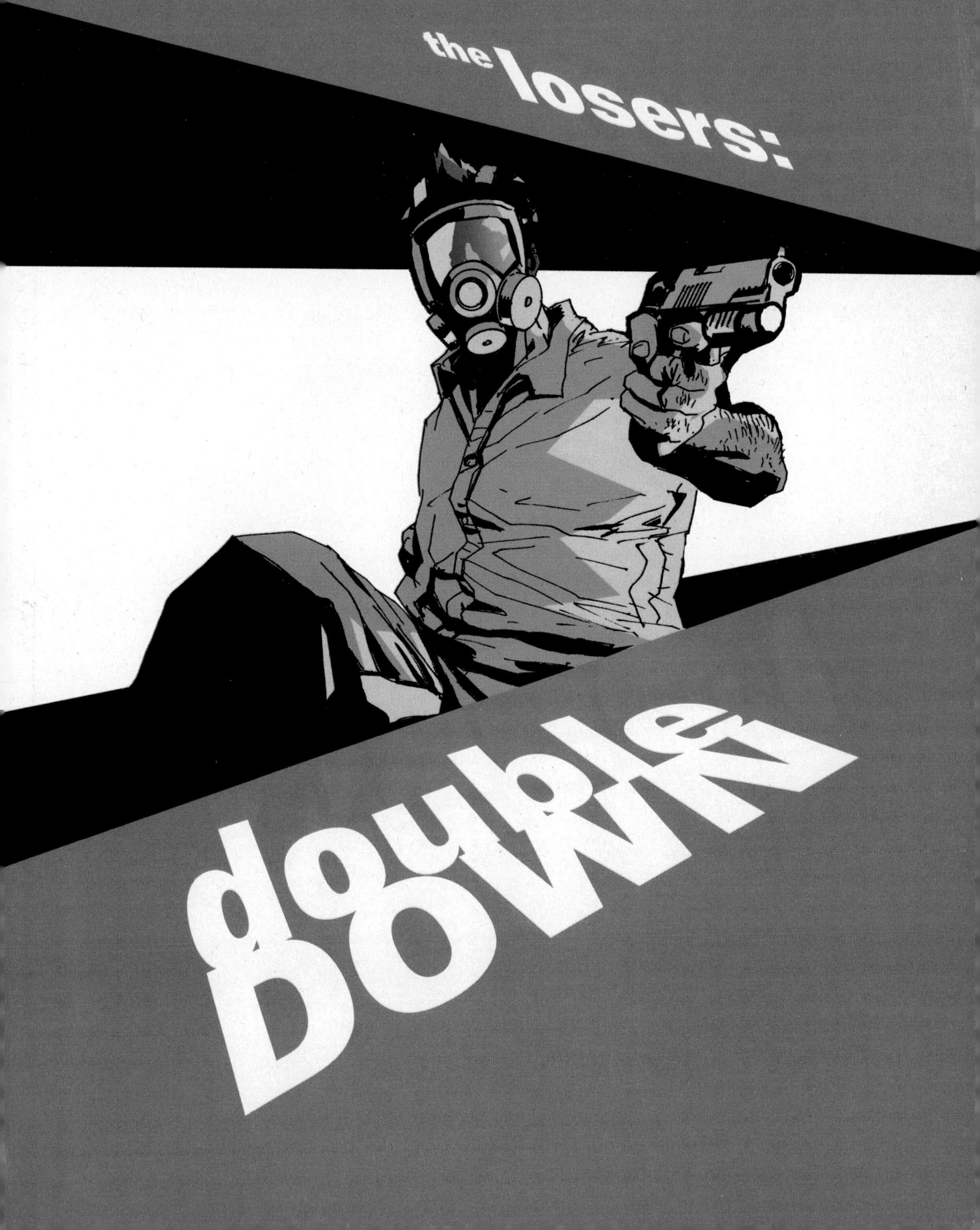
the losers:
double
DOWN

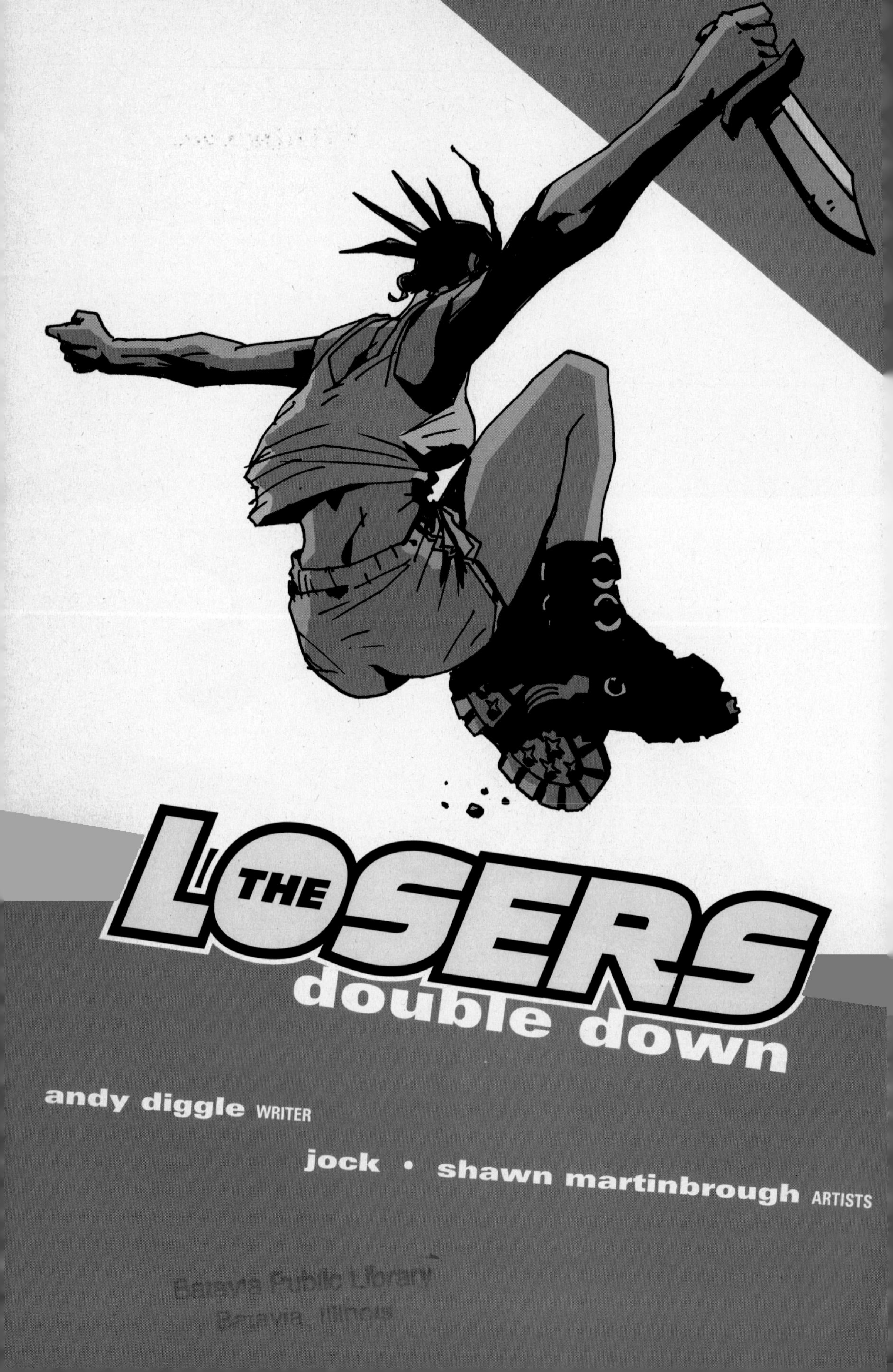

THE LOSERS
double down

andy diggle WRITER

jock • shawn martinbrough ARTISTS

THE LOSERS: DOUBLE DOWN Published by DC Comics. Cover and compilation copyright © 2004 DC Comics. All Rights Reserved. Originally published in single magazine form as THE LOSERS 7-12. Copyright © 2004 DC Comics.
All Rights Reserved. All characters, their distinctive likenesses and related elements featured in this publication are trademarks of DC Comics. The stories, characters and incidents featured in this publication are entirely
fictional. DC Comics does not read or accept unsolicited submissions of ideas, stories or artwork. DC Comics, 1700 Broadway, New York, NY 10019. A Warner Bros. Entertainment Company. Printed in Canada. First Printing.
ISBN: 1-4012-0348-5
Cover illustration by **Jock.**
Publication design by **John J. Hill.**

lee loughridge COLORIST

clem robins LETTERER

jock ORIGINAL SERIES COVERS

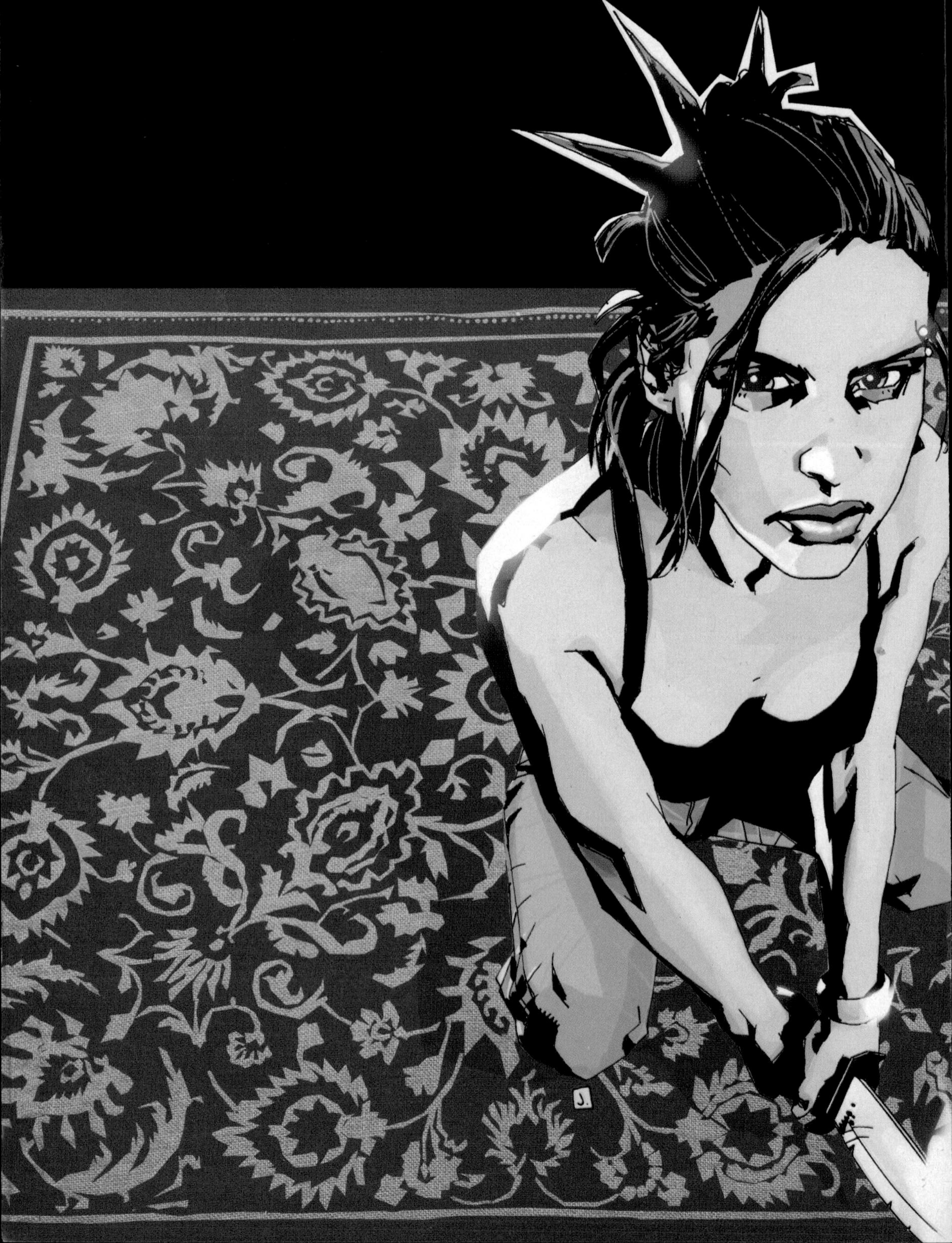

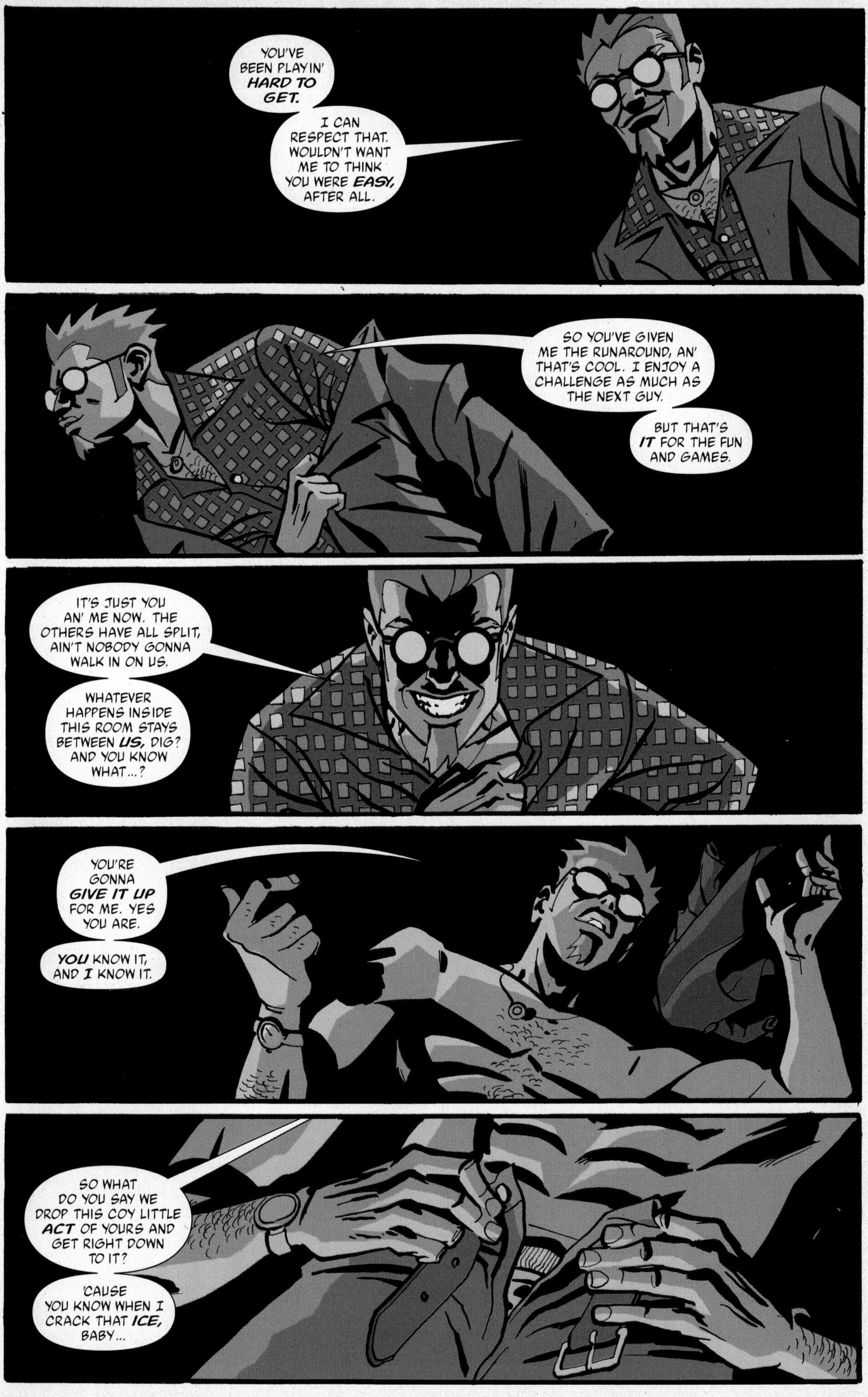
YOU'VE BEEN PLAYIN' HARD TO GET.
I CAN RESPECT THAT. WOULDN'T WANT ME TO THINK YOU WERE EASY, AFTER ALL.
SO YOU'VE GIVEN ME THE RUNAROUND, AN' THAT'S COOL. I ENJOY A CHALLENGE AS MUCH AS THE NEXT GUY.
BUT THAT'S IT FOR THE FUN AND GAMES.
IT'S JUST YOU AN' ME NOW. THE OTHERS HAVE ALL SPLIT, AIN'T NOBODY GONNA WALK IN ON US.
WHATEVER HAPPENS INSIDE THIS ROOM STAYS BETWEEN US, DIG? AND YOU KNOW WHAT...?
YOU'RE GONNA GIVE IT UP FOR ME. YES YOU ARE.
YOU KNOW IT, AND I KNOW IT.
SO WHAT DO YOU SAY WE DROP THIS COY LITTLE ACT OF YOURS AND GET RIGHT DOWN TO IT?
'CAUSE YOU KNOW WHEN I CRACK THAT ICE, BABY...

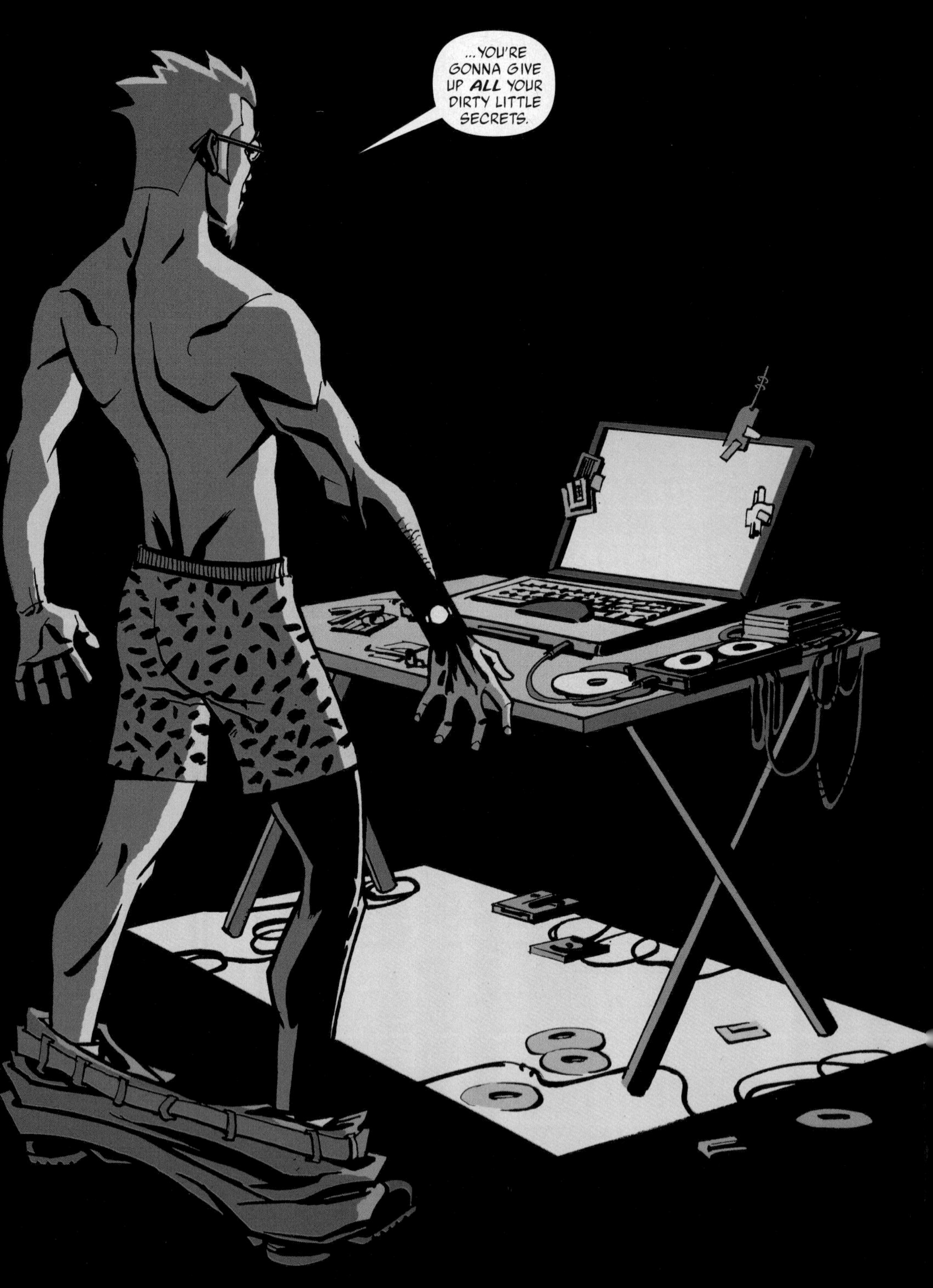
...YOU'RE GONNA GIVE UP ALL YOUR DIRTY LITTLE SECRETS.

DOWNTIME

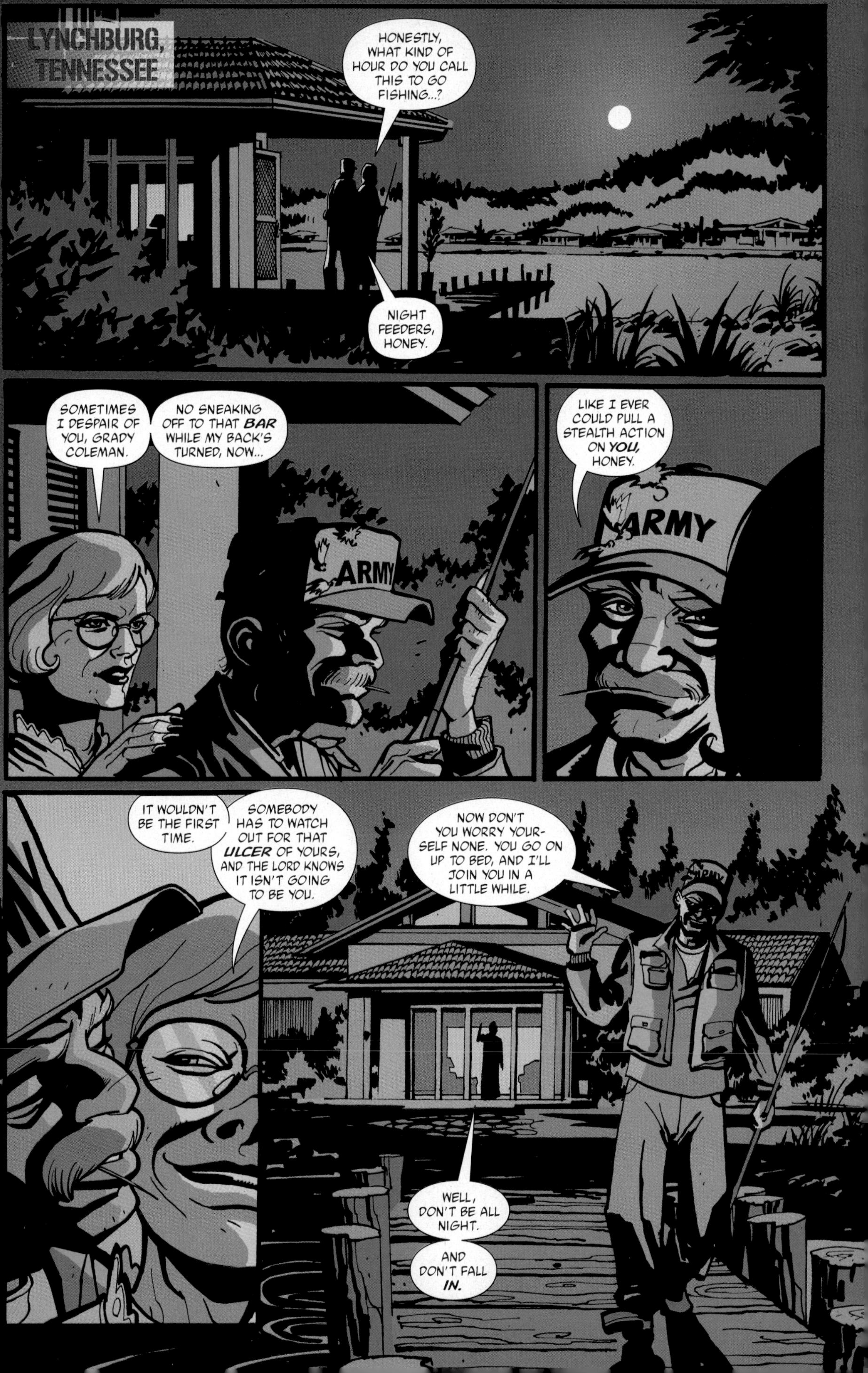
LYNCHBURG, TENNESSEE
HONESTLY, WHAT KIND OF HOUR DO YOU CALL THIS TO GO FISHING...?
NIGHT FEEDERS, HONEY.
SOMETIMES I DESPAIR OF YOU, GRADY COLEMAN.
NO SNEAKING OFF TO THAT **BAR** WHILE MY BACK'S TURNED, NOW...
ARMY
LIKE I EVER COULD PULL A STEALTH ACTION ON ***YOU,*** HONEY.
ARMY
IT WOULDN'T BE THE FIRST TIME.
SOMEBODY HAS TO WATCH OUT FOR THAT ***ULCER*** OF YOURS, AND THE LORD KNOWS IT ISN'T GOING TO BE YOU.
NOW DON'T YOU WORRY YOURSELF NONE. YOU GO ON UP TO BED, AND I'LL JOIN YOU IN A LITTLE WHILE.
WELL, DON'T BE ALL NIGHT.
AND DON'T FALL ***IN.***

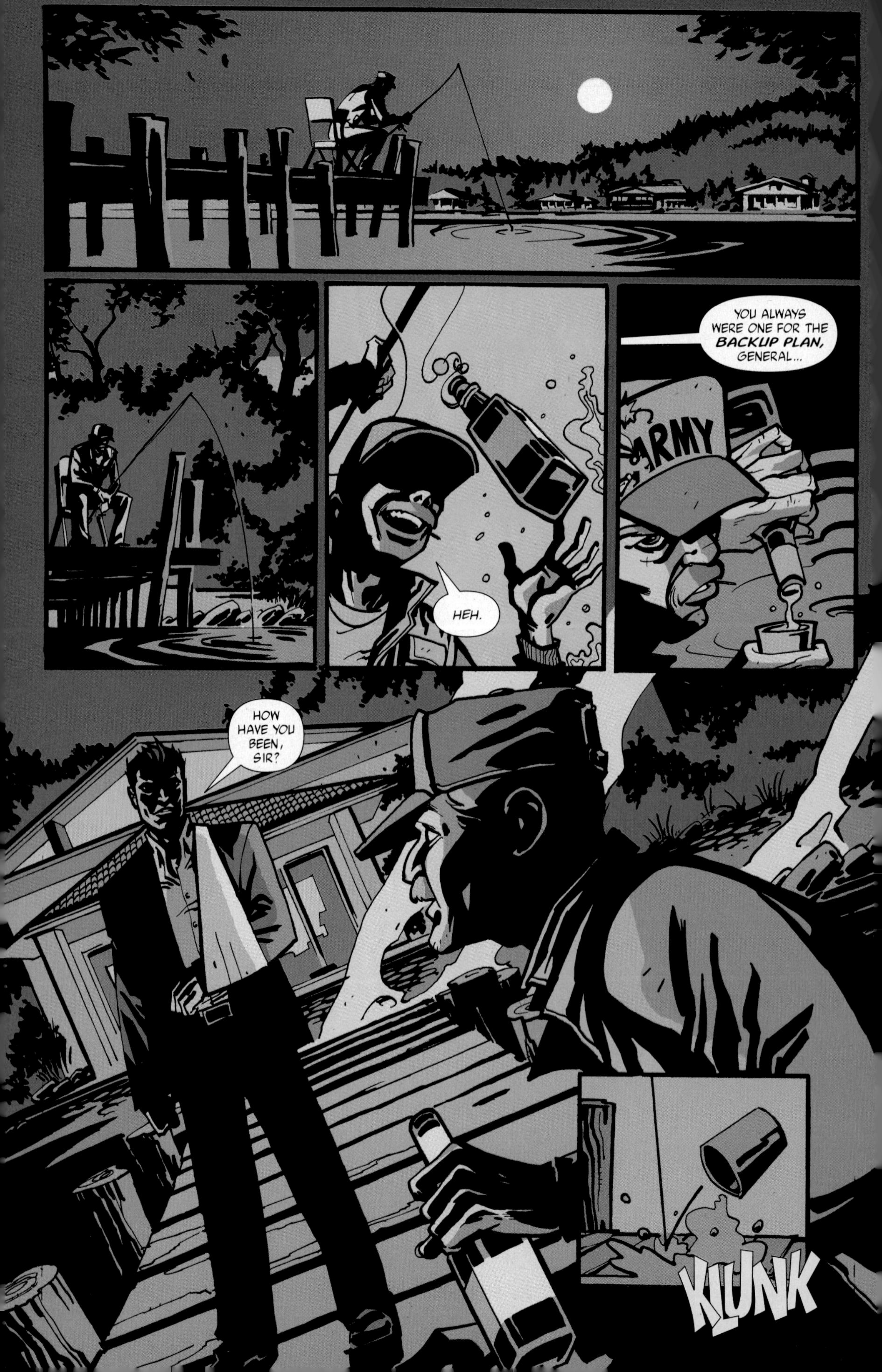
HEH.
YOU ALWAYS WERE ONE FOR THE BACKUP PLAN, GENERAL...
HOW HAVE YOU BEEN, SIR?
ARMY
KLUNK

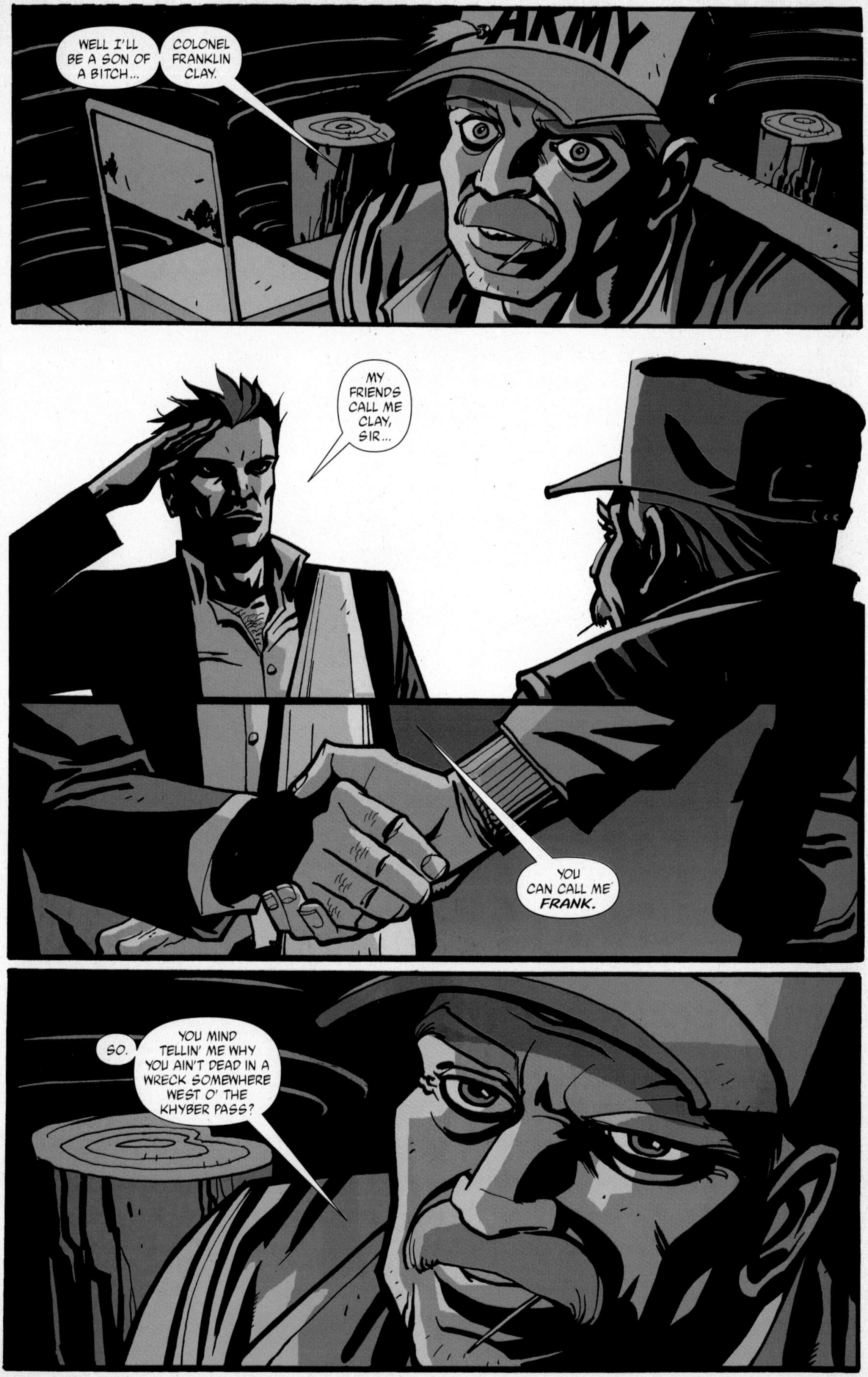
WELL I'LL BE A SON OF A BITCH...
COLONEL FRANKLIN CLAY.
MY FRIENDS CALL ME CLAY, SIR...
YOU CAN CALL ME **FRANK.**
SO.
YOU MIND TELLIN' ME WHY YOU AIN'T DEAD IN A WRECK SOMEWHERE WEST O' THE KHYBER PASS?

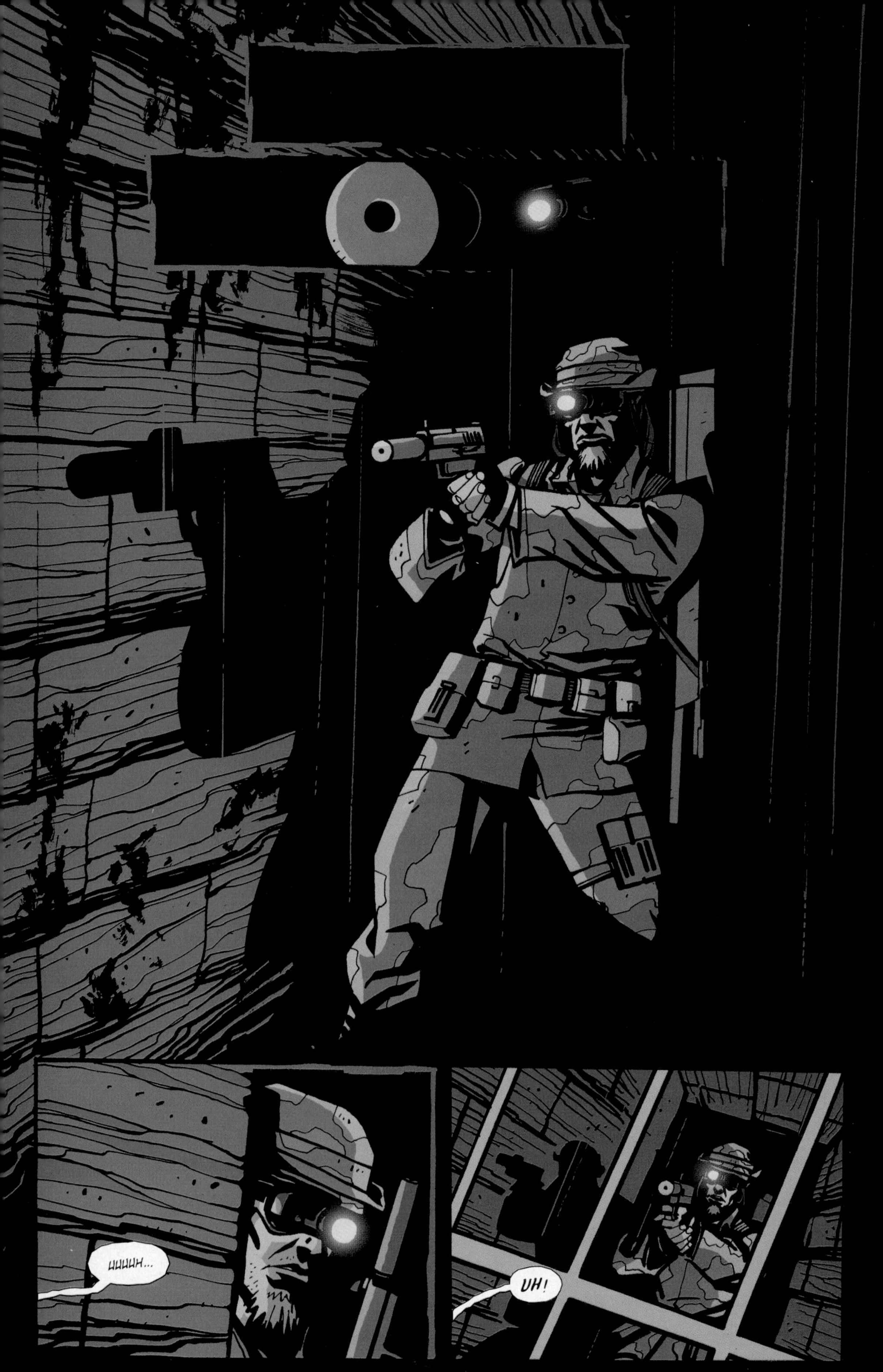
UUUUH...
UH!

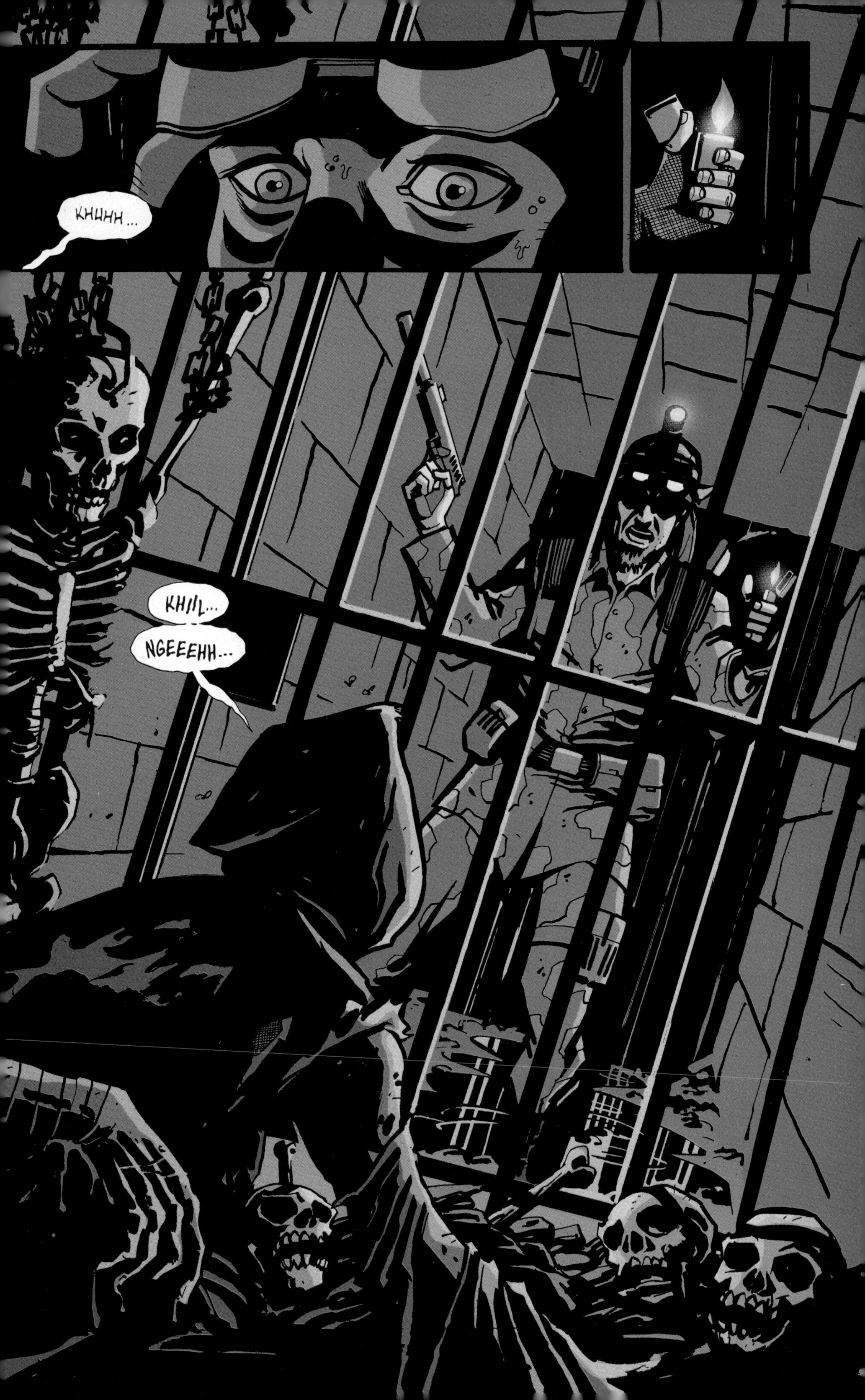
KHHHH...
KHIIL...
NGEEEHH...

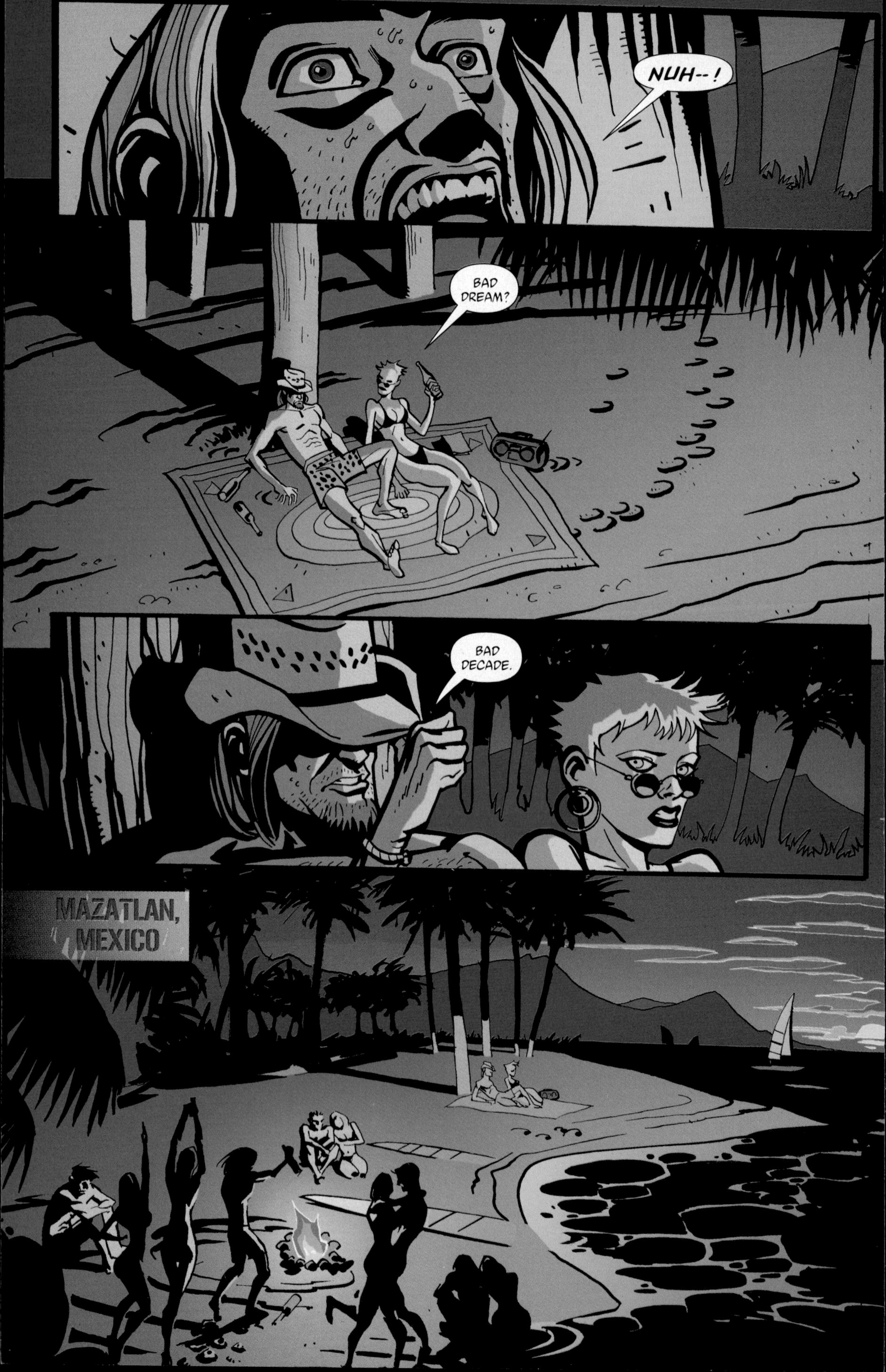
NUH--!
BAD DREAM?
BAD DECADE.
MAZATLAN, MEXICO

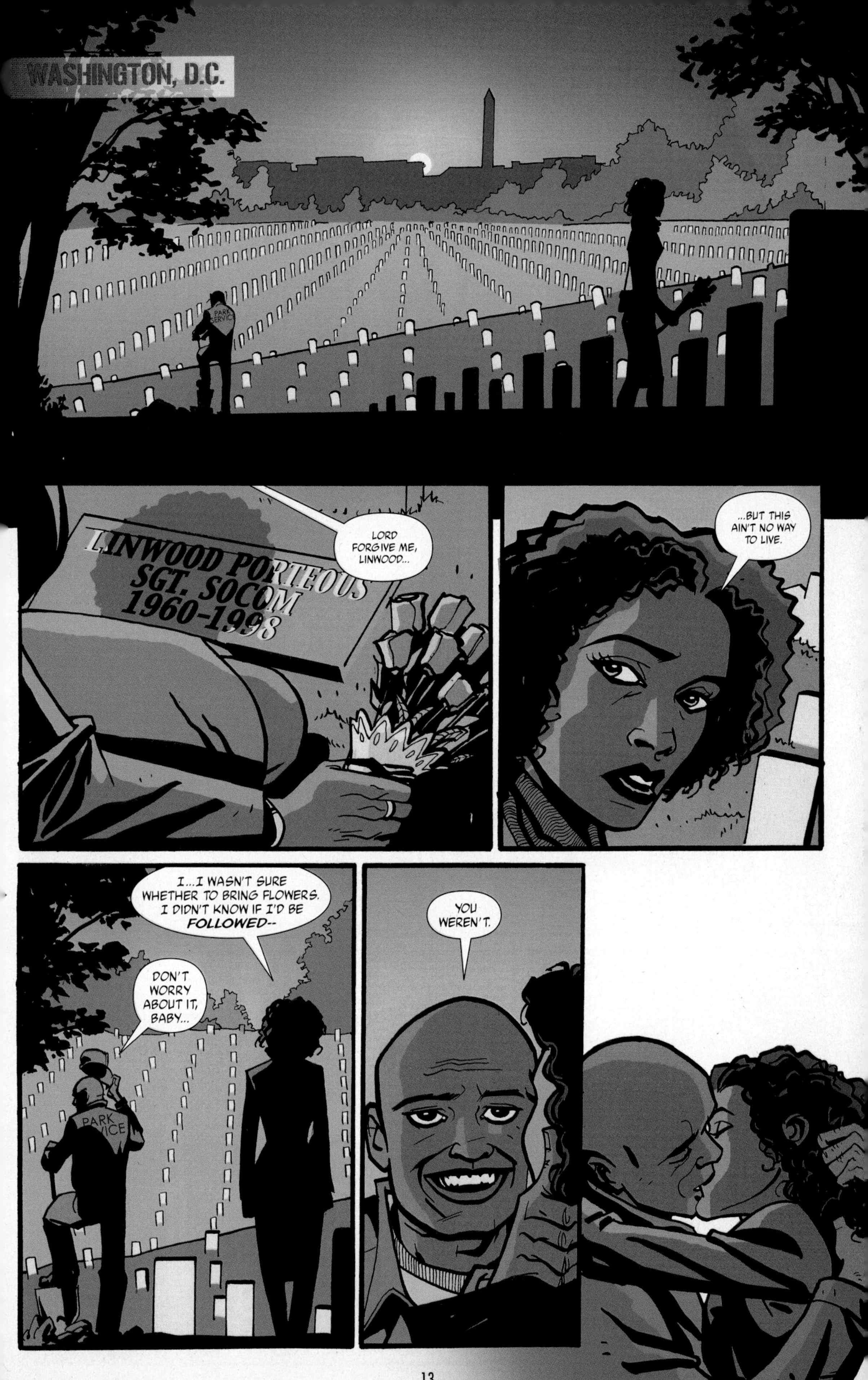
WASHINGTON, D.C.
PARK SERVICE
LINWOOD PORTEOUS SGT. SOCOM 1960-1998
LORD FORGIVE ME, LINWOOD...
...BUT THIS AIN'T NO WAY TO LIVE.
I...I WASN'T SURE WHETHER TO BRING FLOWERS. I DIDN'T KNOW IF I'D BE FOLLOWED--
DON'T WORRY ABOUT IT, BABY...
YOU WEREN'T.

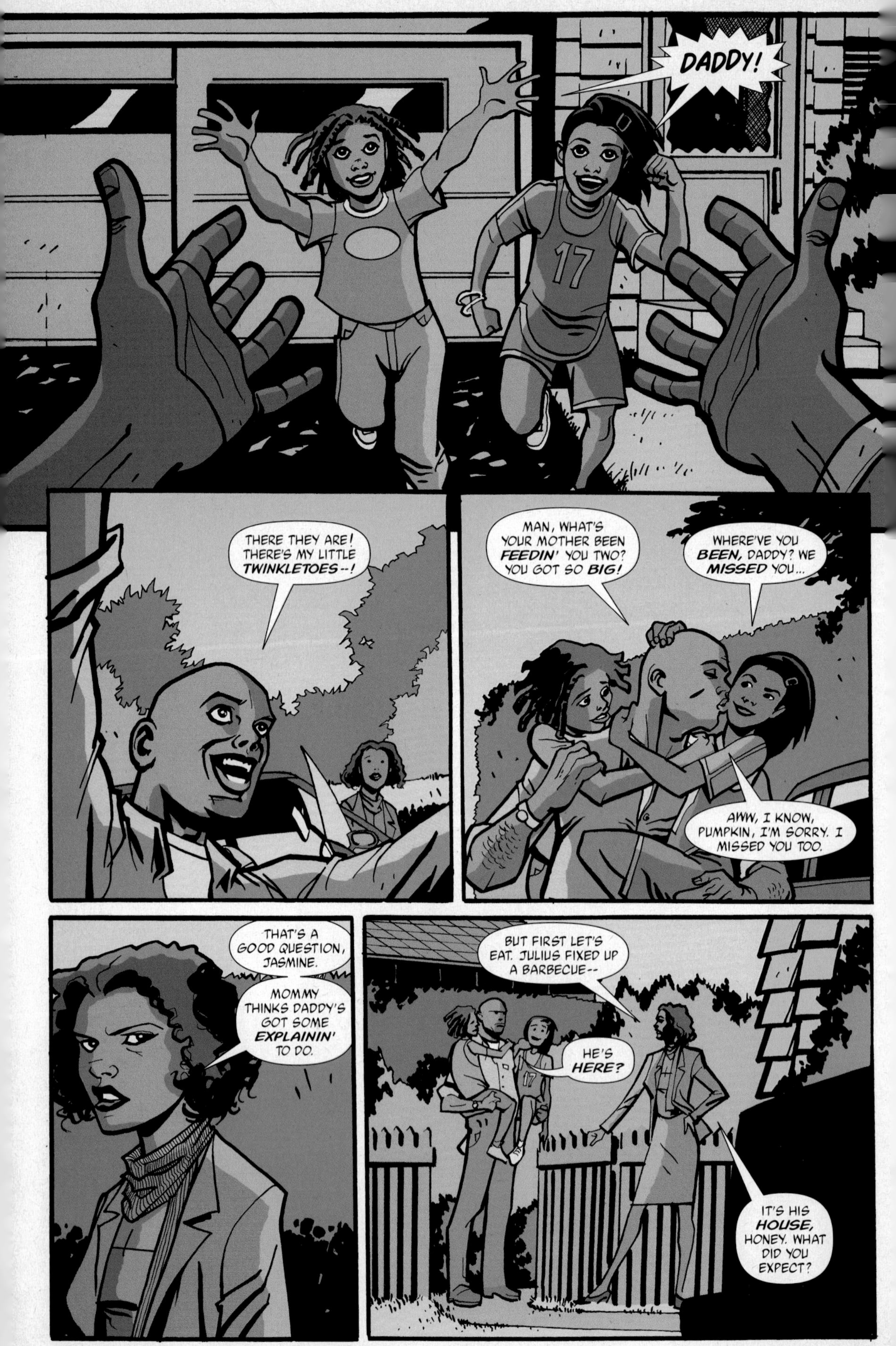
DADDY!
THERE THEY ARE! THERE'S MY LITTLE TWINKLETOES--!
MAN, WHAT'S YOUR MOTHER BEEN FEEDIN' YOU TWO? YOU GOT SO BIG!
WHERE'VE YOU BEEN, DADDY? WE MISSED YOU...
AWW, I KNOW, PUMPKIN, I'M SORRY. I MISSED YOU TOO.
THAT'S A GOOD QUESTION, JASMINE.
MOMMY THINKS DADDY'S GOT SOME EXPLAININ' TO DO.
BUT FIRST LET'S EAT. JULIUS FIXED UP A BARBECUE--
HE'S HERE?
IT'S HIS HOUSE, HONEY. WHAT DID YOU EXPECT?

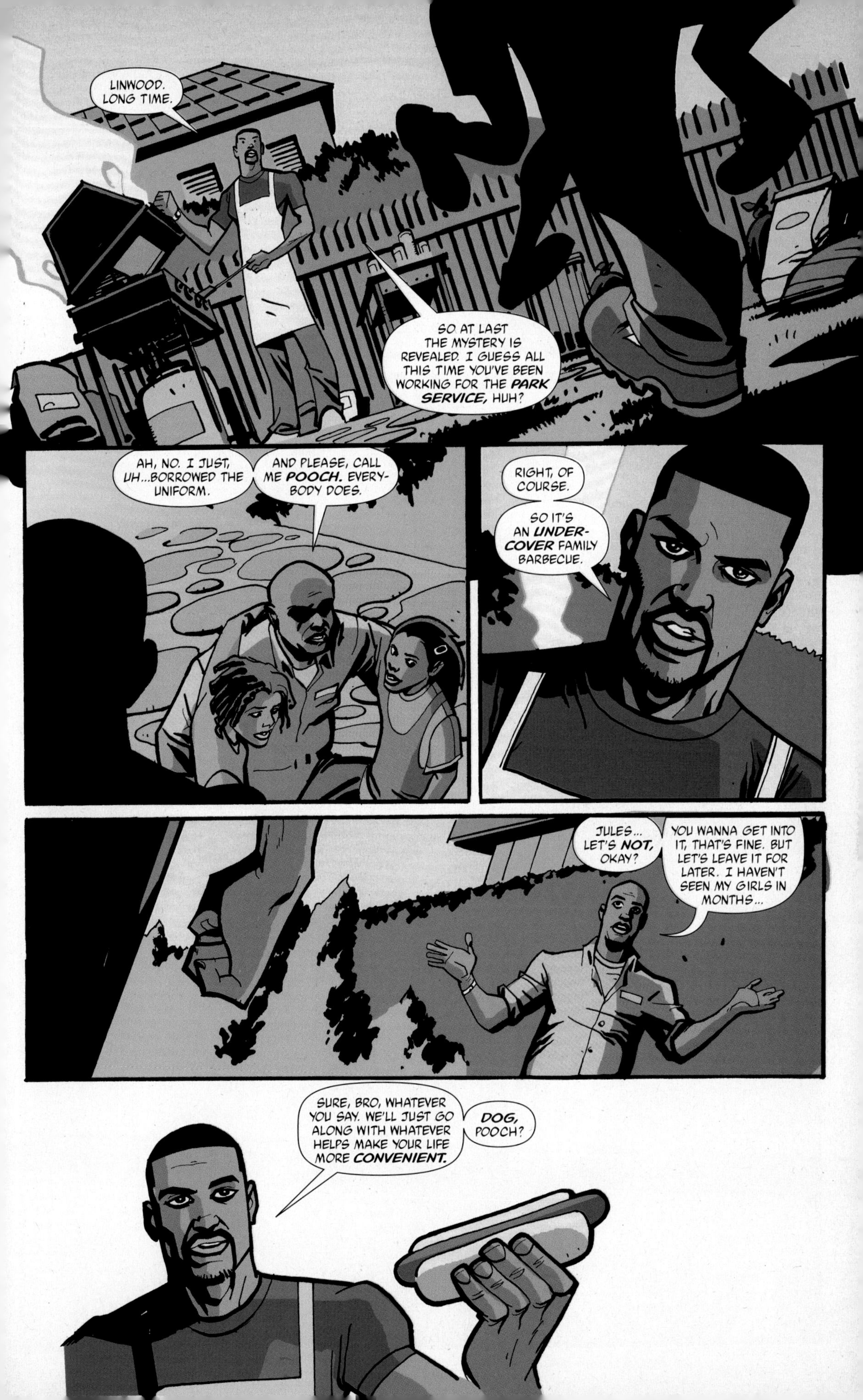
LINWOOD. LONG TIME.
SO AT LAST THE MYSTERY IS REVEALED. I GUESS ALL THIS TIME YOU'VE BEEN WORKING FOR THE **PARK SERVICE,** HUH?
AH, NO. I JUST, UH...BORROWED THE UNIFORM.
AND PLEASE, CALL ME **POOCH.** EVERY-BODY DOES.
RIGHT, OF COURSE.
SO IT'S AN **UNDER-COVER** FAMILY BARBECUE.
JULES... LET'S **NOT,** OKAY?
YOU WANNA GET INTO IT, THAT'S FINE. BUT LET'S LEAVE IT FOR LATER. I HAVEN'T SEEN MY GIRLS IN MONTHS...
SURE, BRO, WHATEVER YOU SAY. WE'LL JUST GO ALONG WITH WHATEVER HELPS MAKE YOUR LIFE MORE **CONVENIENT.**
DOG, POOCH?

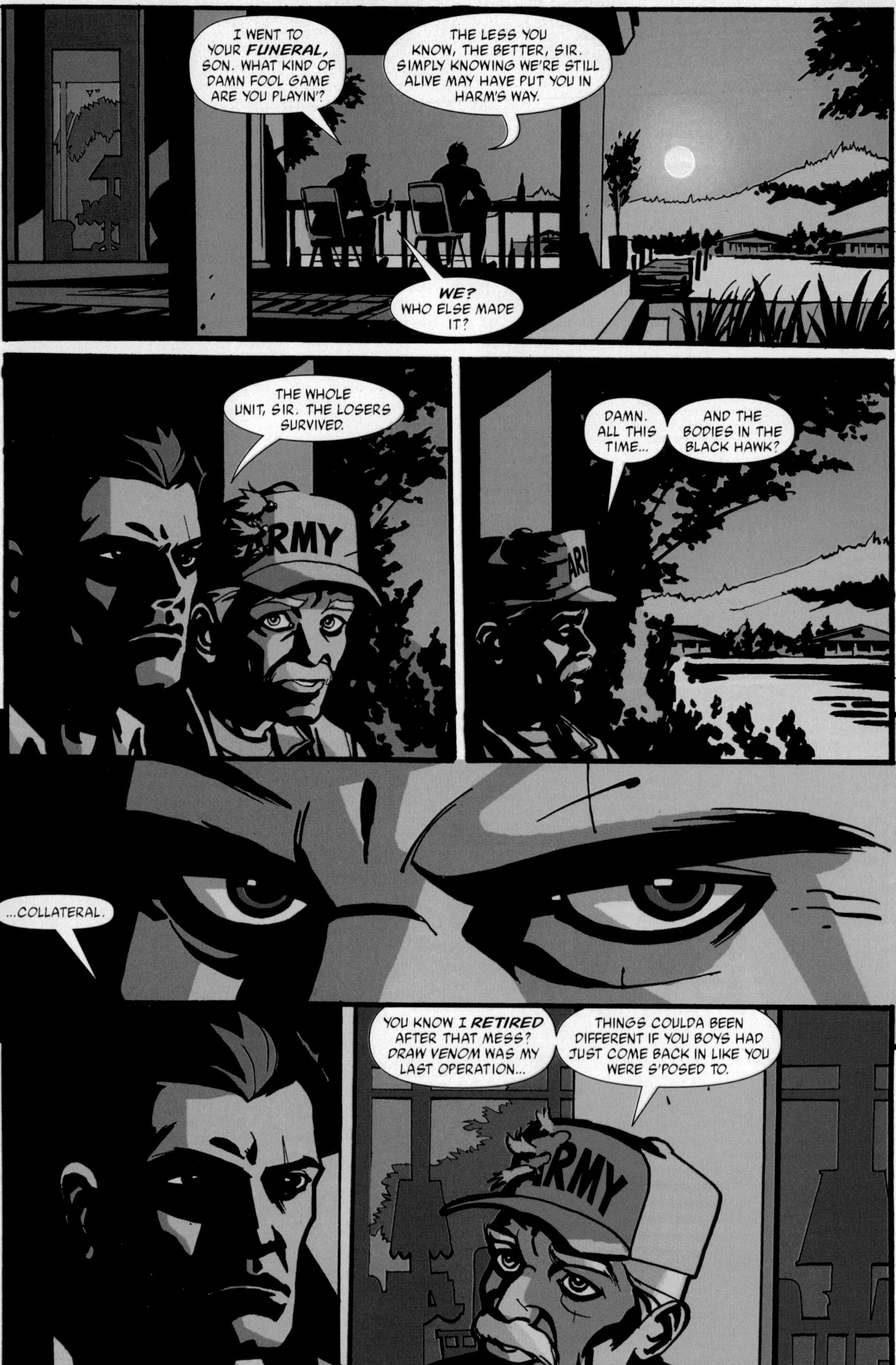
I WENT TO YOUR FUNERAL, SON. WHAT KIND OF DAMN FOOL GAME ARE YOU PLAYIN'?
THE LESS YOU KNOW, THE BETTER, SIR. SIMPLY KNOWING WE'RE STILL ALIVE MAY HAVE PUT YOU IN HARM'S WAY.
WE? WHO ELSE MADE IT?
THE WHOLE UNIT, SIR. THE LOSERS SURVIVED.
ARMY
DAMN. ALL THIS TIME...
AND THE BODIES IN THE BLACK HAWK?
...COLLATERAL.
YOU KNOW I RETIRED AFTER THAT MESS? DRAW VENOM WAS MY LAST OPERATION...
THINGS COULDA BEEN DIFFERENT IF YOU BOYS HAD JUST COME BACK IN LIKE YOU WERE S'POSED TO.
ARMY

WE *COULDN'T* COME BACK IN.

IT WASN'T SOME HAIRY-ASSED TRIBESMAN WITH AN *R.P.G.* BROUGHT DOWN OUR BLACK HAWK, SIR. IT WAS A PAKISTANI *MIRAGE* OUT OF PESHAWAR, ACTING UNDER AGENCY ORDERS.

THAT'S ONE HELL OF AN ALLEGATION, SON. CAN YOU BACK IT UP?

WE INTERCEPTED THE STRIKE CALL.

WE SAW SOMETHING WE SHOULDN'T HAVE. OUR HANDLER DIDN'T WANT IT GETTING OUT.

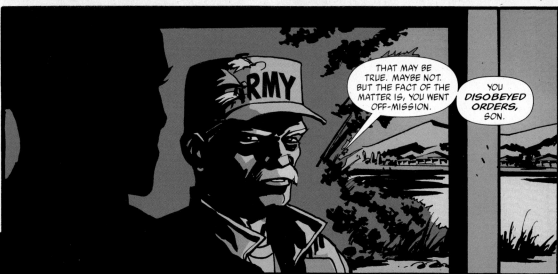

THAT MAY BE TRUE. MAYBE NOT. BUT THE FACT OF THE MATTER IS, YOU WENT OFF-MISSION.

YOU *DISOBEYED ORDERS,* SON.

WITH RESPECT, SIR, MY GRANDFATHER *DIED* FIGHTING AN AXIS THAT WAS "JUST FOLLOWING ORDERS."

EVERY SOLDIER MAKES A CHOICE.

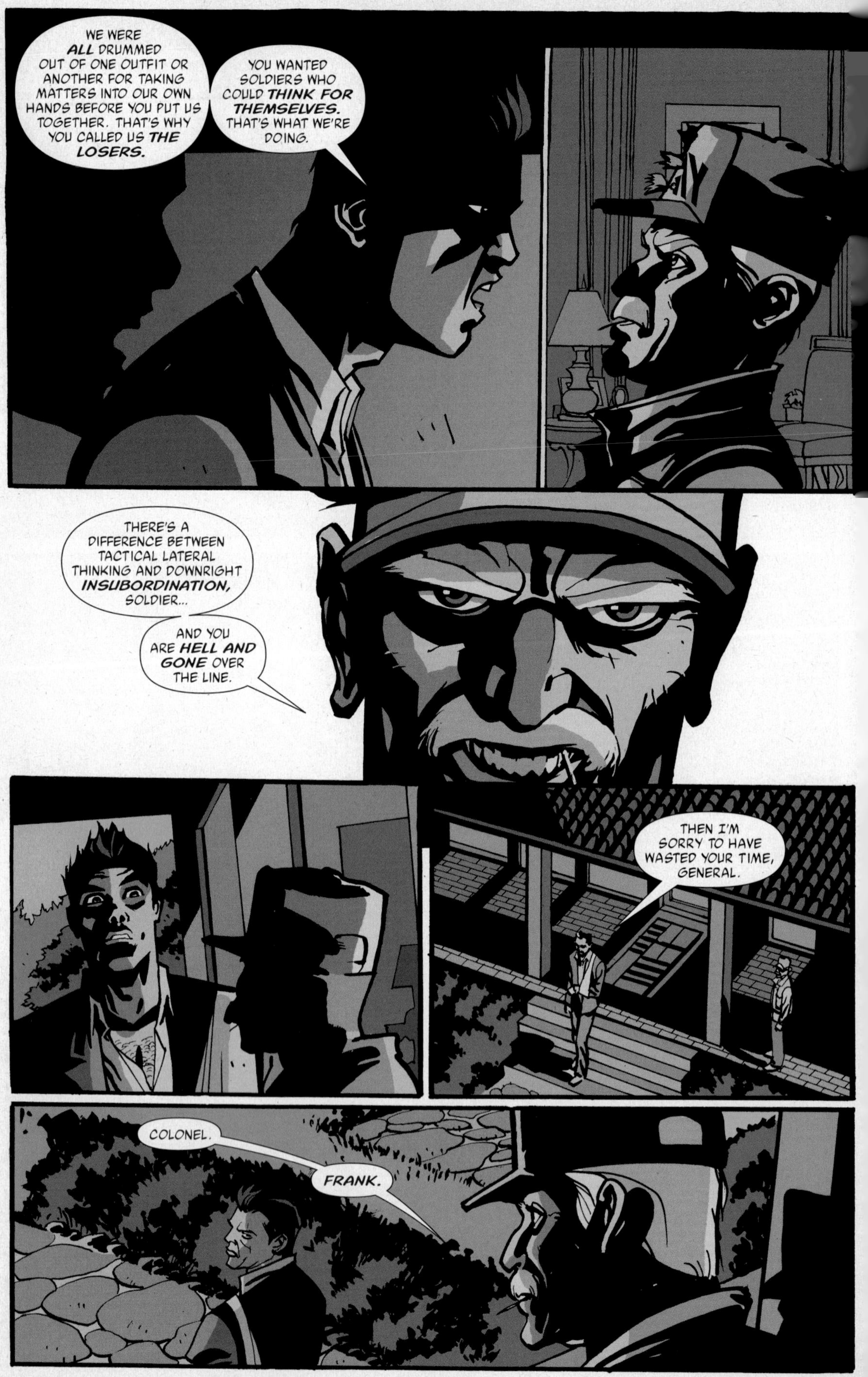
WE WERE ALL DRUMMED OUT OF ONE OUTFIT OR ANOTHER FOR TAKING MATTERS INTO OUR OWN HANDS BEFORE YOU PUT US TOGETHER. THAT'S WHY YOU CALLED US THE LOSERS.
YOU WANTED SOLDIERS WHO COULD THINK FOR THEMSELVES. THAT'S WHAT WE'RE DOING.
THERE'S A DIFFERENCE BETWEEN TACTICAL LATERAL THINKING AND DOWNRIGHT INSUBORDINATION, SOLDIER...
AND YOU ARE HELL AND GONE OVER THE LINE.
THEN I'M SORRY TO HAVE WASTED YOUR TIME, GENERAL.
COLONEL.
FRANK.

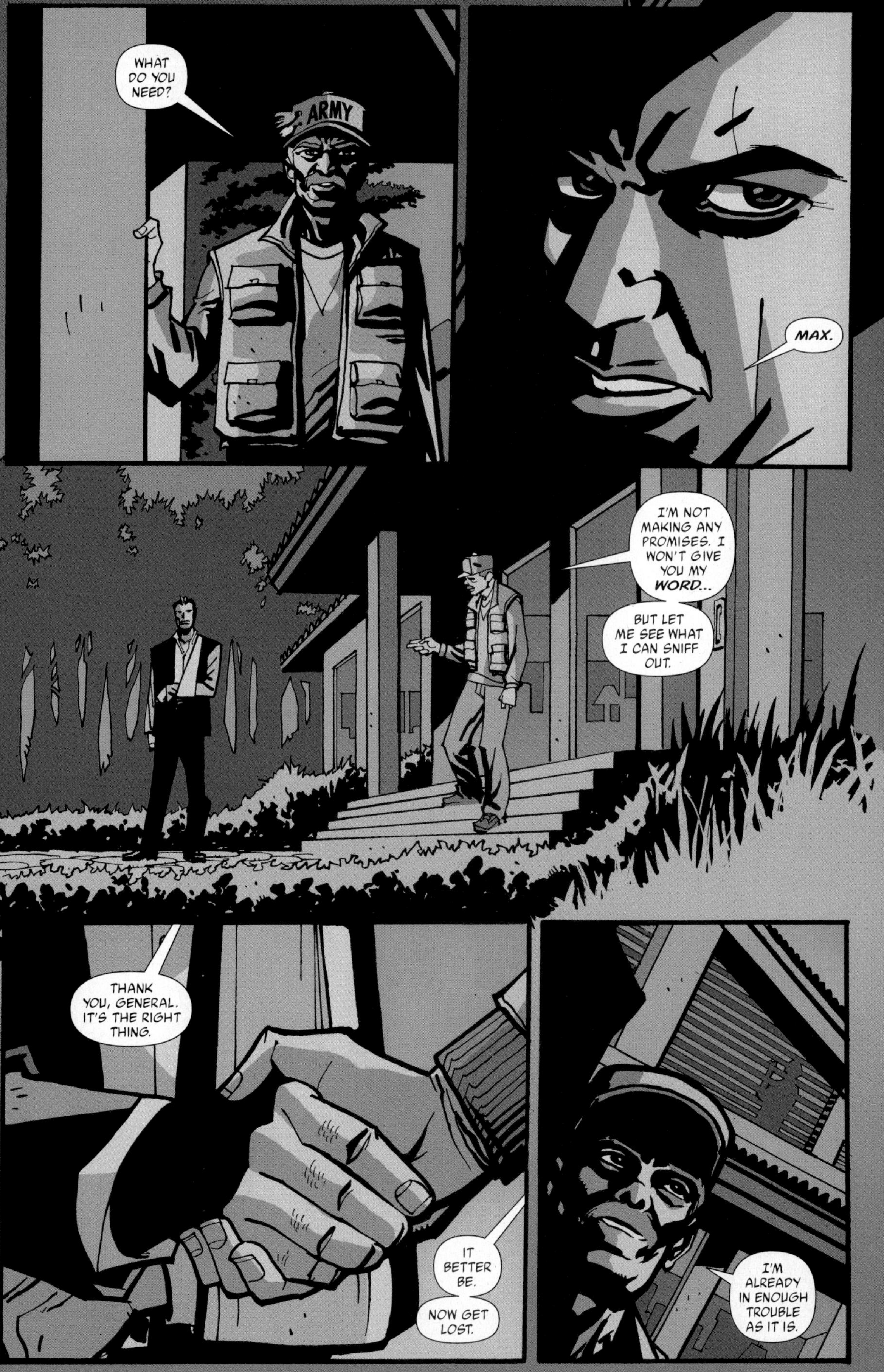
WHAT DO YOU NEED?
MAX.
I'M NOT MAKING ANY PROMISES. I WON'T GIVE YOU MY WORD...
BUT LET ME SEE WHAT I CAN SNIFF OUT.
THANK YOU, GENERAL. IT'S THE RIGHT THING.
IT BETTER BE.
NOW GET LOST.
I'M ALREADY IN ENOUGH TROUBLE AS IT IS.

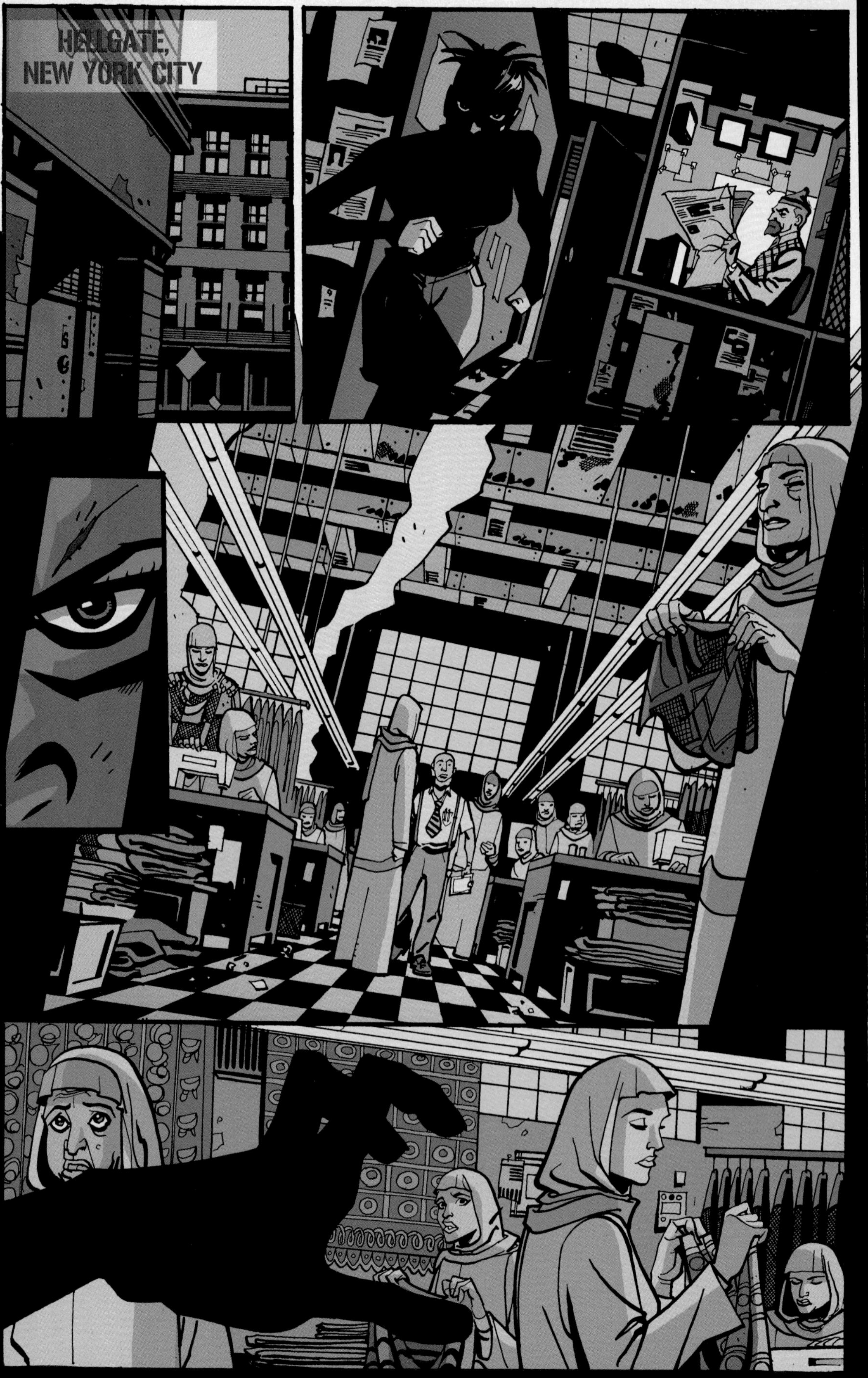
HELLGATE,
NEW YORK CITY

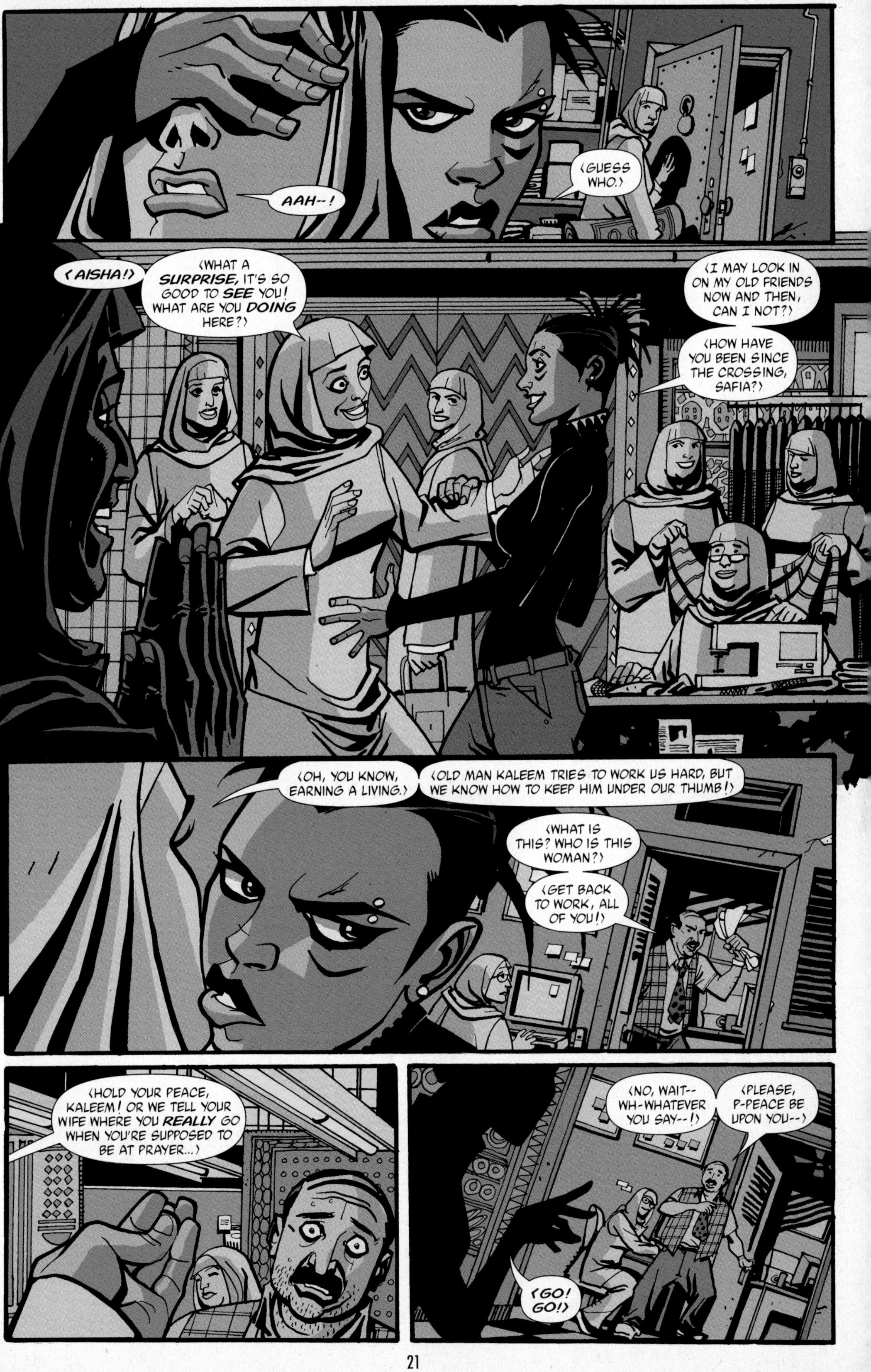
AAH--!
‹GUESS WHO.›
‹AISHA!›
‹WHAT A SURPRISE, IT'S SO GOOD TO SEE YOU! WHAT ARE YOU DOING HERE?›
‹I MAY LOOK IN ON MY OLD FRIENDS NOW AND THEN, CAN I NOT?›
‹HOW HAVE YOU BEEN SINCE THE CROSSING, SAFIA?›
‹OH, YOU KNOW, EARNING A LIVING.›
‹OLD MAN KALEEM TRIES TO WORK US HARD, BUT WE KNOW HOW TO KEEP HIM UNDER OUR THUMB!›
‹WHAT IS THIS? WHO IS THIS WOMAN?›
‹GET BACK TO WORK, ALL OF YOU!›
‹HOLD YOUR PEACE, KALEEM! OR WE TELL YOUR WIFE WHERE YOU REALLY GO WHEN YOU'RE SUPPOSED TO BE AT PRAYER...›
‹NO, WAIT-- WH-WHATEVER YOU SAY--!›
‹PLEASE, P-PEACE BE UPON YOU--›
‹GO! GO!›

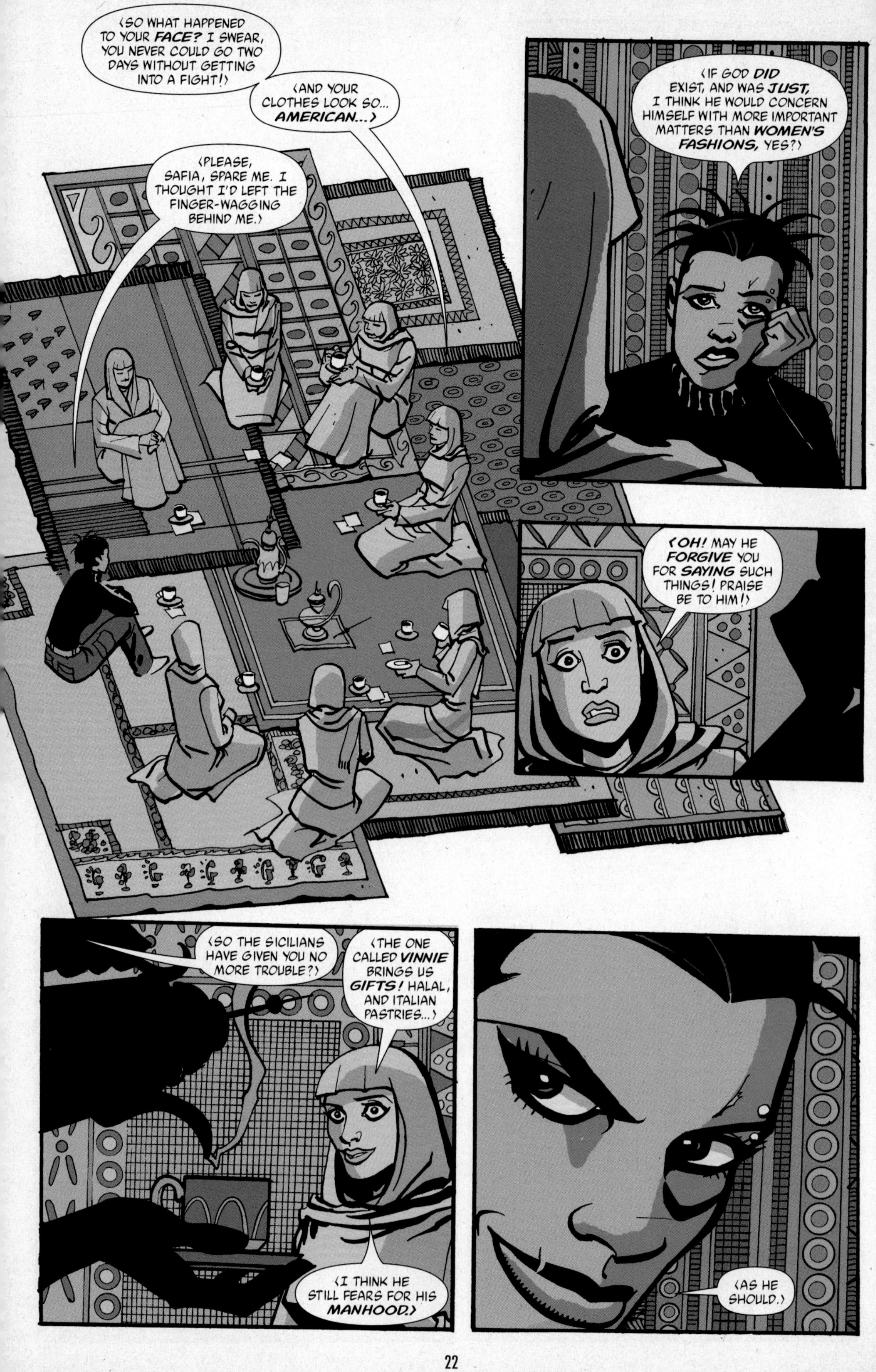
‹SO WHAT HAPPENED TO YOUR FACE? I SWEAR, YOU NEVER COULD GO TWO DAYS WITHOUT GETTING INTO A FIGHT!›
‹AND YOUR CLOTHES LOOK SO... AMERICAN...›
‹PLEASE, SAFIA, SPARE ME. I THOUGHT I'D LEFT THE FINGER-WAGGING BEHIND ME.›
‹IF GOD DID EXIST, AND WAS JUST, I THINK HE WOULD CONCERN HIMSELF WITH MORE IMPORTANT MATTERS THAN WOMEN'S FASHIONS, YES?›
‹OH! MAY HE FORGIVE YOU FOR SAYING SUCH THINGS! PRAISE BE TO HIM!›
‹SO THE SICILIANS HAVE GIVEN YOU NO MORE TROUBLE?›
‹THE ONE CALLED VINNIE BRINGS US GIFTS! HALAL, AND ITALIAN PASTRIES...›
‹I THINK HE STILL FEARS FOR HIS MANHOOD.›
‹AS HE SHOULD.›

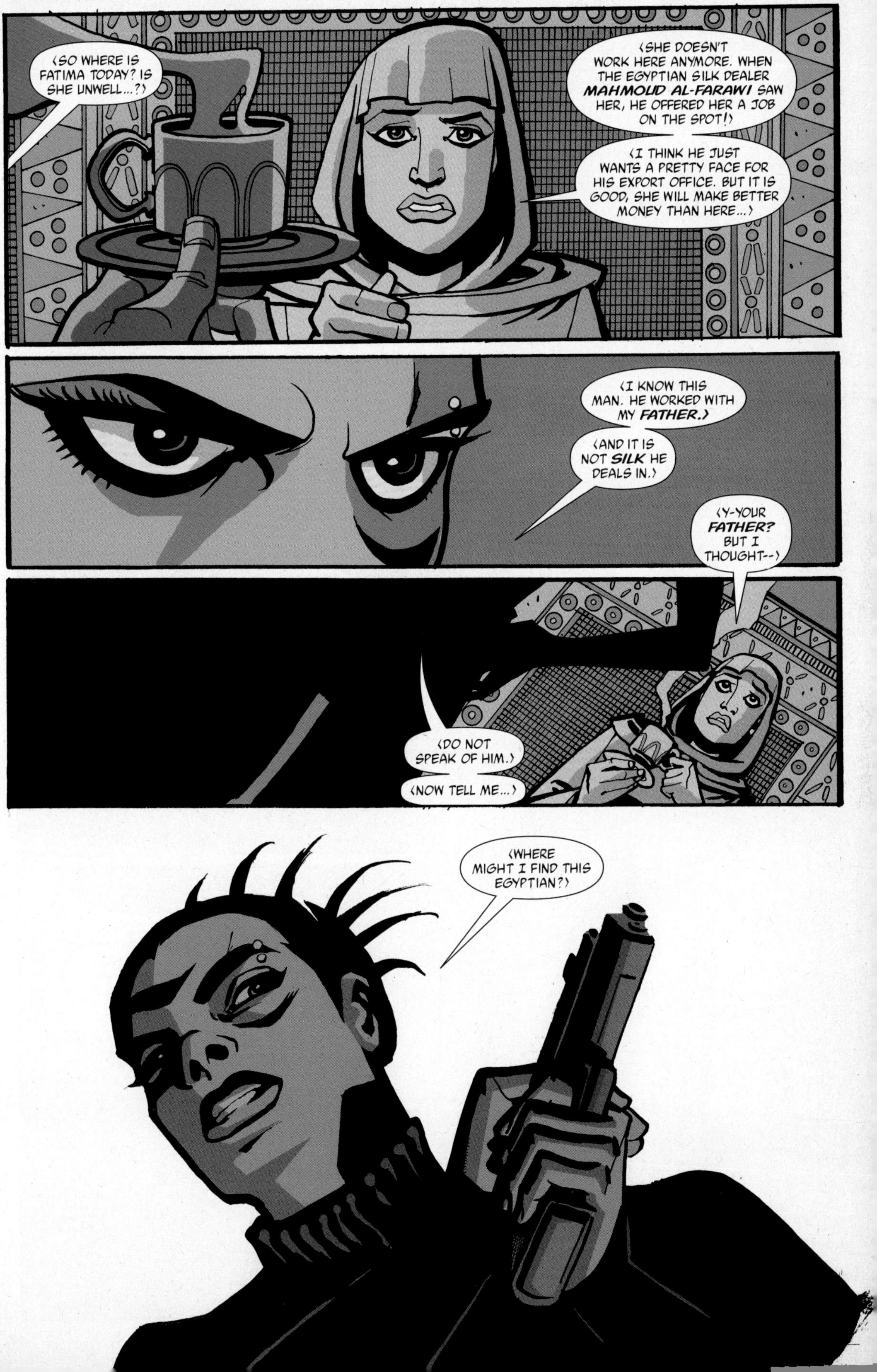
‹SO WHERE IS FATIMA TODAY? IS SHE UNWELL...?›
‹SHE DOESN'T WORK HERE ANYMORE. WHEN THE EGYPTIAN SILK DEALER MAHMOUD AL-FARAWI SAW HER, HE OFFERED HER A JOB ON THE SPOT!›
‹I THINK HE JUST WANTS A PRETTY FACE FOR HIS EXPORT OFFICE. BUT IT IS GOOD, SHE WILL MAKE BETTER MONEY THAN HERE...›
‹I KNOW THIS MAN. HE WORKED WITH MY FATHER.›
‹AND IT IS NOT SILK HE DEALS IN.›
‹Y-YOUR FATHER? BUT I THOUGHT--›
‹DO NOT SPEAK OF HIM.›
‹NOW TELL ME...›
‹WHERE MIGHT I FIND THIS EGYPTIAN?›

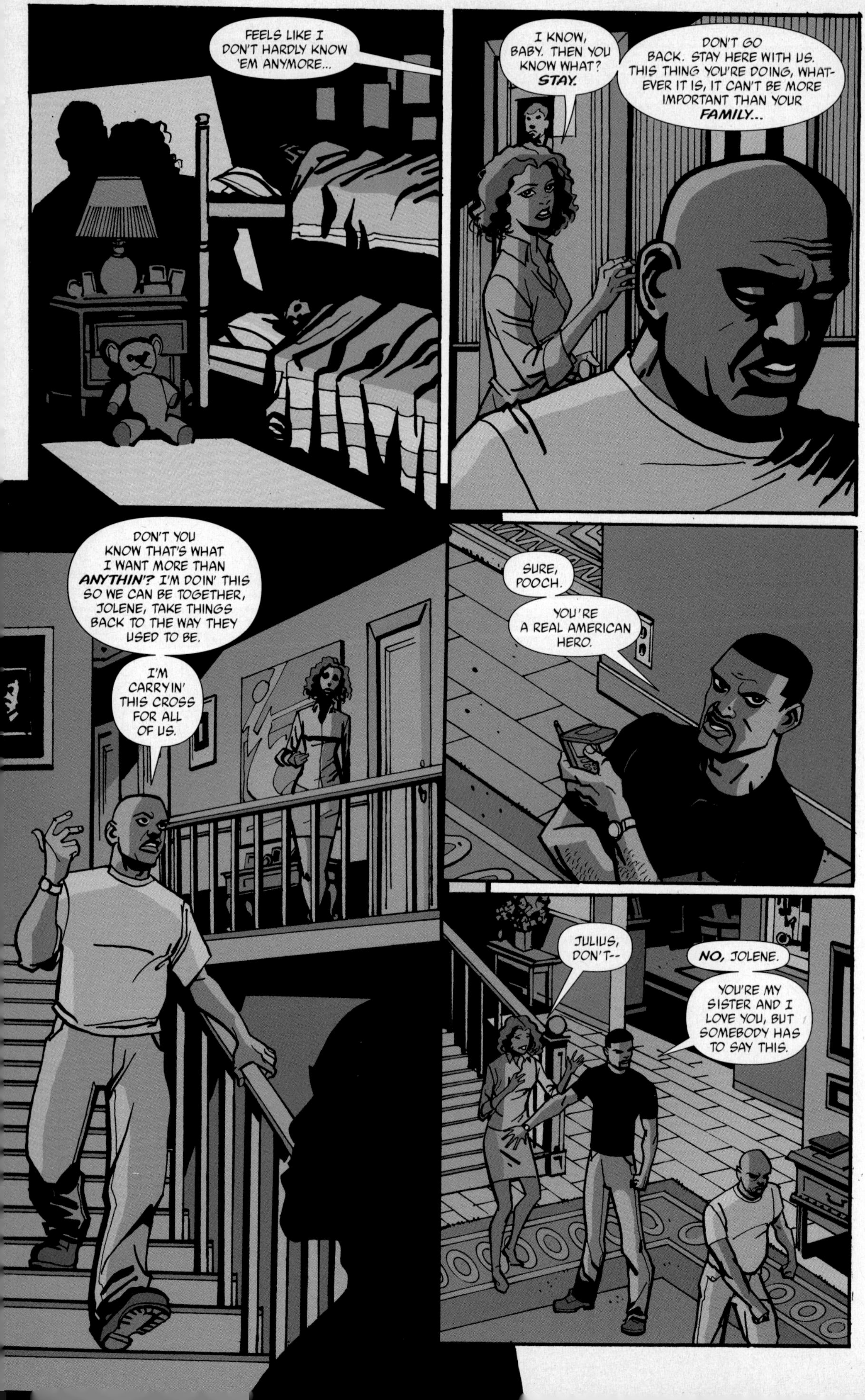

FEELS LIKE I DON'T HARDLY KNOW 'EM ANYMORE...
I KNOW, BABY. THEN YOU KNOW WHAT? STAY.
DON'T GO BACK. STAY HERE WITH US. THIS THING YOU'RE DOING, WHAT-EVER IT IS, IT CAN'T BE MORE IMPORTANT THAN YOUR FAMILY...
DON'T YOU KNOW THAT'S WHAT I WANT MORE THAN ANYTHIN'? I'M DOIN' THIS SO WE CAN BE TOGETHER, JOLENE, TAKE THINGS BACK TO THE WAY THEY USED TO BE.
I'M CARRYIN' THIS CROSS FOR ALL OF US.
SURE, POOCH.
YOU'RE A REAL AMERICAN HERO.
JULIUS, DON'T--
NO, JOLENE.
YOU'RE MY SISTER AND I LOVE YOU, BUT SOMEBODY HAS TO SAY THIS.

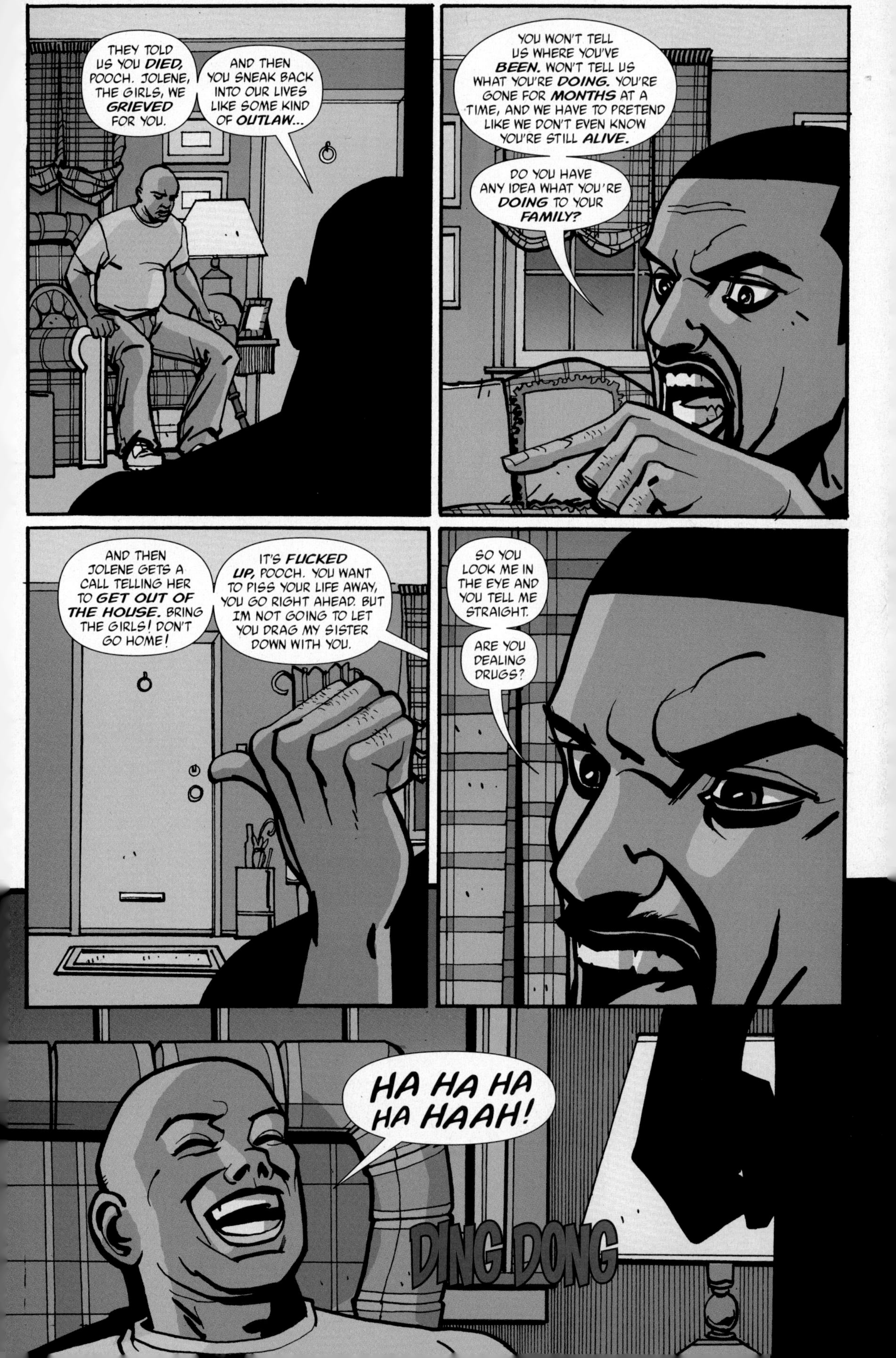
THEY TOLD US YOU DIED, POOCH. JOLENE, THE GIRLS, WE GRIEVED FOR YOU.
AND THEN YOU SNEAK BACK INTO OUR LIVES LIKE SOME KIND OF OUTLAW...
YOU WON'T TELL US WHERE YOU'VE BEEN. WON'T TELL US WHAT YOU'RE DOING. YOU'RE GONE FOR MONTHS AT A TIME, AND WE HAVE TO PRETEND LIKE WE DON'T EVEN KNOW YOU'RE STILL ALIVE.
DO YOU HAVE ANY IDEA WHAT YOU'RE DOING TO YOUR FAMILY?
AND THEN JOLENE GETS A CALL TELLING HER TO GET OUT OF THE HOUSE. BRING THE GIRLS! DON'T GO HOME!
IT'S FUCKED UP, POOCH. YOU WANT TO PISS YOUR LIFE AWAY, YOU GO RIGHT AHEAD. BUT IM NOT GOING TO LET YOU DRAG MY SISTER DOWN WITH YOU.
SO YOU LOOK ME IN THE EYE AND YOU TELL ME STRAIGHT.
ARE YOU DEALING DRUGS?
HA HA HA HA HAAH!
DING DONG

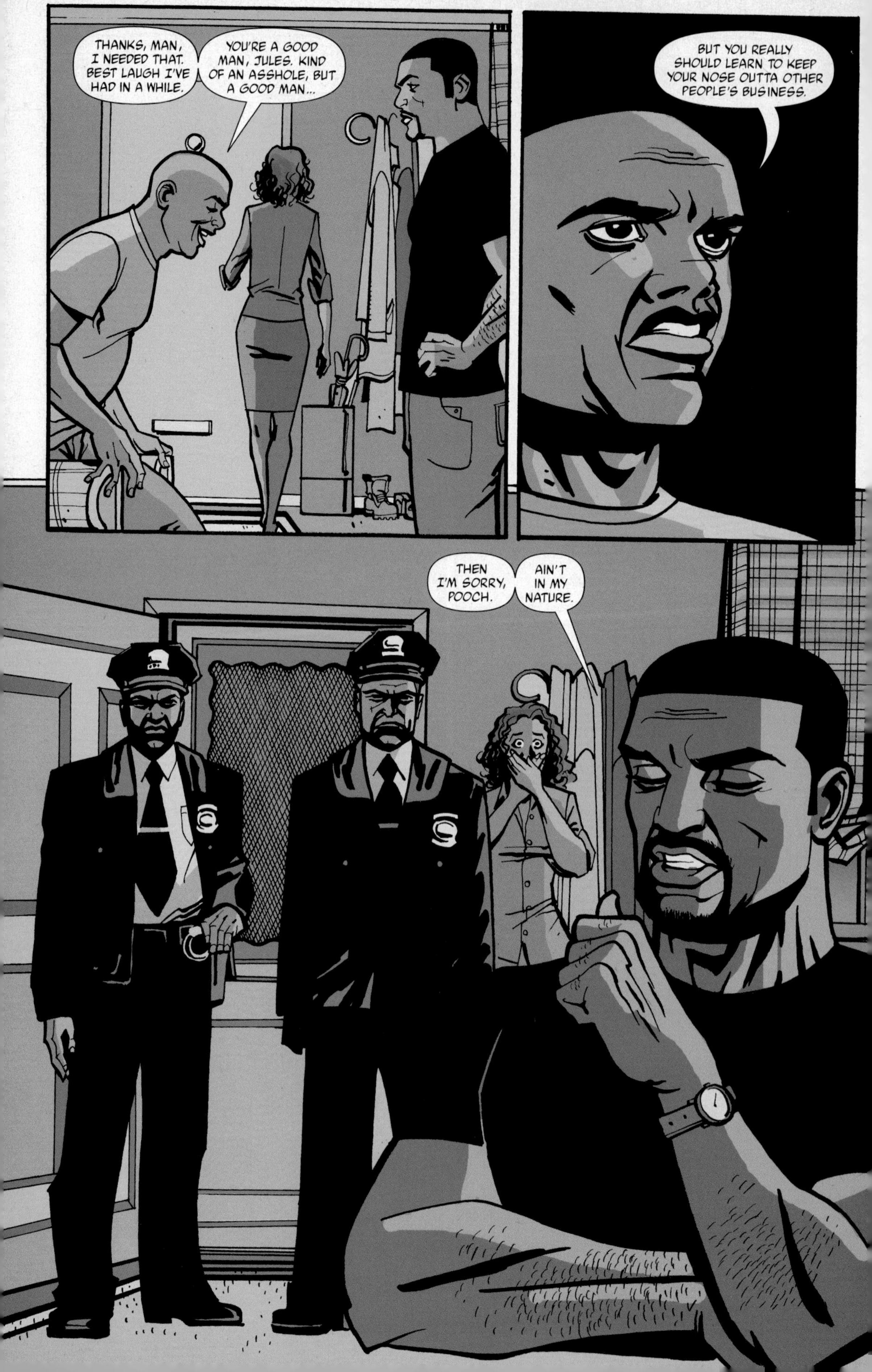
THANKS, MAN, I NEEDED THAT. BEST LAUGH I'VE HAD IN A WHILE.
YOU'RE A GOOD MAN, JULES. KIND OF AN ASSHOLE, BUT A GOOD MAN...
BUT YOU REALLY SHOULD LEARN TO KEEP YOUR NOSE OUTTA OTHER PEOPLE'S BUSINESS.
THEN I'M SORRY, POOCH.
AIN'T IN MY NATURE.

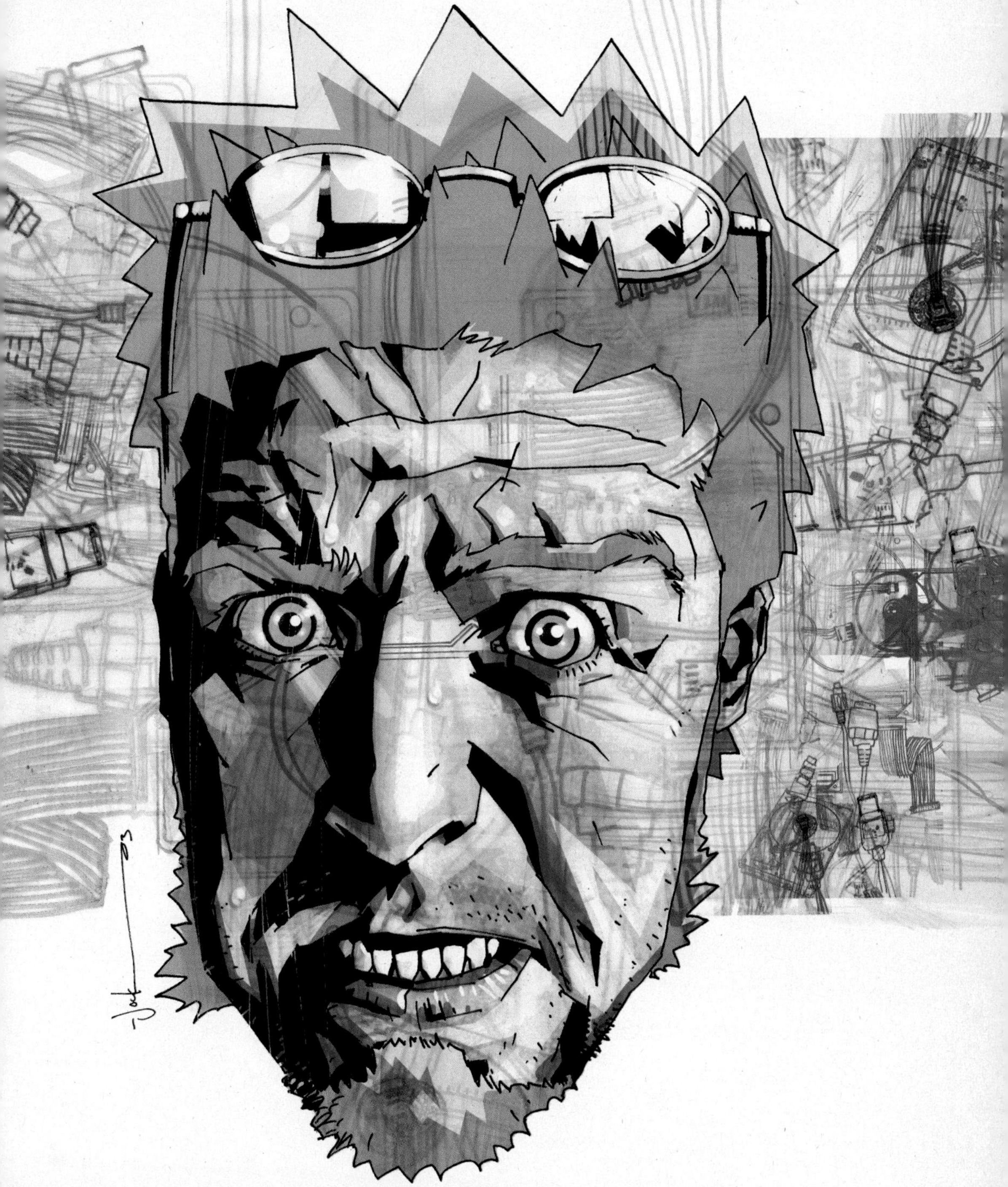

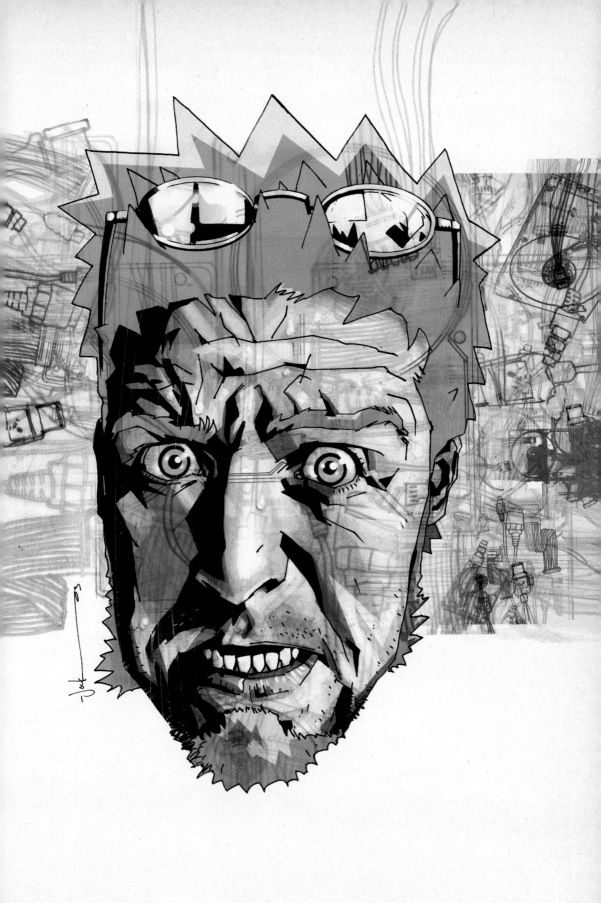

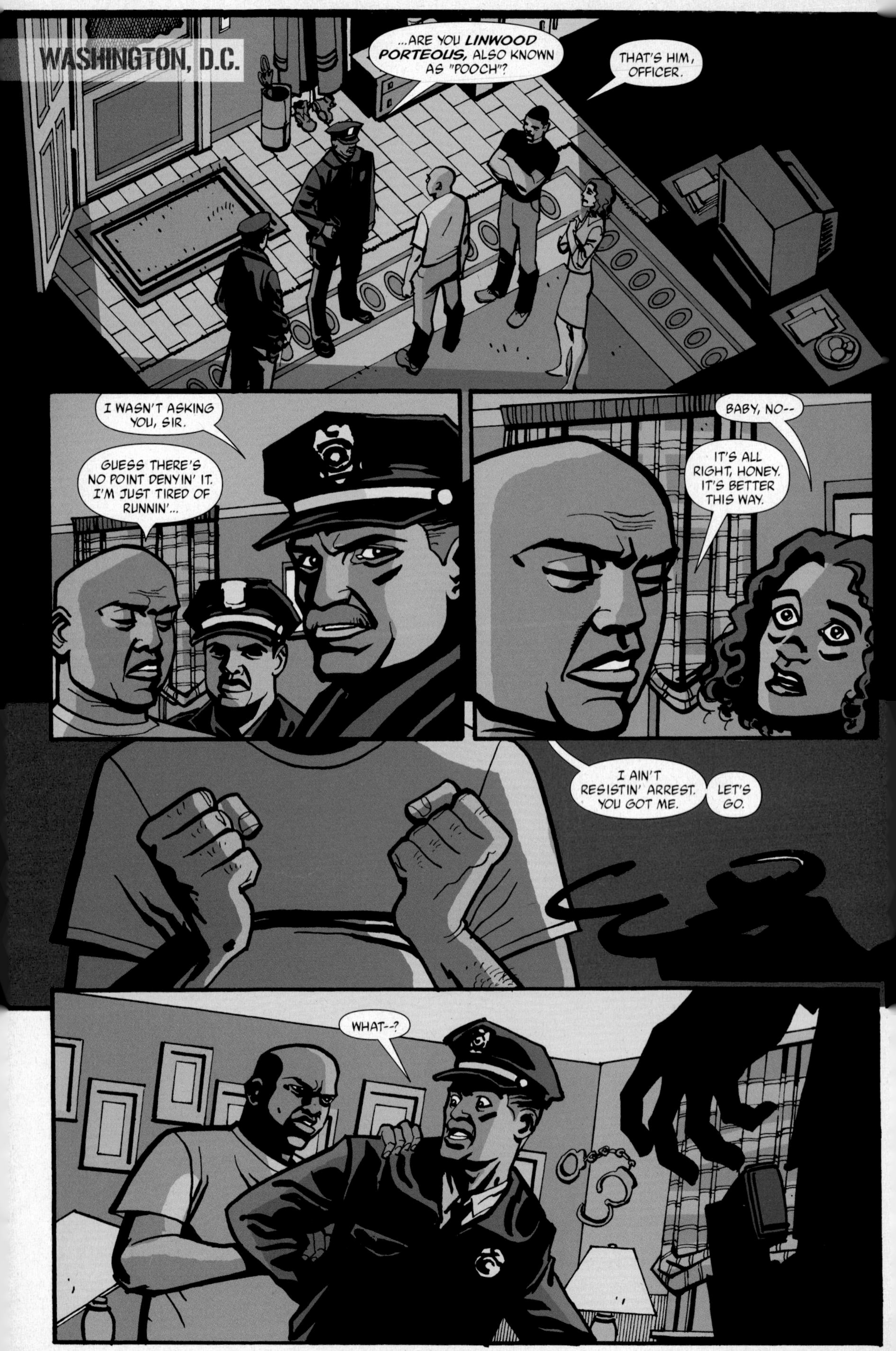
WASHINGTON, D.C.
...ARE YOU LINWOOD PORTEOUS, ALSO KNOWN AS "POOCH"?
THAT'S HIM, OFFICER.
I WASN'T ASKING YOU, SIR.
GUESS THERE'S NO POINT DENYIN' IT. I'M JUST TIRED OF RUNNIN'...
BABY, NO--
IT'S ALL RIGHT, HONEY. IT'S BETTER THIS WAY.
I AIN'T RESISTIN' ARREST. YOU GOT ME.
LET'S GO.
WHAT--?

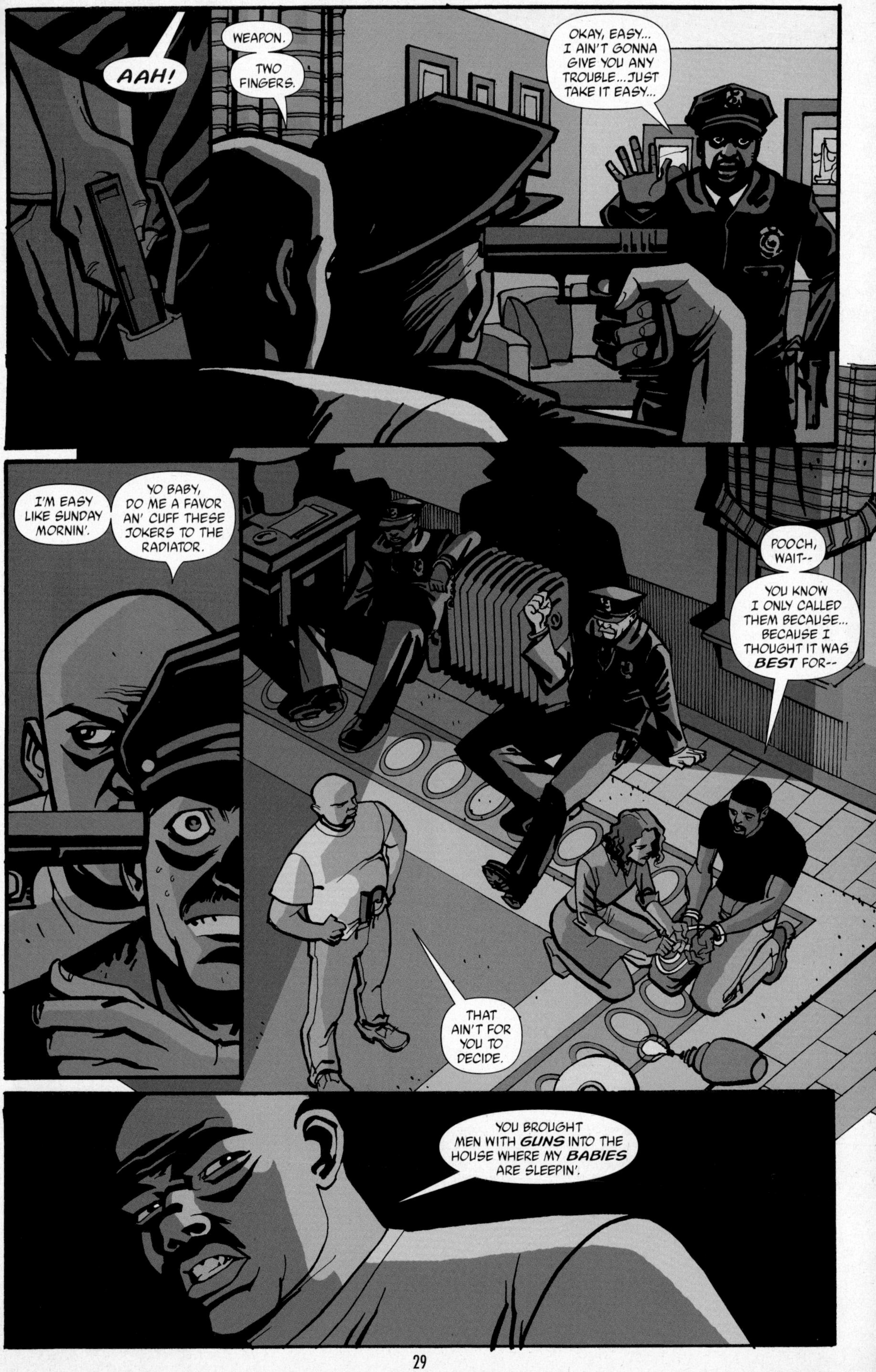
AAH!
WEAPON.
TWO FINGERS.
OKAY, EASY... I AIN'T GONNA GIVE YOU ANY TROUBLE...JUST TAKE IT EASY...
I'M EASY LIKE SUNDAY MORNIN'.
YO BABY, DO ME A FAVOR AN' CUFF THESE JOKERS TO THE RADIATOR.
POOCH, WAIT--
YOU KNOW I ONLY CALLED THEM BECAUSE... BECAUSE I THOUGHT IT WAS **BEST** FOR--
THAT AIN'T FOR YOU TO DECIDE.
YOU BROUGHT MEN WITH **GUNS** INTO THE HOUSE WHERE MY **BABIES** ARE SLEEPIN'.

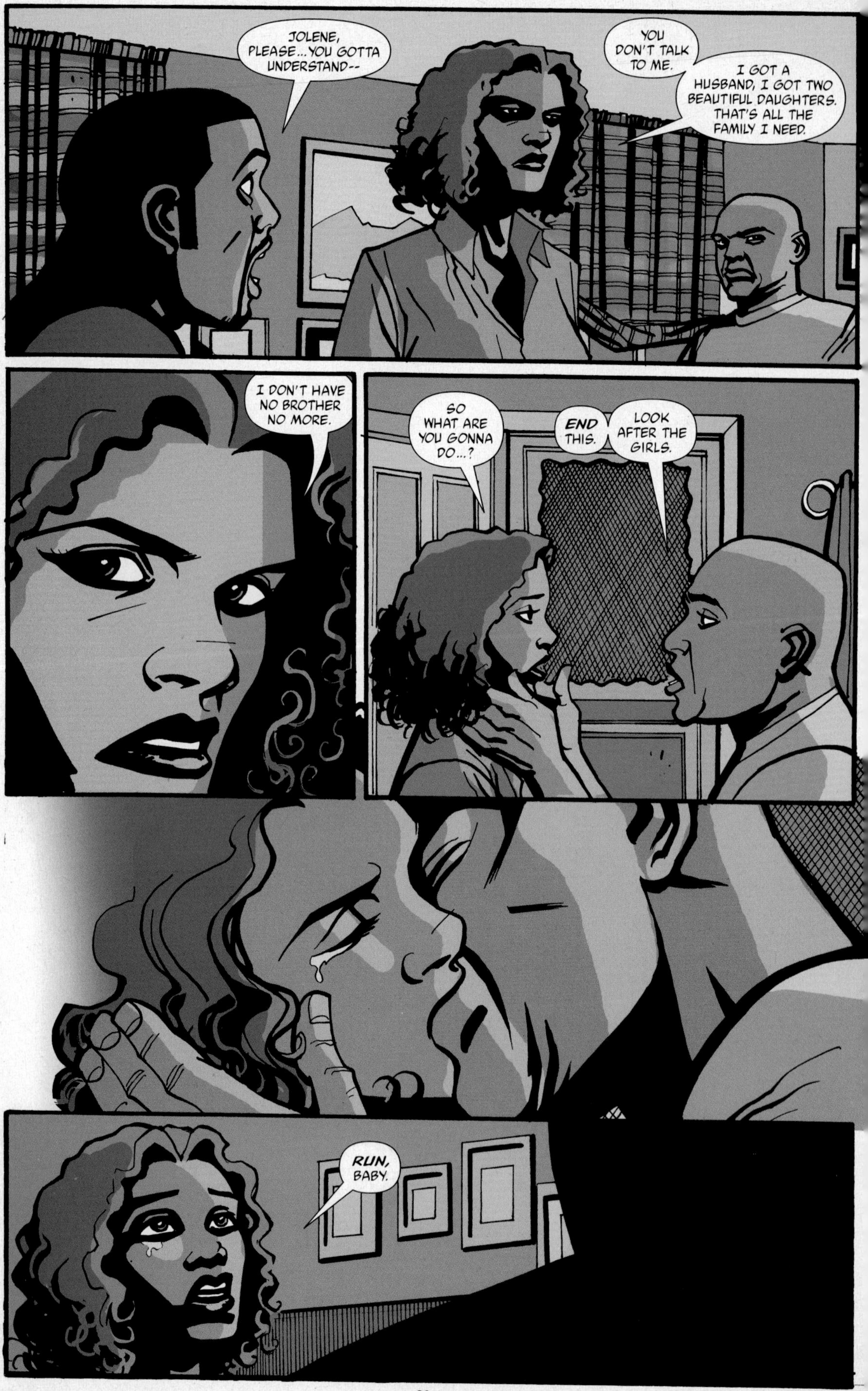
JOLENE, PLEASE...YOU GOTTA UNDERSTAND--
YOU DON'T TALK TO ME.
I GOT A HUSBAND, I GOT TWO BEAUTIFUL DAUGHTERS. THAT'S ALL THE FAMILY I NEED.
I DON'T HAVE NO BROTHER NO MORE.
SO WHAT ARE YOU GONNA DO...?
END THIS.
LOOK AFTER THE GIRLS.
RUN, BABY.

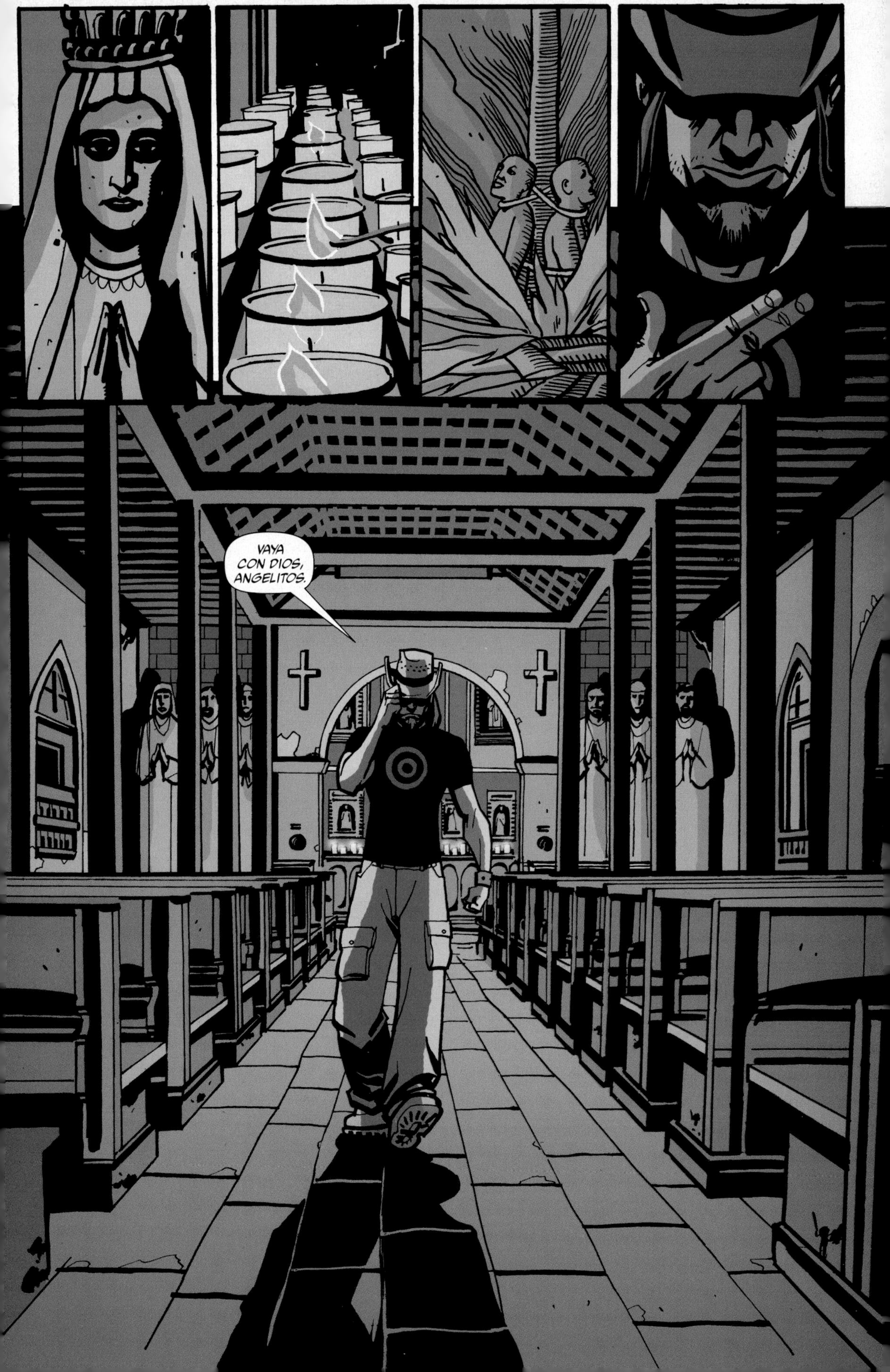
VAYA CON DIOS, ANGELITOS.

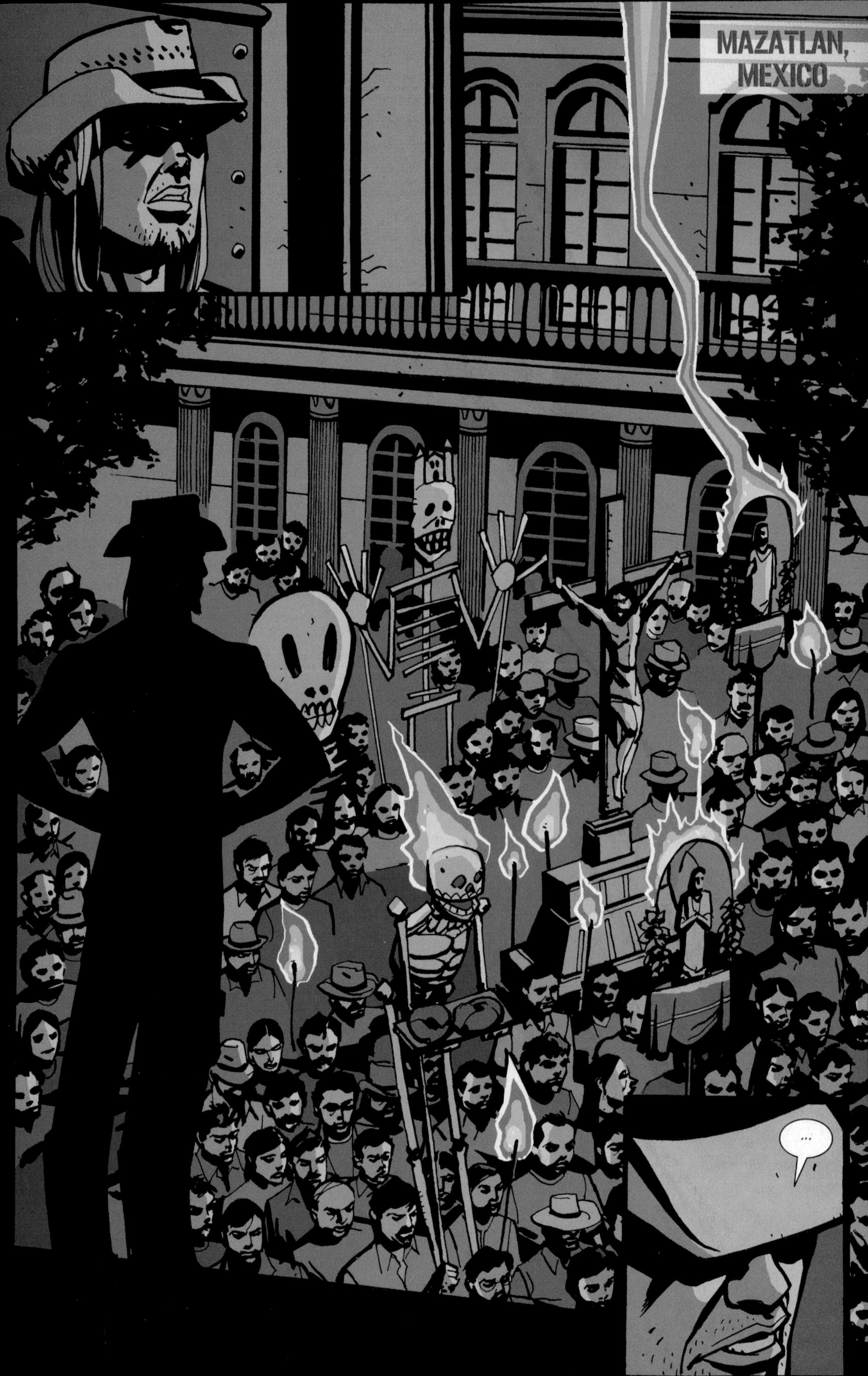
MAZATLAN, MEXICO
...

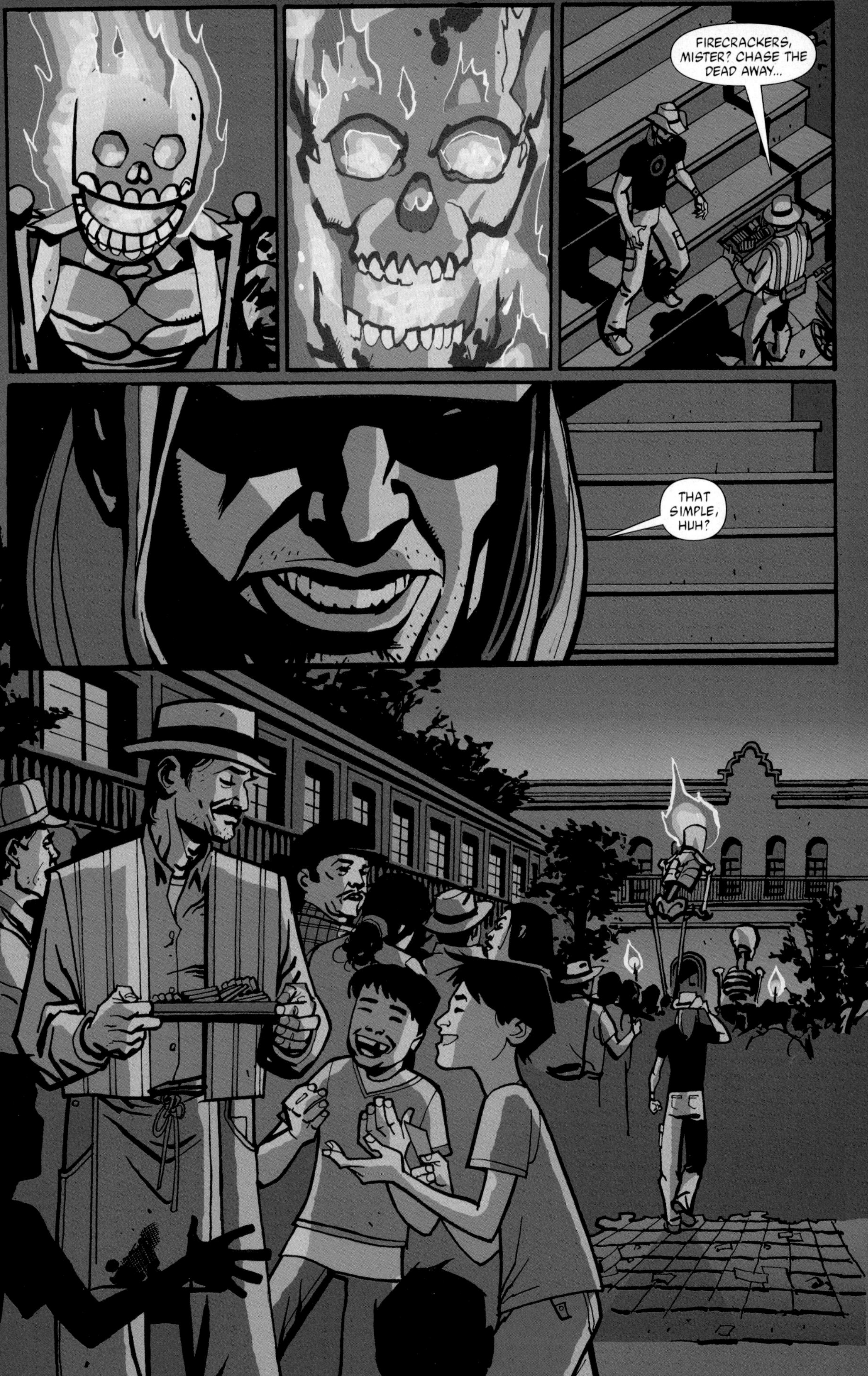
FIRECRACKERS, MISTER? CHASE THE DEAD AWAY...
THAT SIMPLE, HUH?

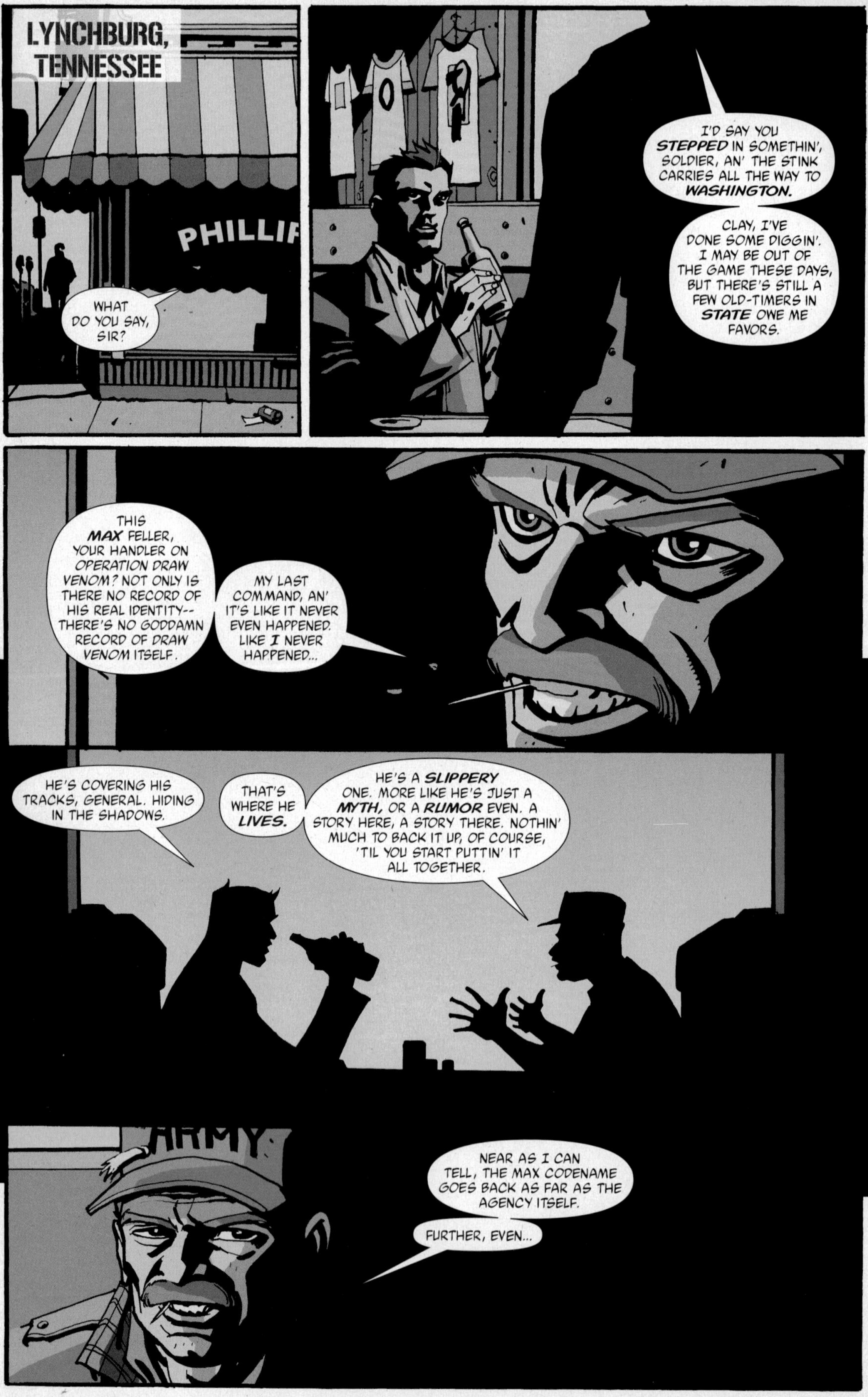

LYNCHBURG, TENNESSEE
PHILLIP
WHAT DO YOU SAY, SIR?
I'D SAY YOU STEPPED IN SOMETHIN', SOLDIER, AN' THE STINK CARRIES ALL THE WAY TO WASHINGTON.
CLAY, I'VE DONE SOME DIGGIN'. I MAY BE OUT OF THE GAME THESE DAYS, BUT THERE'S STILL A FEW OLD-TIMERS IN STATE OWE ME FAVORS.
THIS MAX FELLER, YOUR HANDLER ON OPERATION DRAW VENOM? NOT ONLY IS THERE NO RECORD OF HIS REAL IDENTITY-- THERE'S NO GODDAMN RECORD OF DRAW VENOM ITSELF.
MY LAST COMMAND, AN' IT'S LIKE IT NEVER EVEN HAPPENED. LIKE I NEVER HAPPENED...
HE'S COVERING HIS TRACKS, GENERAL. HIDING IN THE SHADOWS.
THAT'S WHERE HE LIVES.
HE'S A SLIPPERY ONE. MORE LIKE HE'S JUST A MYTH, OR A RUMOR EVEN. A STORY HERE, A STORY THERE. NOTHIN' MUCH TO BACK IT UP, OF COURSE, 'TIL YOU START PUTTIN' IT ALL TOGETHER.
ARMY
NEAR AS I CAN TELL, THE MAX CODENAME GOES BACK AS FAR AS THE AGENCY ITSELF.
FURTHER, EVEN...

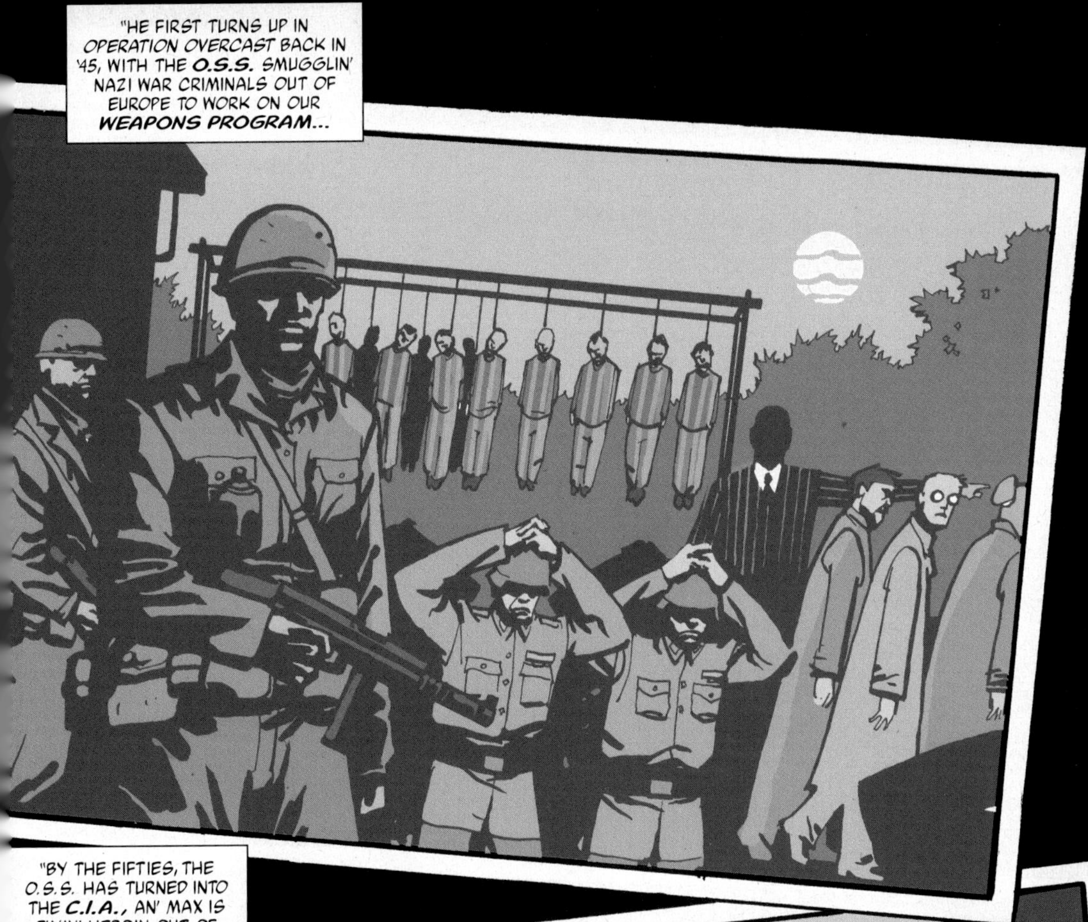
"HE FIRST TURNS UP IN OPERATION OVERCAST BACK IN '45, WITH THE O.S.S. SMUGGLIN' NAZI WAR CRIMINALS OUT OF EUROPE TO WORK ON OUR WEAPONS PROGRAM...

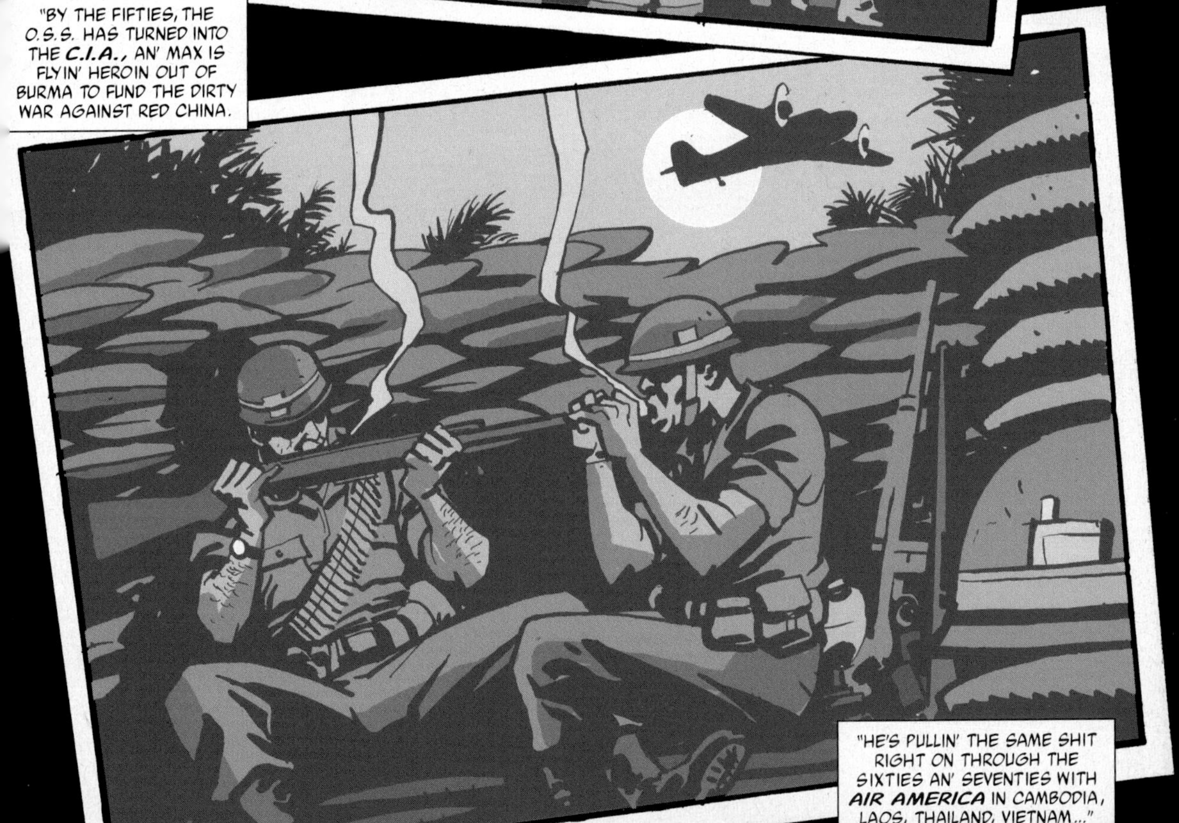
"BY THE FIFTIES, THE O.S.S. HAS TURNED INTO THE C.I.A., AN' MAX IS FLYIN' HEROIN OUT OF BURMA TO FUND THE DIRTY WAR AGAINST RED CHINA.
"HE'S PULLIN' THE SAME SHIT RIGHT ON THROUGH THE SIXTIES AN' SEVENTIES WITH AIR AMERICA IN CAMBODIA, LAOS, THAILAND, VIETNAM..."

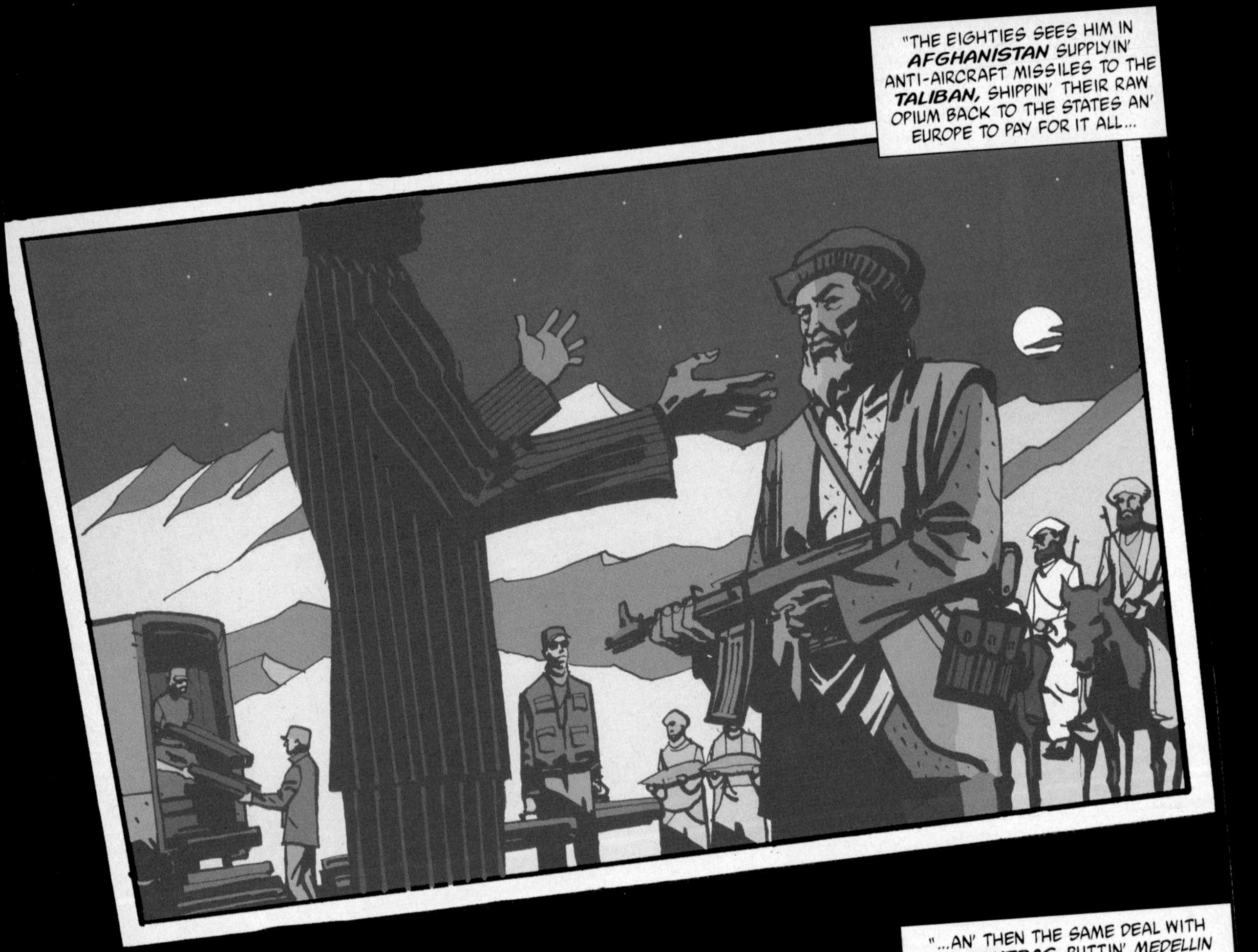
"THE EIGHTIES SEES HIM IN AFGHANISTAN SUPPLYIN' ANTI-AIRCRAFT MISSILES TO THE TALIBAN, SHIPPIN' THEIR RAW OPIUM BACK TO THE STATES AN' EUROPE TO PAY FOR IT ALL...

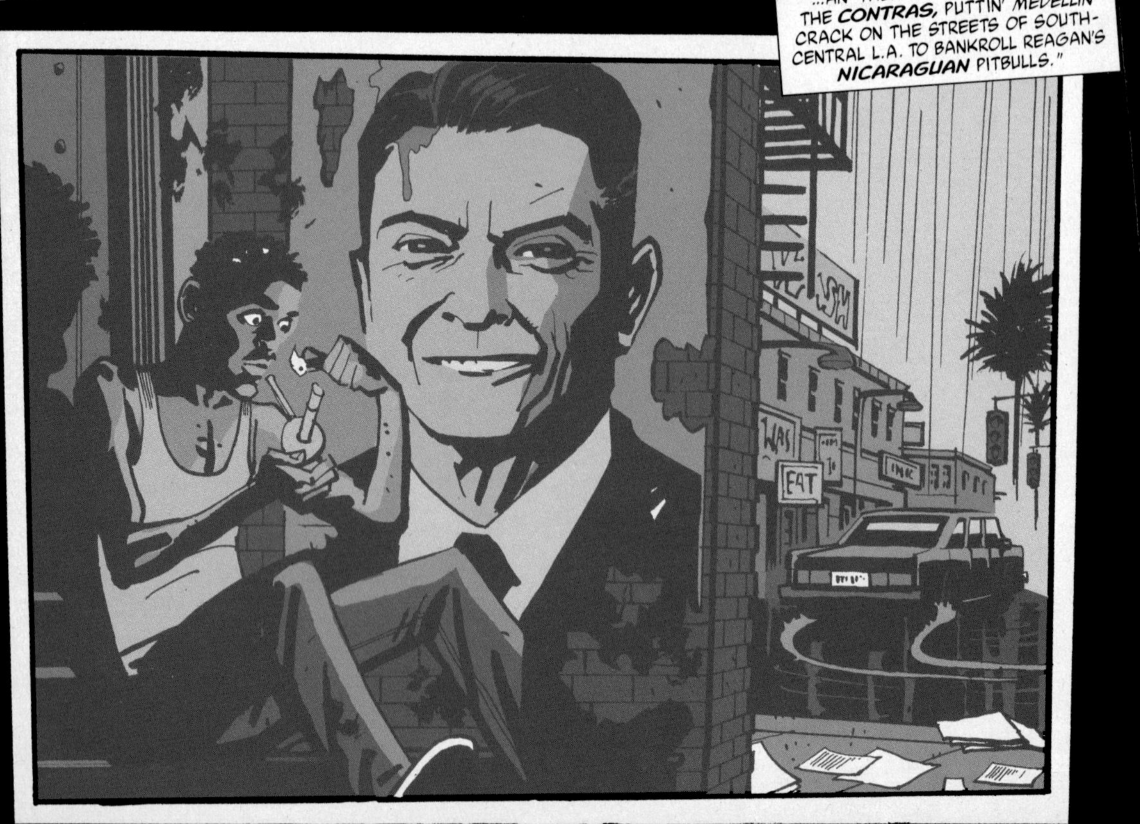
"...AN' THEN THE SAME DEAL WITH THE CONTRAS, PUTTIN' MEDELLIN CRACK ON THE STREETS OF SOUTH-CENTRAL L.A. TO BANKROLL REAGAN'S NICARAGUAN PITBULLS."
EAT

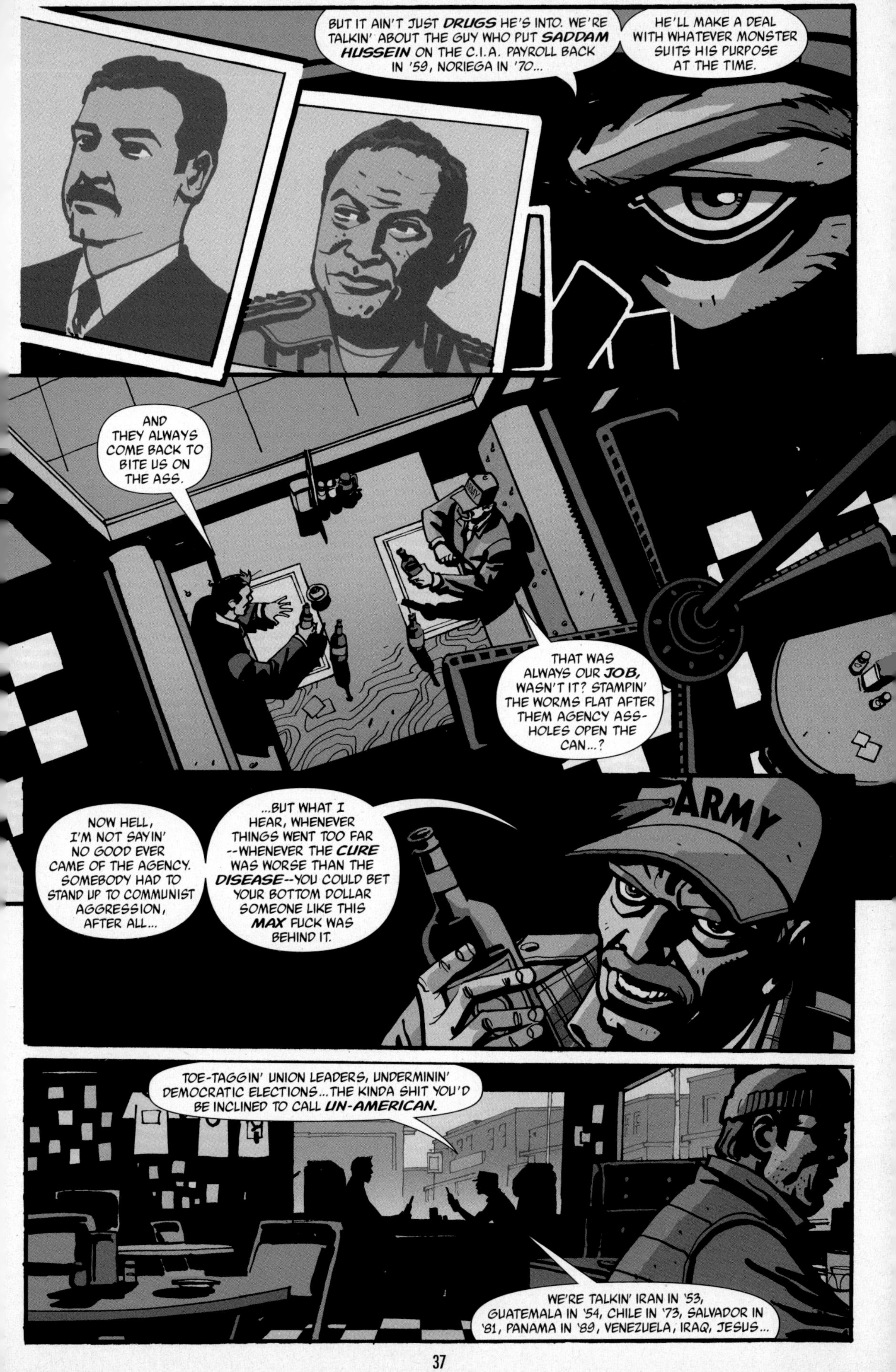
BUT IT AIN'T JUST DRUGS HE'S INTO. WE'RE TALKIN' ABOUT THE GUY WHO PUT SADDAM HUSSEIN ON THE C.I.A. PAYROLL BACK IN '59, NORIEGA IN '70...
HE'LL MAKE A DEAL WITH WHATEVER MONSTER SUITS HIS PURPOSE AT THE TIME.
AND THEY ALWAYS COME BACK TO BITE US ON THE ASS.
ARMY
THAT WAS ALWAYS OUR JOB, WASN'T IT? STAMPIN' THE WORMS FLAT AFTER THEM AGENCY ASS-HOLES OPEN THE CAN...?
NOW HELL, I'M NOT SAYIN' NO GOOD EVER CAME OF THE AGENCY. SOMEBODY HAD TO STAND UP TO COMMUNIST AGGRESSION, AFTER ALL...
...BUT WHAT I HEAR, WHENEVER THINGS WENT TOO FAR --WHENEVER THE CURE WAS WORSE THAN THE DISEASE--YOU COULD BET YOUR BOTTOM DOLLAR SOMEONE LIKE THIS MAX FUCK WAS BEHIND IT.
ARMY
TOE-TAGGIN' UNION LEADERS, UNDERMININ' DEMOCRATIC ELECTIONS...THE KINDA SHIT YOU'D BE INCLINED TO CALL UN-AMERICAN.
WE'RE TALKIN' IRAN IN '53, GUATEMALA IN '54, CHILE IN '73, SALVADOR IN '81, PANAMA IN '89, VENEZUELA, IRAQ, JESUS...

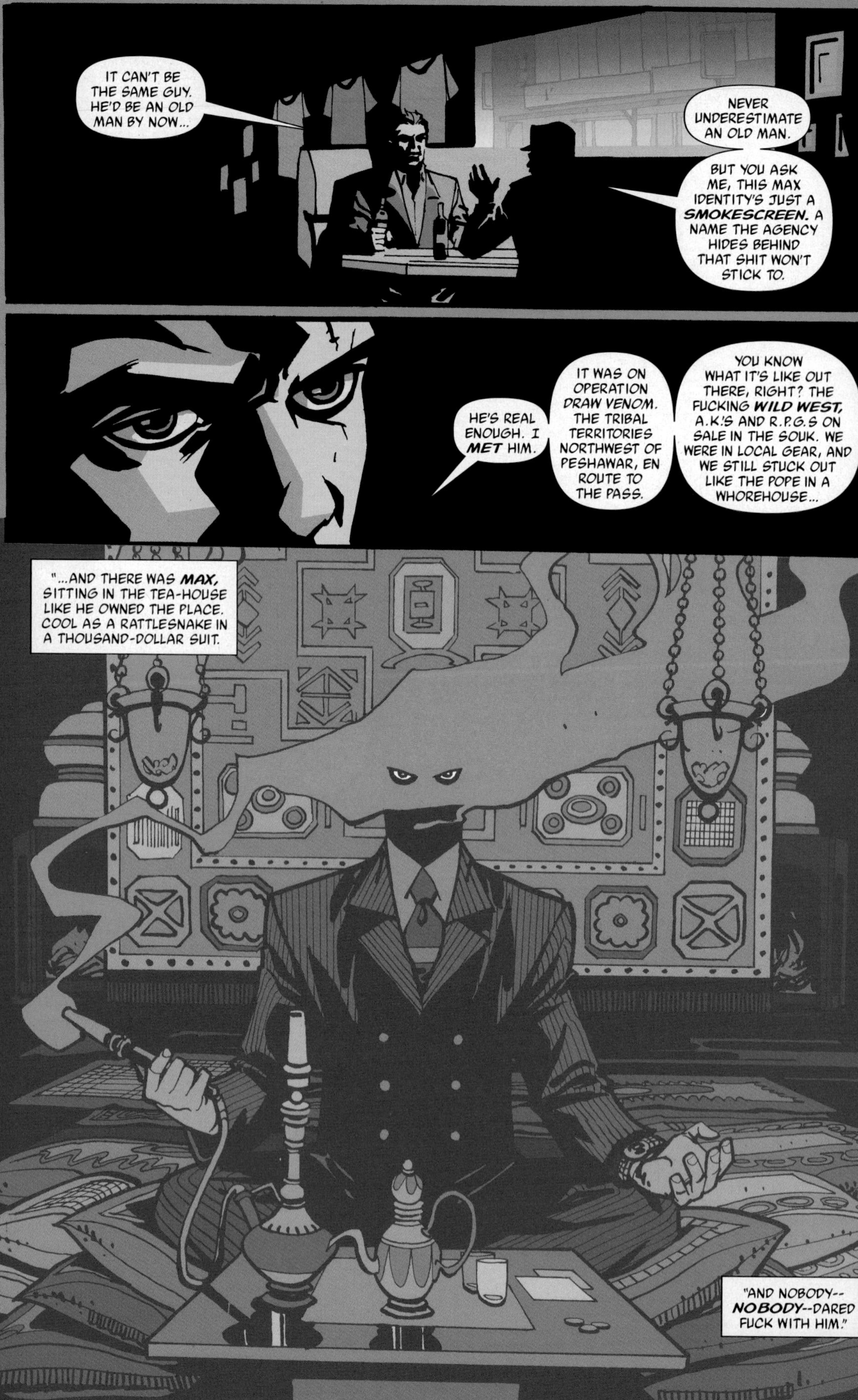
IT CAN'T BE THE SAME GUY. HE'D BE AN OLD MAN BY NOW...
NEVER UNDERESTIMATE AN OLD MAN.
BUT YOU ASK ME, THIS MAX IDENTITY'S JUST A **SMOKESCREEN.** A NAME THE AGENCY HIDES BEHIND THAT SHIT WON'T STICK TO.
HE'S REAL ENOUGH. I **MET** HIM.
IT WAS ON OPERATION *DRAW VENOM.* THE TRIBAL TERRITORIES NORTHWEST OF PESHAWAR, EN ROUTE TO THE PASS.
YOU KNOW WHAT IT'S LIKE OUT THERE, RIGHT? THE FUCKING **WILD WEST,** A.K.'S AND R.P.G.S ON SALE IN THE SOUK. WE WERE IN LOCAL GEAR, AND WE STILL STUCK OUT LIKE THE POPE IN A WHOREHOUSE...
"...AND THERE WAS **MAX,** SITTING IN THE TEA-HOUSE LIKE HE OWNED THE PLACE. COOL AS A RATTLESNAKE IN A THOUSAND-DOLLAR SUIT.
"AND NOBODY-- **NOBODY**--DARED FUCK WITH HIM."

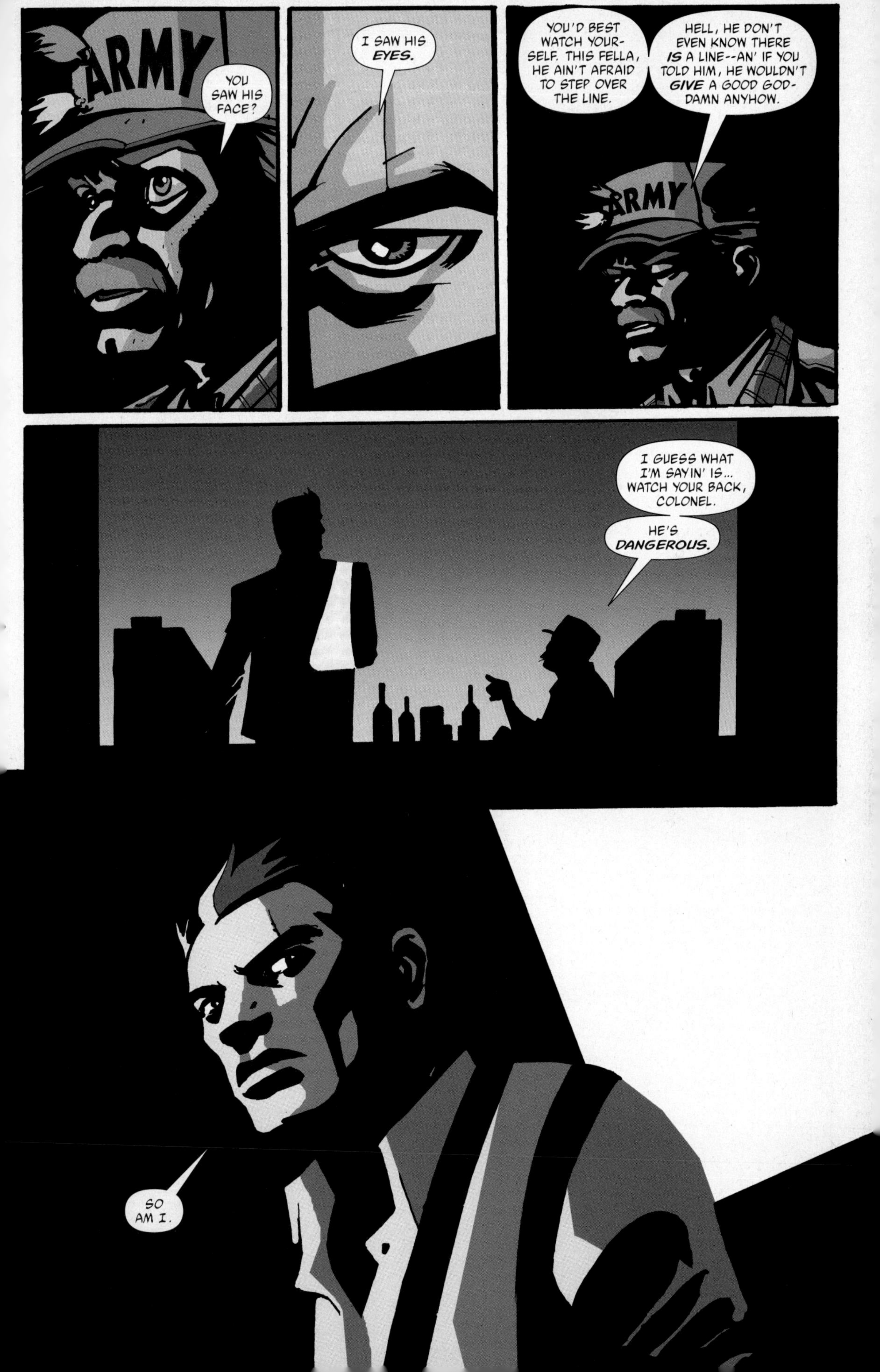
YOU SAW HIS FACE?
I SAW HIS *EYES.*
YOU'D BEST WATCH YOURSELF. THIS FELLA, HE AIN'T AFRAID TO STEP OVER THE LINE.
HELL, HE DON'T EVEN KNOW THERE *IS* A LINE--AN' IF YOU TOLD HIM, HE WOULDN'T *GIVE* A GOOD GOD-DAMN ANYHOW.
I GUESS WHAT I'M SAYIN' IS... WATCH YOUR BACK, COLONEL.
HE'S *DANGEROUS.*
SO AM I.

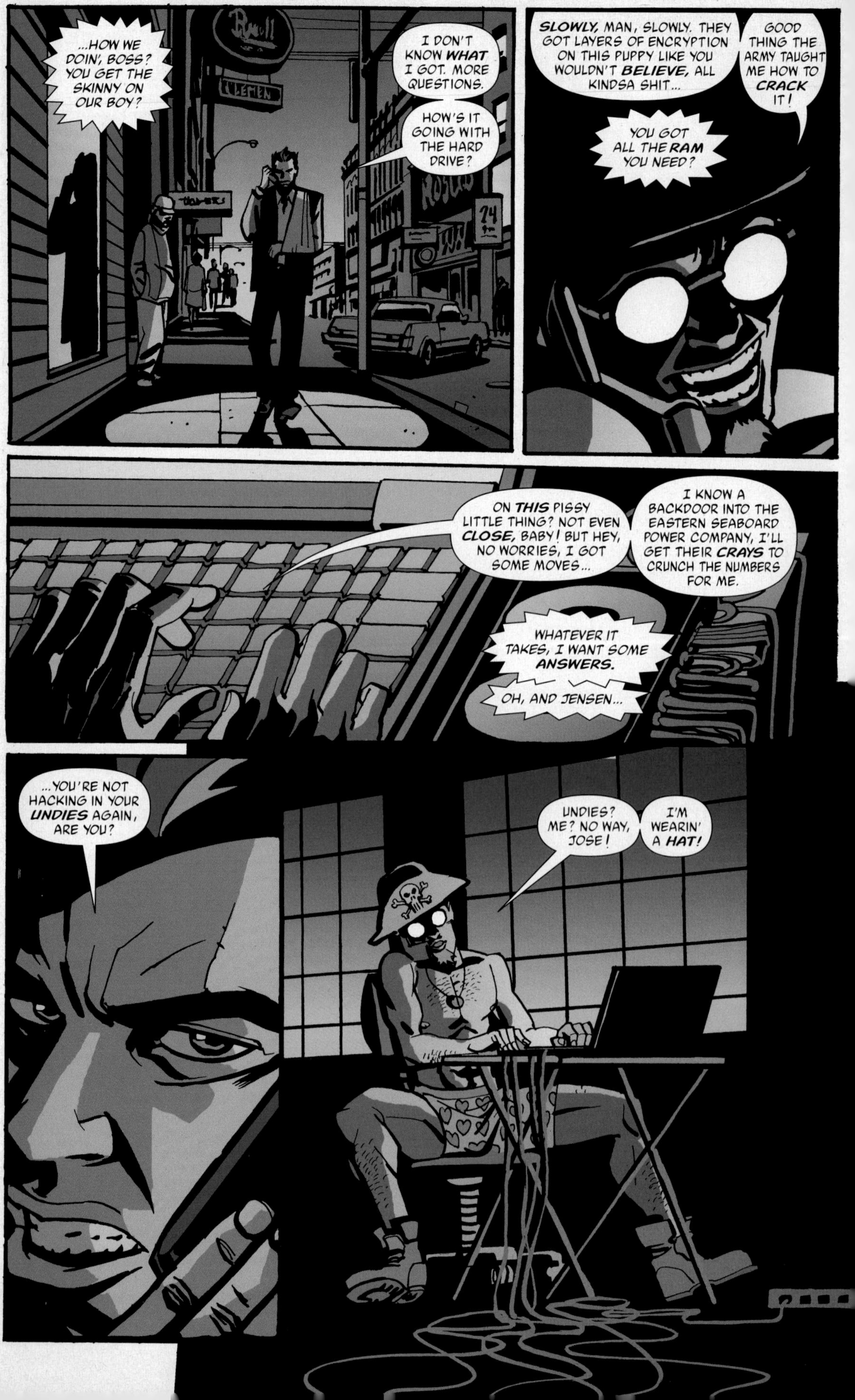
...HOW WE DOIN', BOSS? YOU GET THE SKINNY ON OUR BOY?
I DON'T KNOW WHAT I GOT. MORE QUESTIONS.
HOW'S IT GOING WITH THE HARD DRIVE?
SLOWLY, MAN, SLOWLY. THEY GOT LAYERS OF ENCRYPTION ON THIS PUPPY LIKE YOU WOULDN'T BELIEVE, ALL KINDSA SHIT...
GOOD THING THE ARMY TAUGHT ME HOW TO CRACK IT!
YOU GOT ALL THE RAM YOU NEED?
ON THIS PISSY LITTLE THING? NOT EVEN CLOSE, BABY! BUT HEY, NO WORRIES, I GOT SOME MOVES...
I KNOW A BACKDOOR INTO THE EASTERN SEABOARD POWER COMPANY, I'LL GET THEIR CRAYS TO CRUNCH THE NUMBERS FOR ME.
WHATEVER IT TAKES, I WANT SOME ANSWERS.
OH, AND JENSEN...
...YOU'RE NOT HACKING IN YOUR UNDIES AGAIN, ARE YOU?
UNDIES? ME? NO WAY, JOSE!
I'M WEARIN' A HAT!

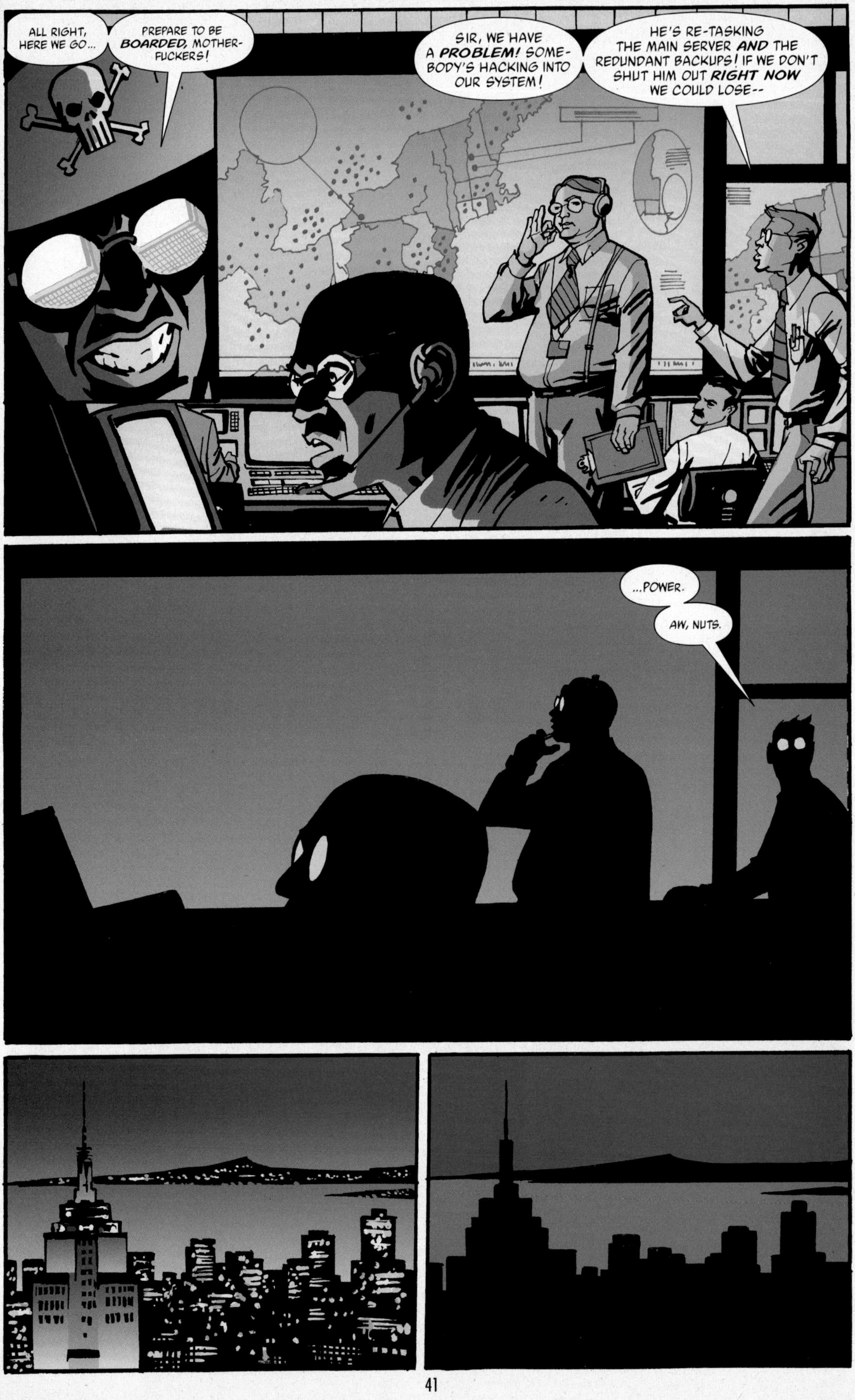
ALL RIGHT, HERE WE GO...
PREPARE TO BE BOARDED, MOTHER-FUCKERS!
SIR, WE HAVE A PROBLEM! SOMEBODY'S HACKING INTO OUR SYSTEM!
HE'S RE-TASKING THE MAIN SERVER AND THE REDUNDANT BACKUPS! IF WE DON'T SHUT HIM OUT RIGHT NOW WE COULD LOSE--
...POWER.
AW, NUTS.

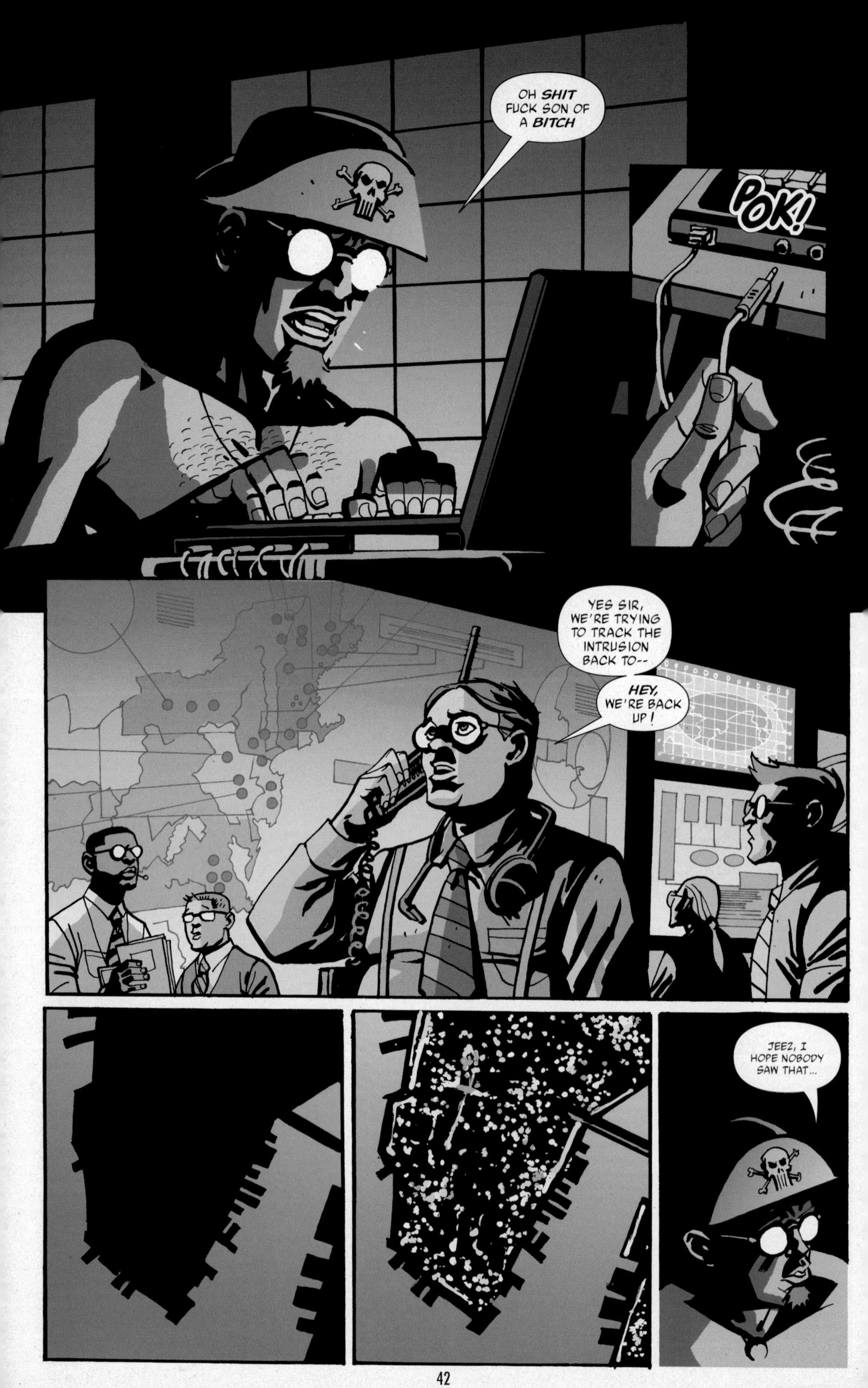
OH SHIT FUCK SON OF A BITCH
POK!
YES SIR, WE'RE TRYING TO TRACK THE INTRUSION BACK TO--
HEY, WE'RE BACK UP!
JEEZ, I HOPE NOBODY SAW THAT...

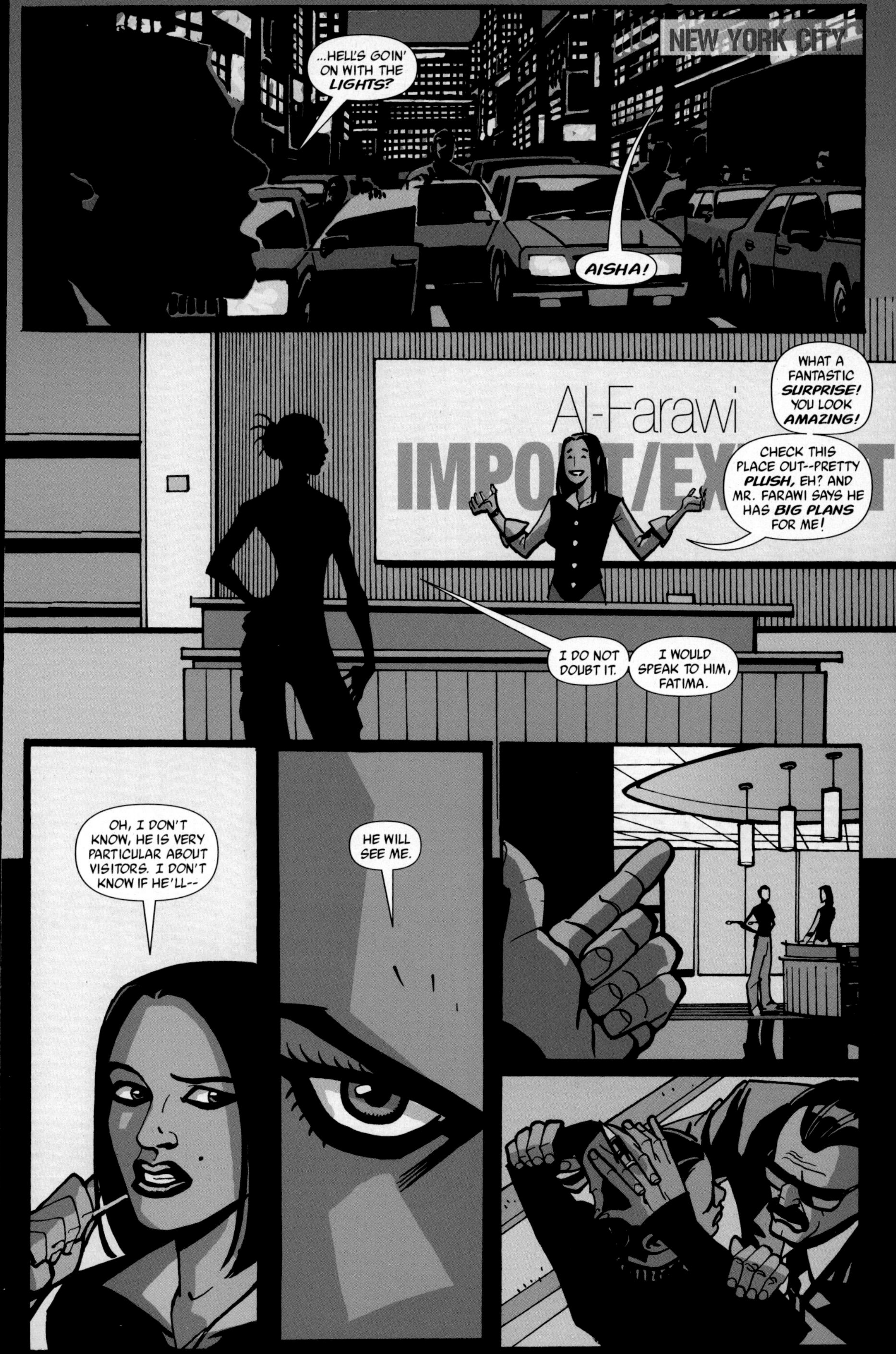
NEW YORK CITY
...HELL'S GOIN' ON WITH THE LIGHTS?
AISHA!
Al-Farawi IMPORT/EXPORT
WHAT A FANTASTIC SURPRISE! YOU LOOK AMAZING!
CHECK THIS PLACE OUT--PRETTY PLUSH, EH? AND MR. FARAWI SAYS HE HAS BIG PLANS FOR ME!
I DO NOT DOUBT IT.
I WOULD SPEAK TO HIM, FATIMA.
OH, I DON'T KNOW, HE IS VERY PARTICULAR ABOUT VISITORS. I DON'T KNOW IF HE'LL--
HE WILL SEE ME.

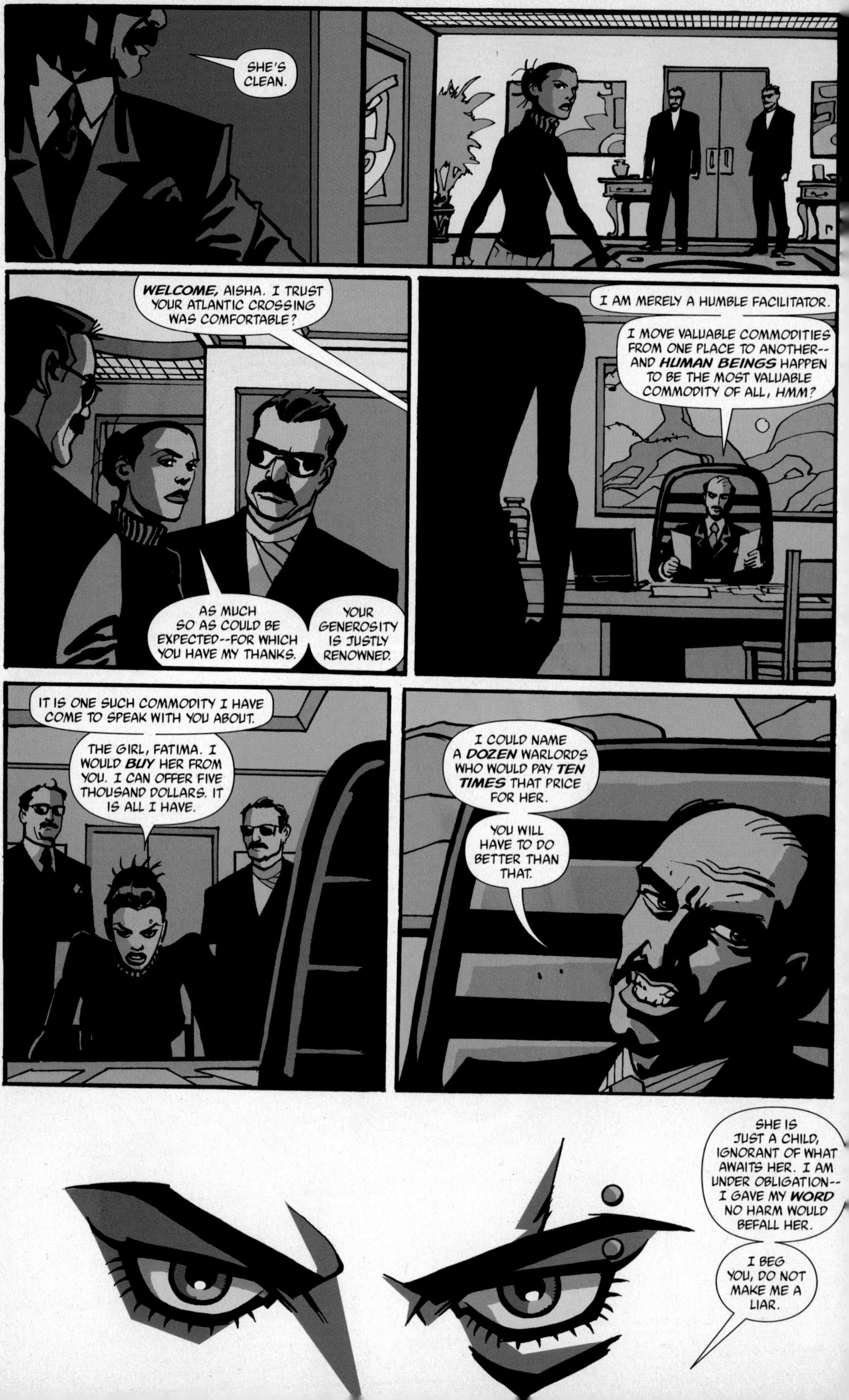
SHE'S CLEAN.
WELCOME, AISHA. I TRUST YOUR ATLANTIC CROSSING WAS COMFORTABLE?
AS MUCH SO AS COULD BE EXPECTED--FOR WHICH YOU HAVE MY THANKS.
YOUR GENEROSITY IS JUSTLY RENOWNED.
I AM MERELY A HUMBLE FACILITATOR.
I MOVE VALUABLE COMMODITIES FROM ONE PLACE TO ANOTHER--AND HUMAN BEINGS HAPPEN TO BE THE MOST VALUABLE COMMODITY OF ALL, HMM?
IT IS ONE SUCH COMMODITY I HAVE COME TO SPEAK WITH YOU ABOUT.
THE GIRL, FATIMA. I WOULD BUY HER FROM YOU. I CAN OFFER FIVE THOUSAND DOLLARS. IT IS ALL I HAVE.
I COULD NAME A DOZEN WARLORDS WHO WOULD PAY TEN TIMES THAT PRICE FOR HER.
YOU WILL HAVE TO DO BETTER THAN THAT.
SHE IS JUST A CHILD, IGNORANT OF WHAT AWAITS HER. I AM UNDER OBLIGATION--I GAVE MY WORD NO HARM WOULD BEFALL HER.
I BEG YOU, DO NOT MAKE ME A LIAR.

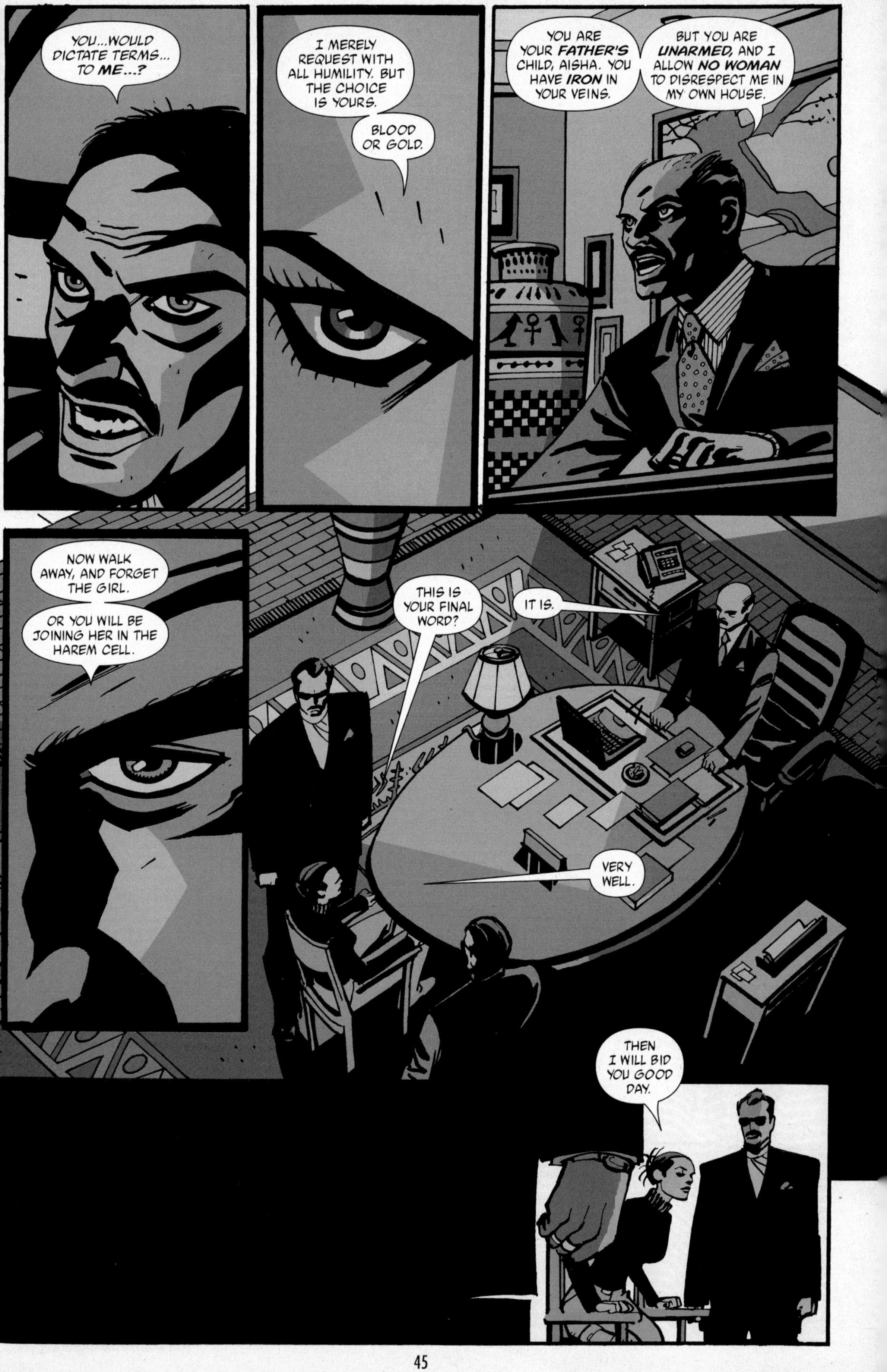
YOU...WOULD DICTATE TERMS... TO ME...?
I MERELY REQUEST WITH ALL HUMILITY. BUT THE CHOICE IS YOURS.
BLOOD OR GOLD.
YOU ARE YOUR FATHER'S CHILD, AISHA. YOU HAVE IRON IN YOUR VEINS.
BUT YOU ARE UNARMED, AND I ALLOW NO WOMAN TO DISRESPECT ME IN MY OWN HOUSE.
NOW WALK AWAY, AND FORGET THE GIRL.
OR YOU WILL BE JOINING HER IN THE HAREM CELL.
THIS IS YOUR FINAL WORD?
IT IS.
VERY WELL.
THEN I WILL BID YOU GOOD DAY.

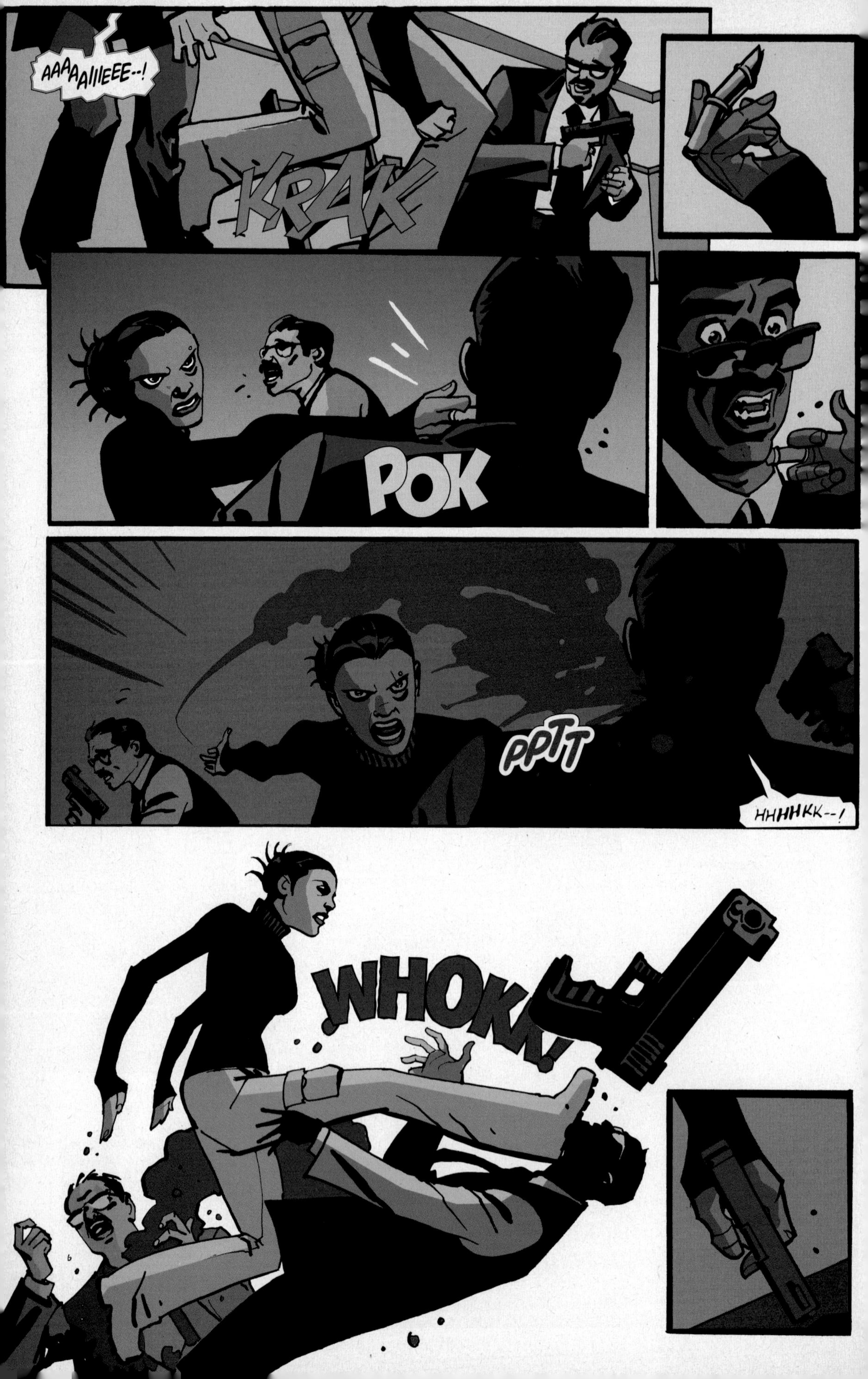
AAAAAIIIEEE--!
KRAK
POK
PPTT
HHHHKK--!
WHOKK!

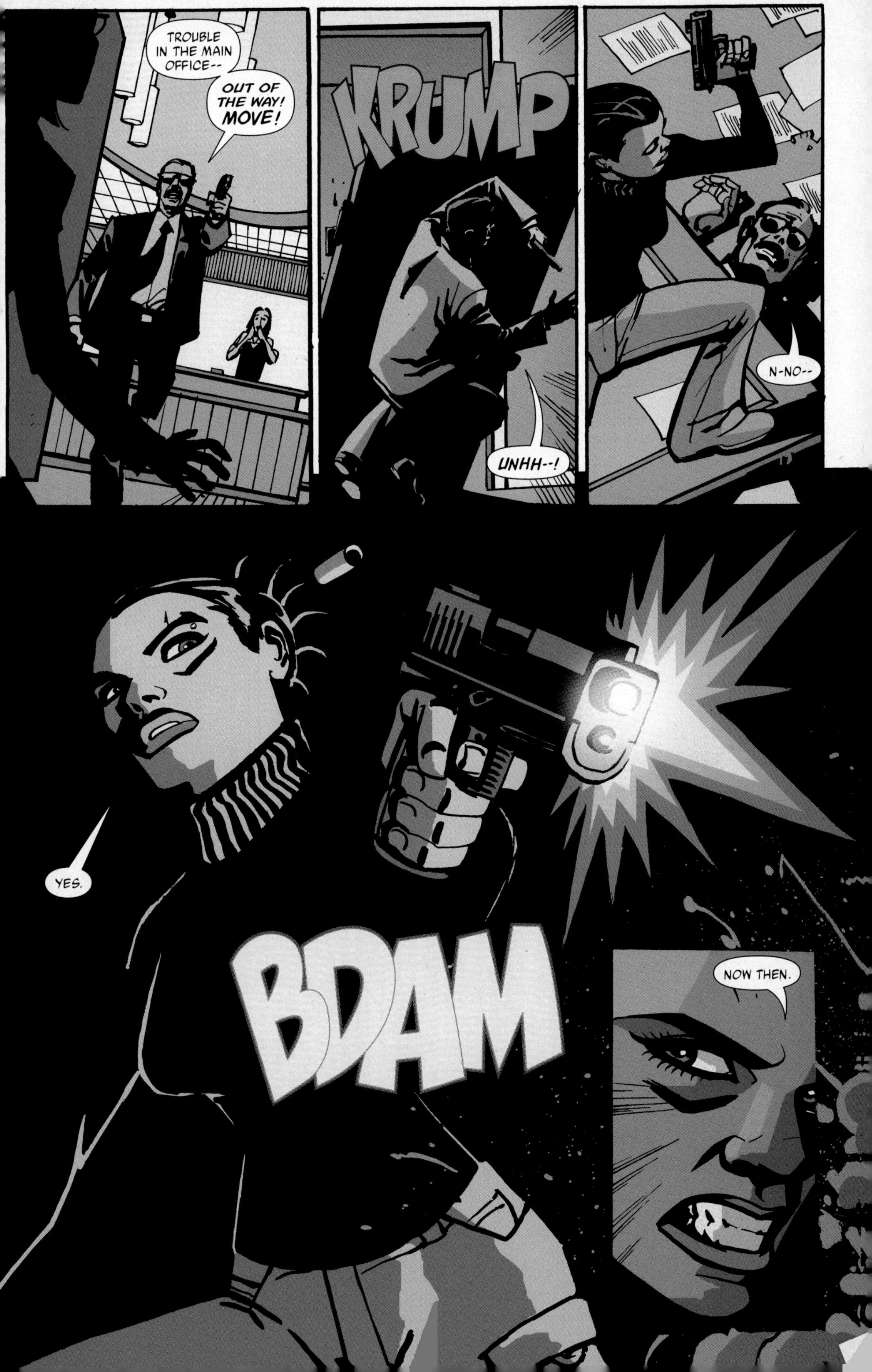
TROUBLE IN THE MAIN OFFICE--
OUT OF THE WAY! MOVE!
KRUMP
UNHH--!
N-NO--
YES.
BDAM
NOW THEN.

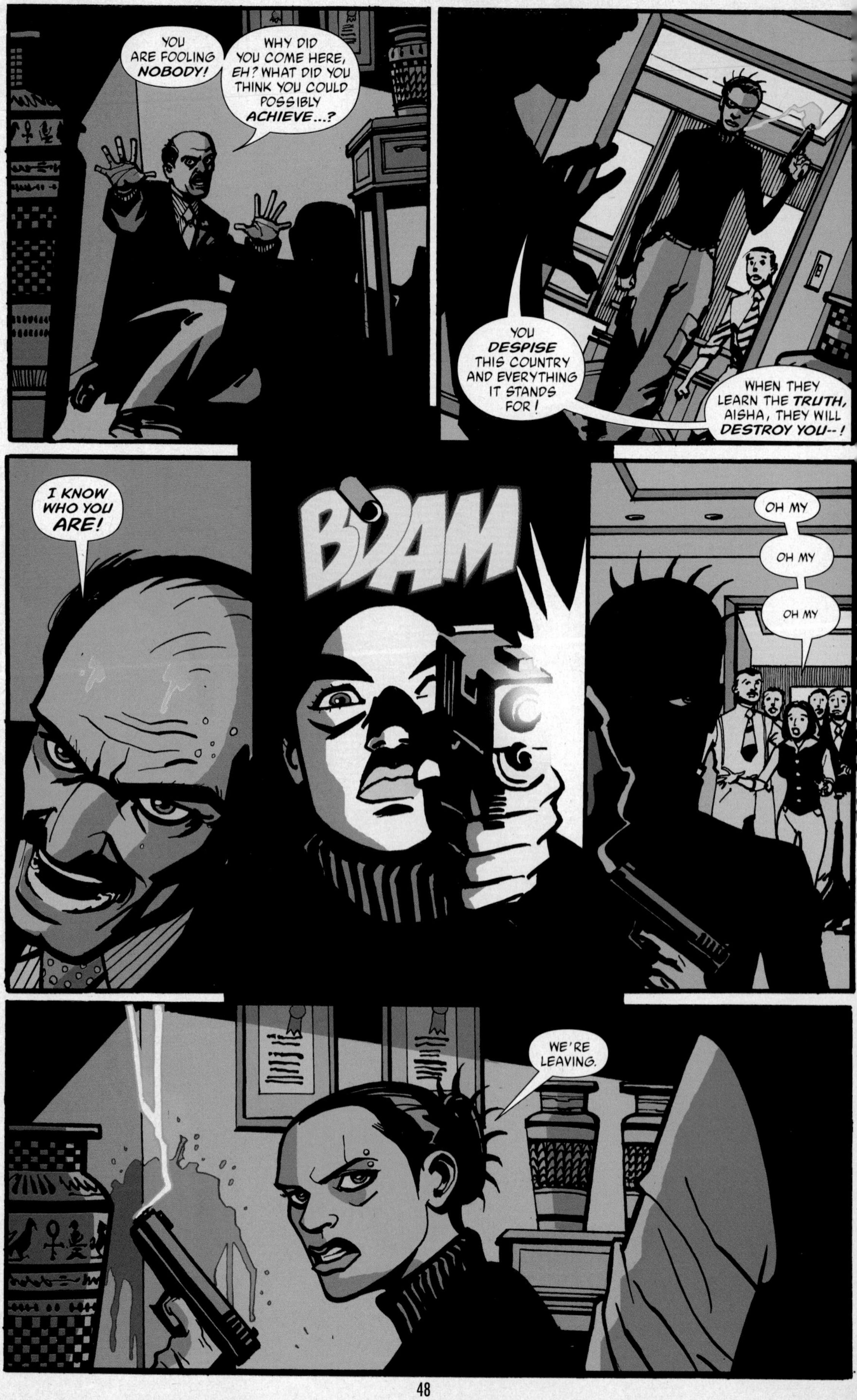
YOU ARE FOOLING NOBODY!
WHY DID YOU COME HERE, EH? WHAT DID YOU THINK YOU COULD POSSIBLY ACHIEVE...?
YOU DESPISE THIS COUNTRY AND EVERYTHING IT STANDS FOR!
WHEN THEY LEARN THE TRUTH, AISHA, THEY WILL DESTROY YOU--!
I KNOW WHO YOU ARE!
BLAM
OH MY
OH MY
OH MY
WE'RE LEAVING.

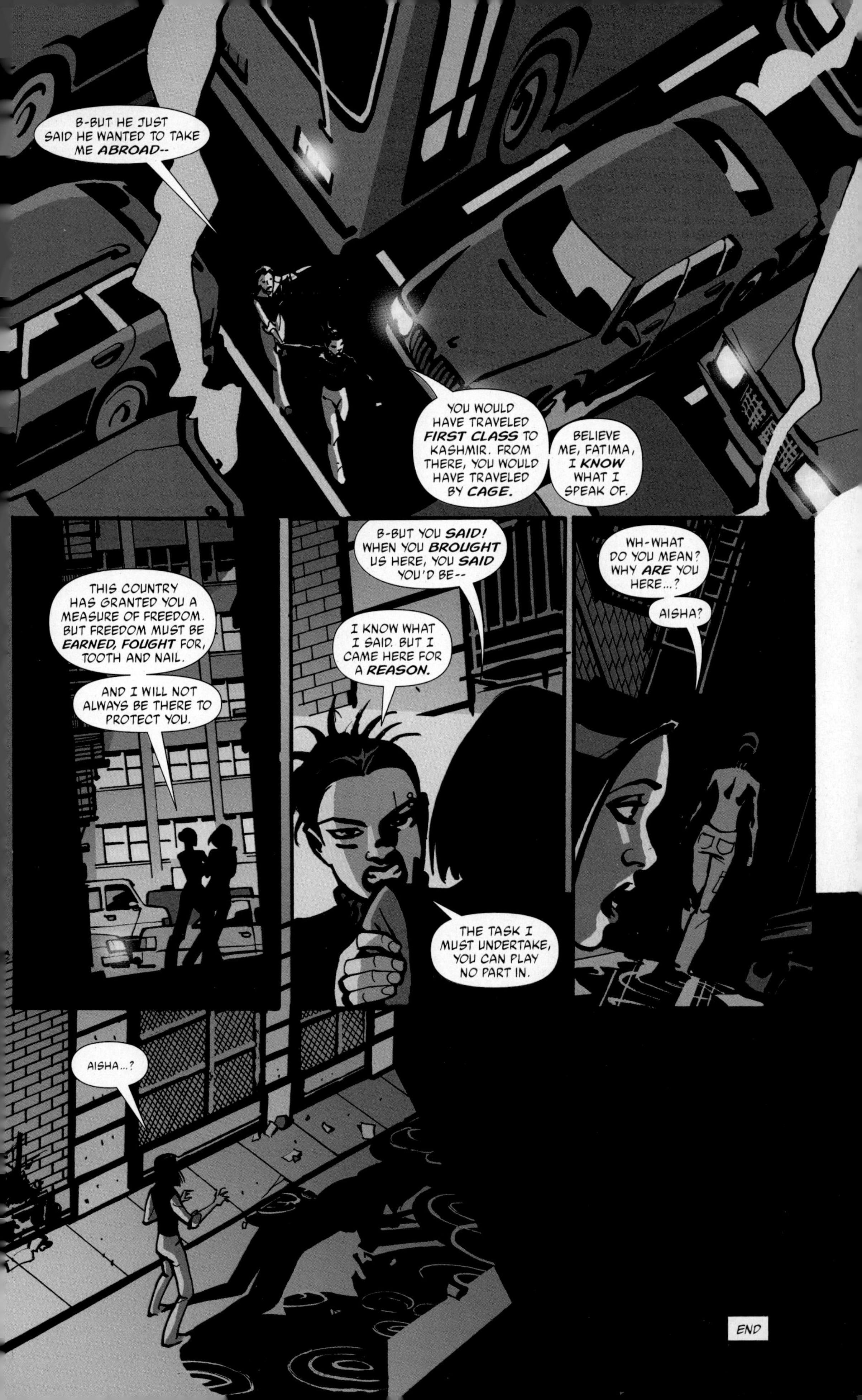
B-BUT HE JUST SAID HE WANTED TO TAKE ME ABROAD--
YOU WOULD HAVE TRAVELED FIRST CLASS TO KASHMIR. FROM THERE, YOU WOULD HAVE TRAVELED BY CAGE.
BELIEVE ME, FATIMA, I KNOW WHAT I SPEAK OF.
THIS COUNTRY HAS GRANTED YOU A MEASURE OF FREEDOM. BUT FREEDOM MUST BE EARNED, FOUGHT FOR, TOOTH AND NAIL.
AND I WILL NOT ALWAYS BE THERE TO PROTECT YOU.
B-BUT YOU SAID! WHEN YOU BROUGHT US HERE, YOU SAID YOU'D BE--
I KNOW WHAT I SAID. BUT I CAME HERE FOR A REASON.
THE TASK I MUST UNDERTAKE, YOU CAN PLAY NO PART IN.
WH-WHAT DO YOU MEAN? WHY ARE YOU HERE...?
AISHA?
AISHA...?
END

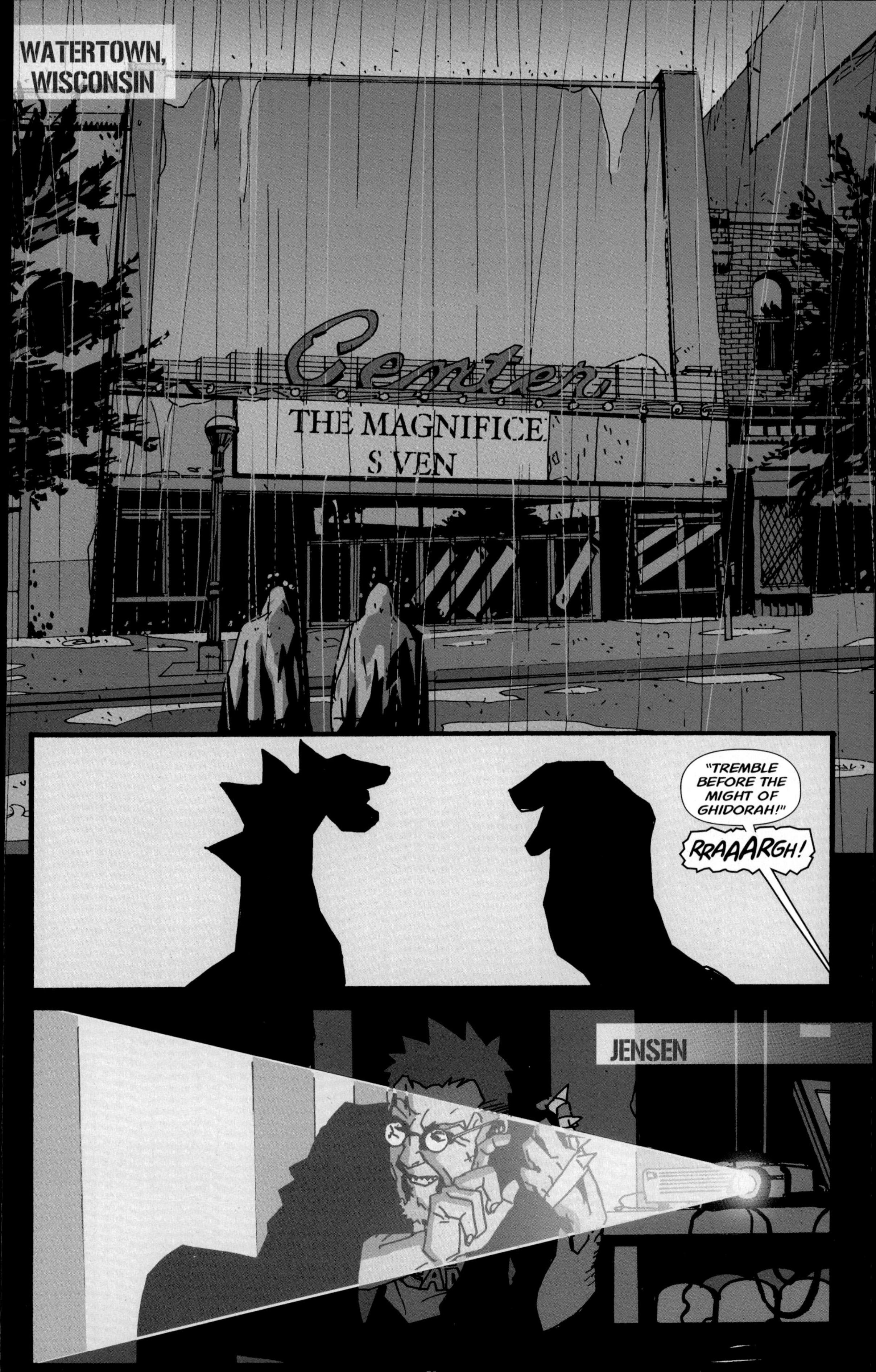
WATERTOWN, WISCONSIN
Center
THE MAGNIFICE
S VEN
"TREMBLE BEFORE THE MIGHT OF GHIDORAH!"
RRAAARGH!
JENSEN

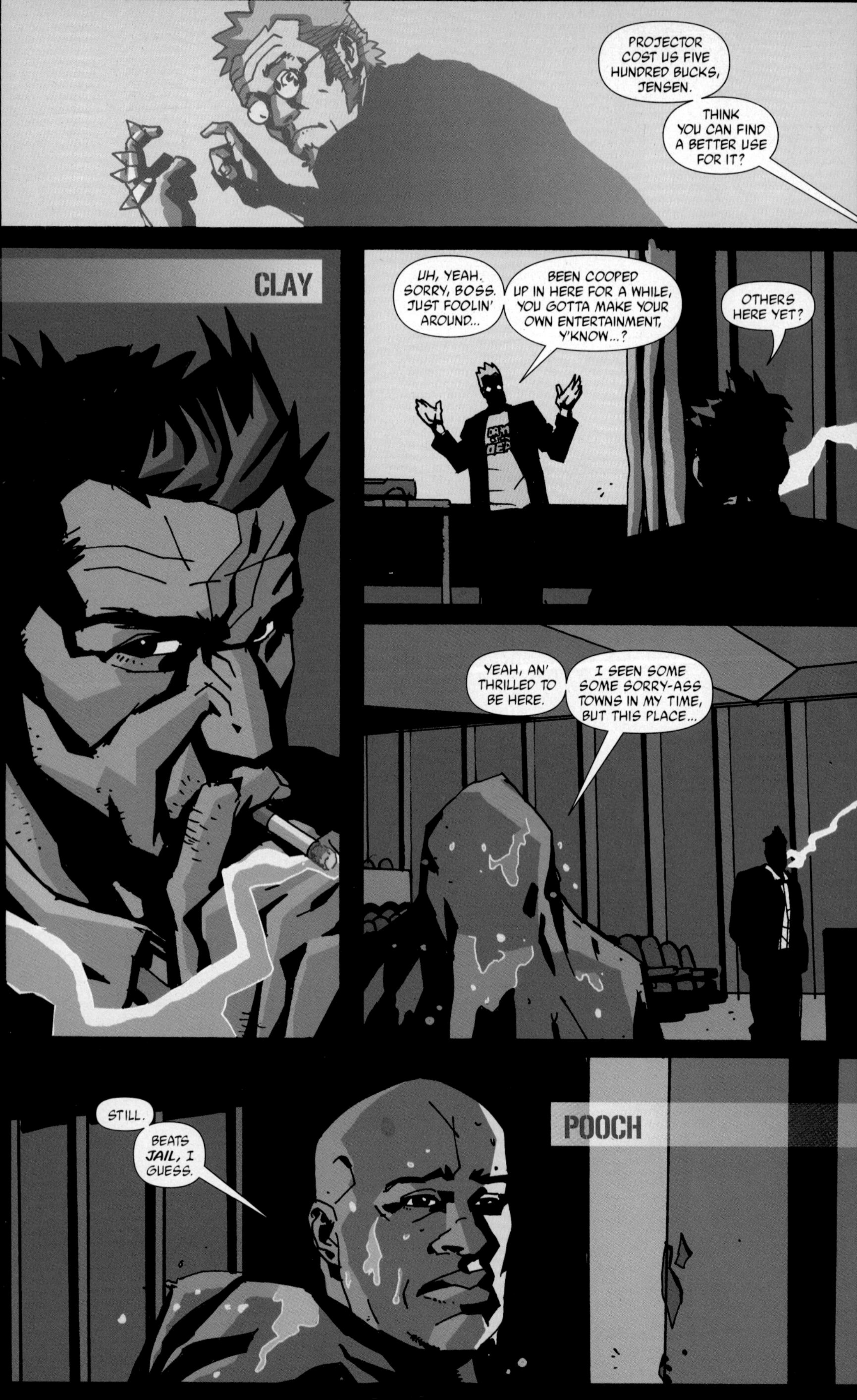

PROJECTOR COST US FIVE HUNDRED BUCKS, JENSEN.
THINK YOU CAN FIND A BETTER USE FOR IT?
CLAY
UH, YEAH. SORRY, BOSS. JUST FOOLIN' AROUND...
BEEN COOPED UP IN HERE FOR A WHILE, YOU GOTTA MAKE YOUR OWN ENTERTAINMENT, Y'KNOW...?
OTHERS HERE YET?
YEAH, AN' THRILLED TO BE HERE.
I SEEN SOME SOME SORRY-ASS TOWNS IN MY TIME, BUT THIS PLACE...
STILL.
BEATS JAIL, I GUESS.
POOCH

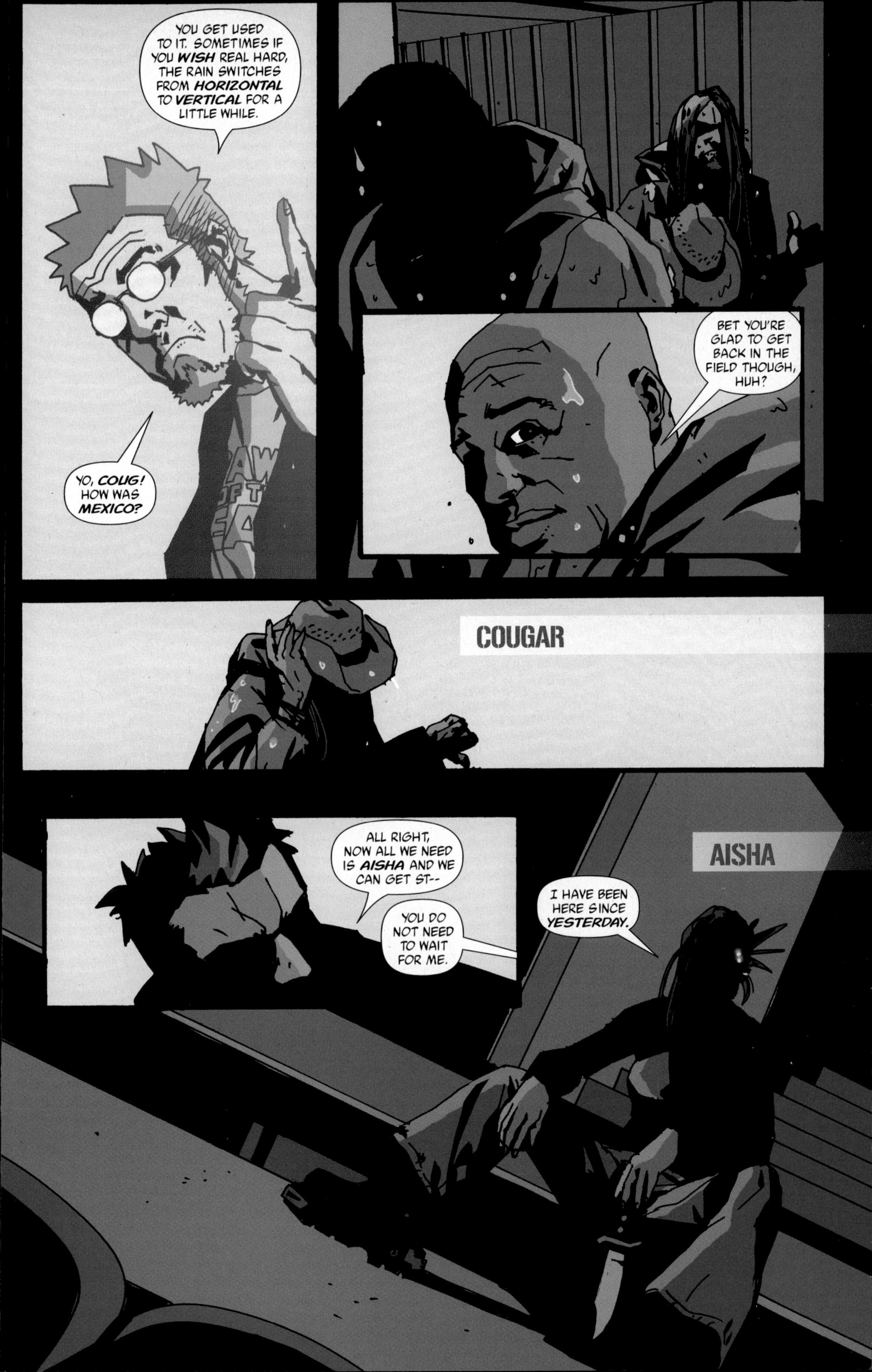
YOU GET USED TO IT. SOMETIMES IF YOU **WISH** REAL HARD, THE RAIN SWITCHES FROM **HORIZONTAL** TO **VERTICAL** FOR A LITTLE WHILE.
YO, **COUG!** HOW WAS **MEXICO?**
BET YOU'RE GLAD TO GET BACK IN THE FIELD THOUGH, HUH?
COUGAR
ALL RIGHT, NOW ALL WE NEED IS **AISHA** AND WE CAN GET ST--
YOU DO NOT NEED TO WAIT FOR ME.
AISHA
I HAVE BEEN HERE SINCE **YESTERDAY.**

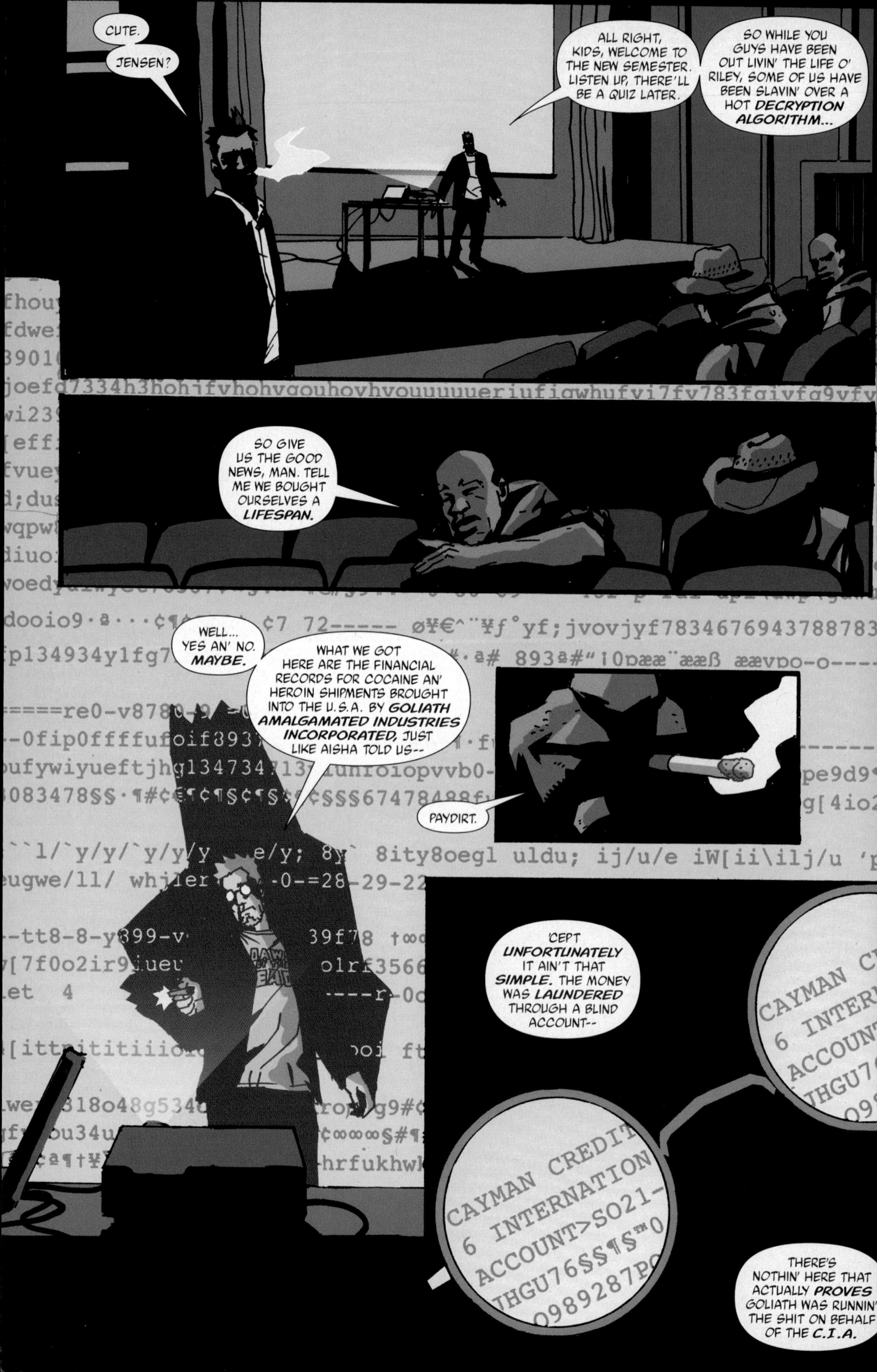
CUTE.
JENSEN?
ALL RIGHT, KIDS, WELCOME TO THE NEW SEMESTER. LISTEN UP, THERE'LL BE A QUIZ LATER.
SO WHILE YOU GUYS HAVE BEEN OUT LIVIN' THE LIFE O' RILEY, SOME OF US HAVE BEEN SLAVIN' OVER A HOT DECRYPTION ALGORITHM...
SO GIVE US THE GOOD NEWS, MAN. TELL ME WE BOUGHT OURSELVES A LIFESPAN.
WELL... YES AN' NO. MAYBE.
WHAT WE GOT HERE ARE THE FINANCIAL RECORDS FOR COCAINE AN' HEROIN SHIPMENTS BROUGHT INTO THE U.S.A. BY GOLIATH AMALGAMATED INDUSTRIES INCORPORATED, JUST LIKE AISHA TOLD US--
PAYDIRT.
'CEPT UNFORTUNATELY IT AIN'T THAT SIMPLE. THE MONEY WAS LAUNDERED THROUGH A BLIND ACCOUNT--
CAYMAN CREDIT
6 INTERNATION
ACCOUNT>SO21-
THERE'S NOTHIN' HERE THAT ACTUALLY PROVES GOLIATH WAS RUNNIN' THE SHIT ON BEHALF OF THE C.I.A.

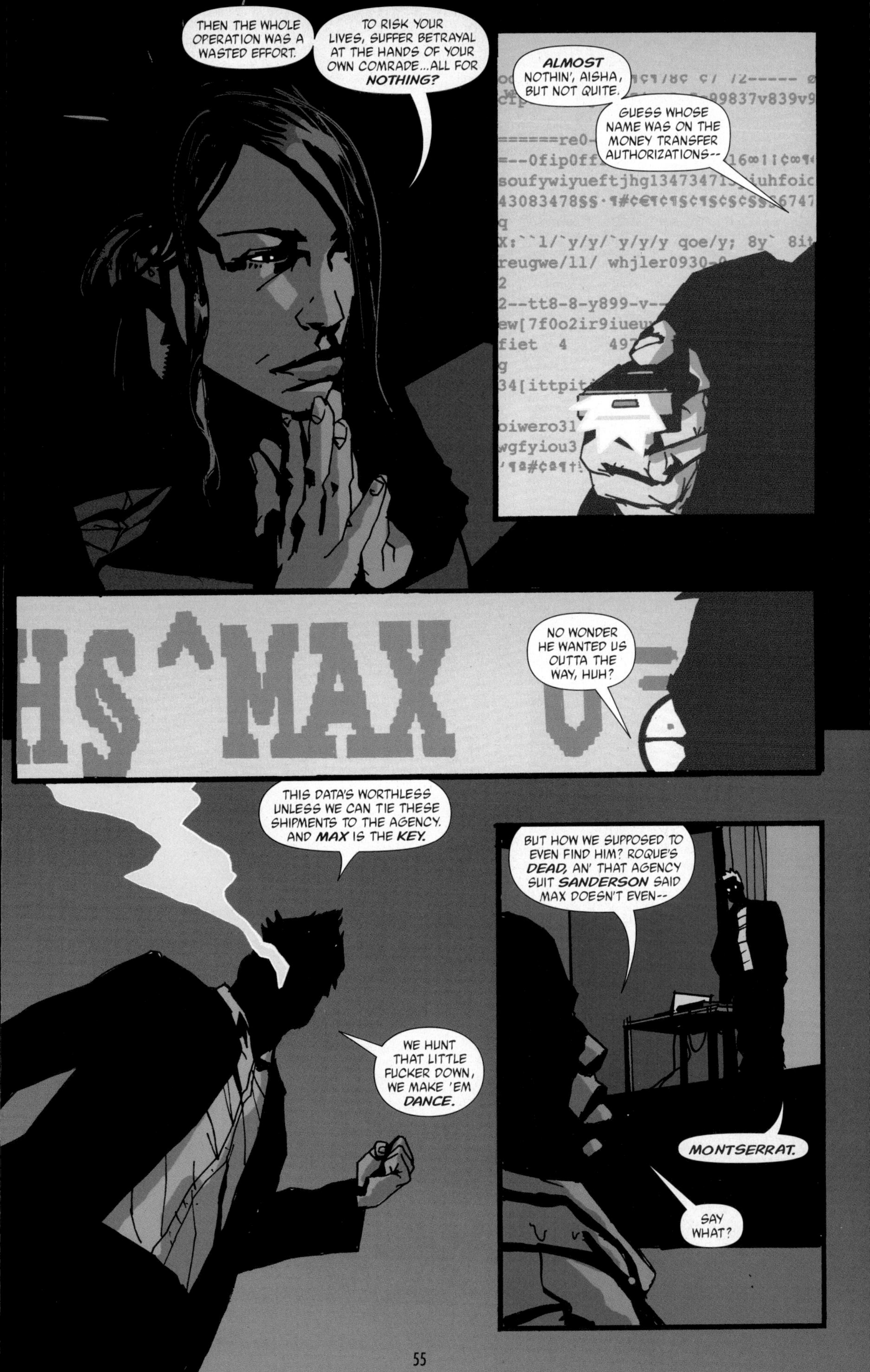
THEN THE WHOLE OPERATION WAS A WASTED EFFORT.
TO RISK YOUR LIVES, SUFFER BETRAYAL AT THE HANDS OF YOUR OWN COMRADE...ALL FOR NOTHING?
ALMOST NOTHIN', AISHA, BUT NOT QUITE.
GUESS WHOSE NAME WAS ON THE MONEY TRANSFER AUTHORIZATIONS--
HS^MAX
NO WONDER HE WANTED US OUTTA THE WAY, HUH?
THIS DATA'S WORTHLESS UNLESS WE CAN TIE THESE SHIPMENTS TO THE AGENCY. AND MAX IS THE KEY.
WE HUNT THAT LITTLE FUCKER DOWN, WE MAKE 'EM DANCE.
BUT HOW WE SUPPOSED TO EVEN FIND HIM? ROQUE'S DEAD, AN' THAT AGENCY SUIT SANDERSON SAID MAX DOESN'T EVEN--
MONTSERRAT.
SAY WHAT?

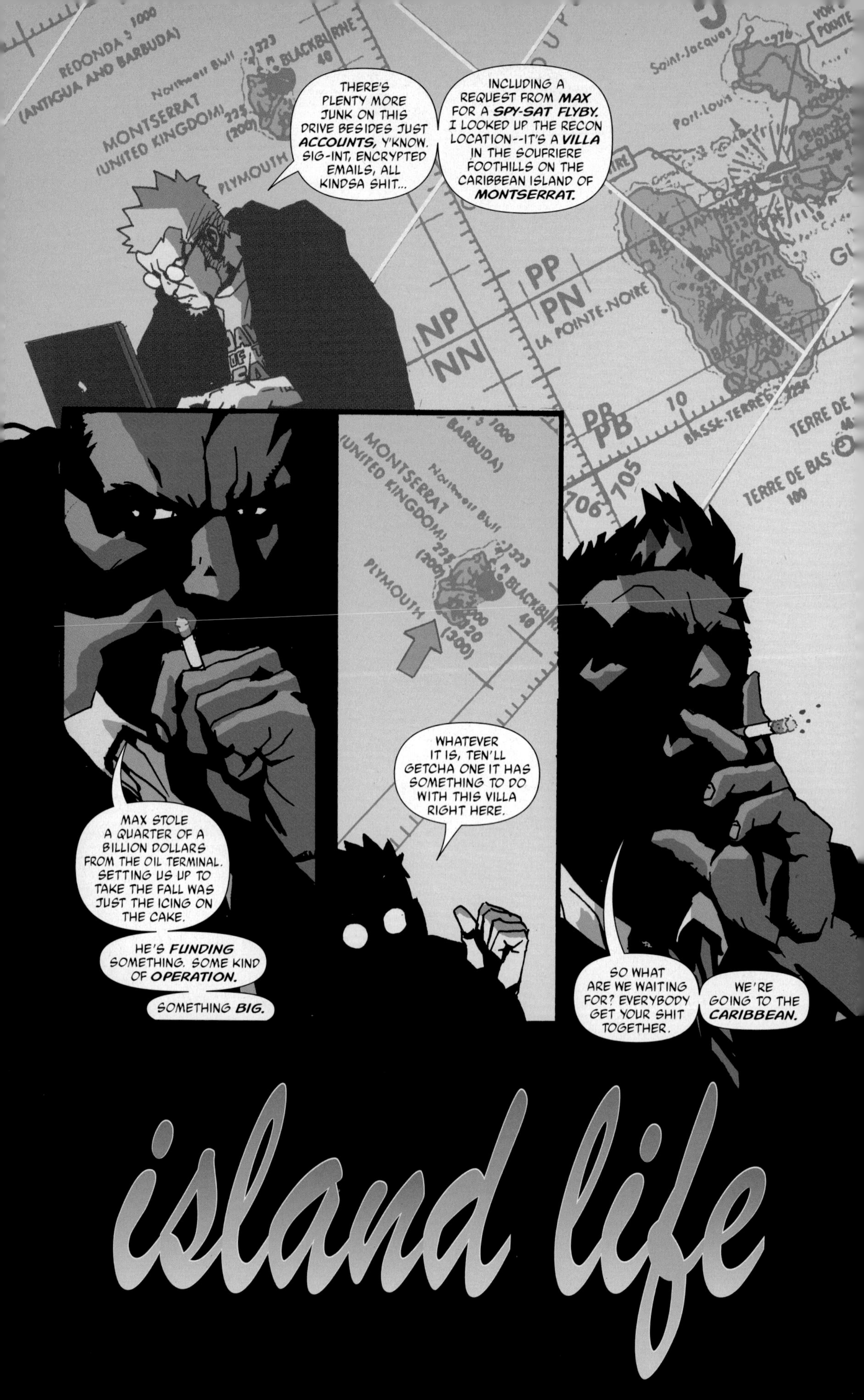
THERE'S PLENTY MORE JUNK ON THIS DRIVE BESIDES JUST ACCOUNTS, Y'KNOW. SIG-INT, ENCRYPTED EMAILS, ALL KINDSA SHIT...
INCLUDING A REQUEST FROM MAX FOR A SPY-SAT FLYBY. I LOOKED UP THE RECON LOCATION--IT'S A VILLA IN THE SOUFRIERE FOOTHILLS ON THE CARIBBEAN ISLAND OF MONTSERRAT.
MAX STOLE A QUARTER OF A BILLION DOLLARS FROM THE OIL TERMINAL. SETTING US UP TO TAKE THE FALL WAS JUST THE ICING ON THE CAKE.
HE'S FUNDING SOMETHING. SOME KIND OF OPERATION.
SOMETHING BIG.
WHATEVER IT IS, TEN'LL GETCHA ONE IT HAS SOMETHING TO DO WITH THIS VILLA RIGHT HERE.
SO WHAT ARE WE WAITING FOR? EVERYBODY GET YOUR SHIT TOGETHER.
WE'RE GOING TO THE CARIBBEAN.
island life

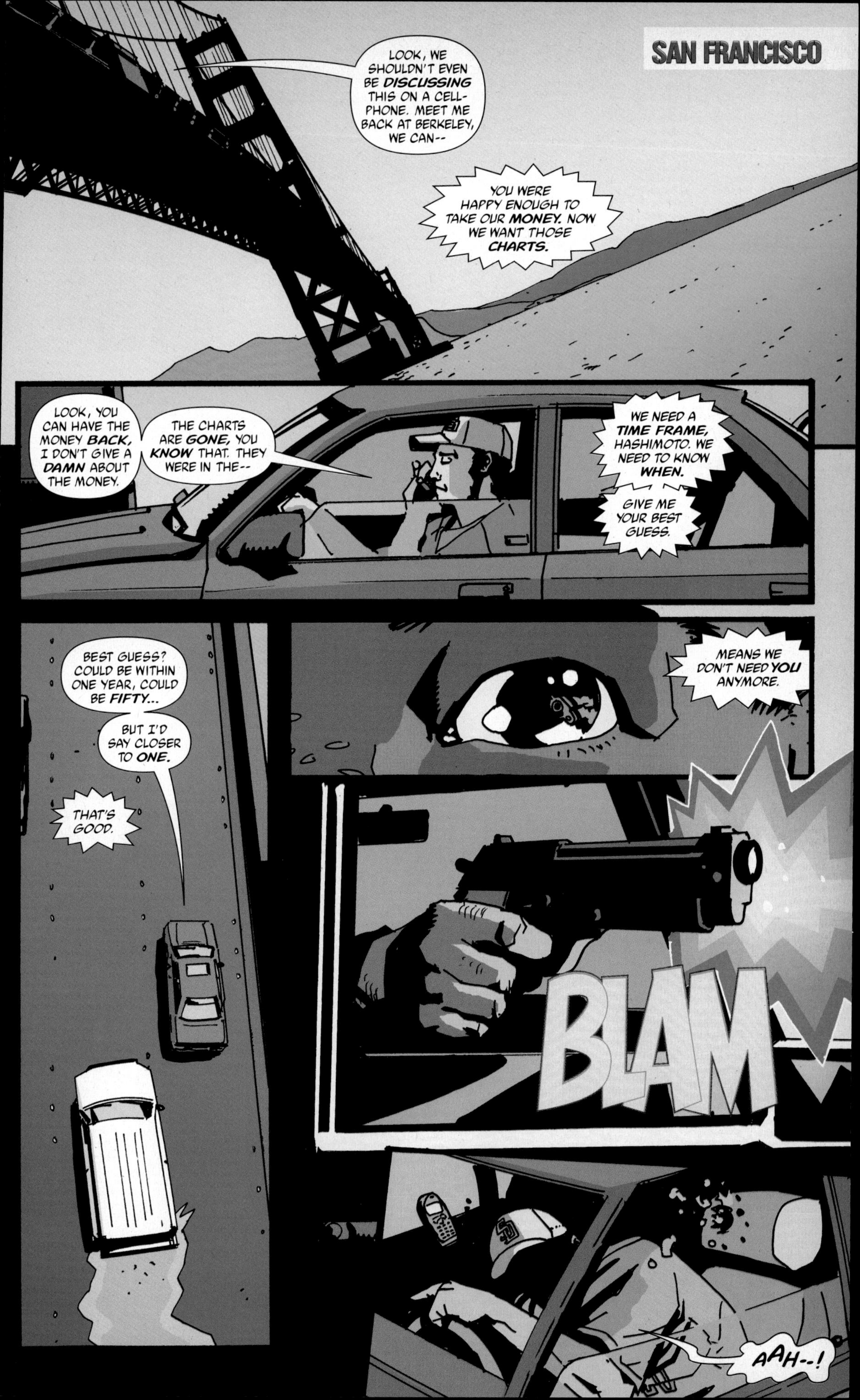
SAN FRANCISCO
LOOK, WE SHOULDN'T EVEN BE DISCUSSING THIS ON A CELL-PHONE. MEET ME BACK AT BERKELEY, WE CAN--
YOU WERE HAPPY ENOUGH TO TAKE OUR MONEY. NOW WE WANT THOSE CHARTS.
LOOK, YOU CAN HAVE THE MONEY BACK, I DON'T GIVE A DAMN ABOUT THE MONEY.
THE CHARTS ARE GONE, YOU KNOW THAT. THEY WERE IN THE--
WE NEED A TIME FRAME, HASHIMOTO. WE NEED TO KNOW WHEN.
GIVE ME YOUR BEST GUESS.
BEST GUESS? COULD BE WITHIN ONE YEAR, COULD BE FIFTY...
BUT I'D SAY CLOSER TO ONE.
THAT'S GOOD.
MEANS WE DON'T NEED YOU ANYMORE.
BLAM
AAH--!

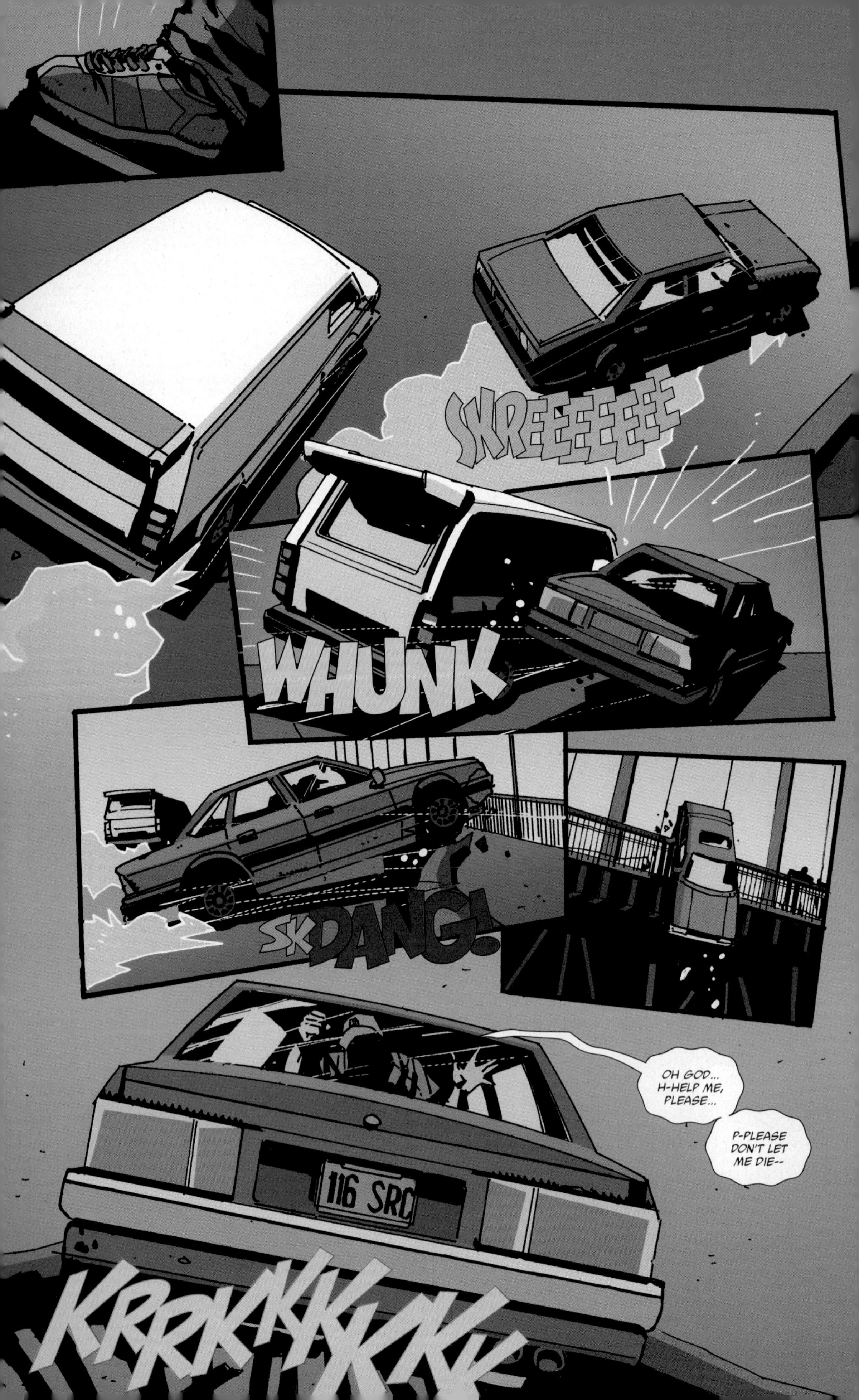

SKREEEEEEE
WHUNK
SKDANG!
OH GOD... H-HELP ME, PLEASE...
P-PLEASE DON'T LET ME DIE--
116 SRC
KRRKKKKKK

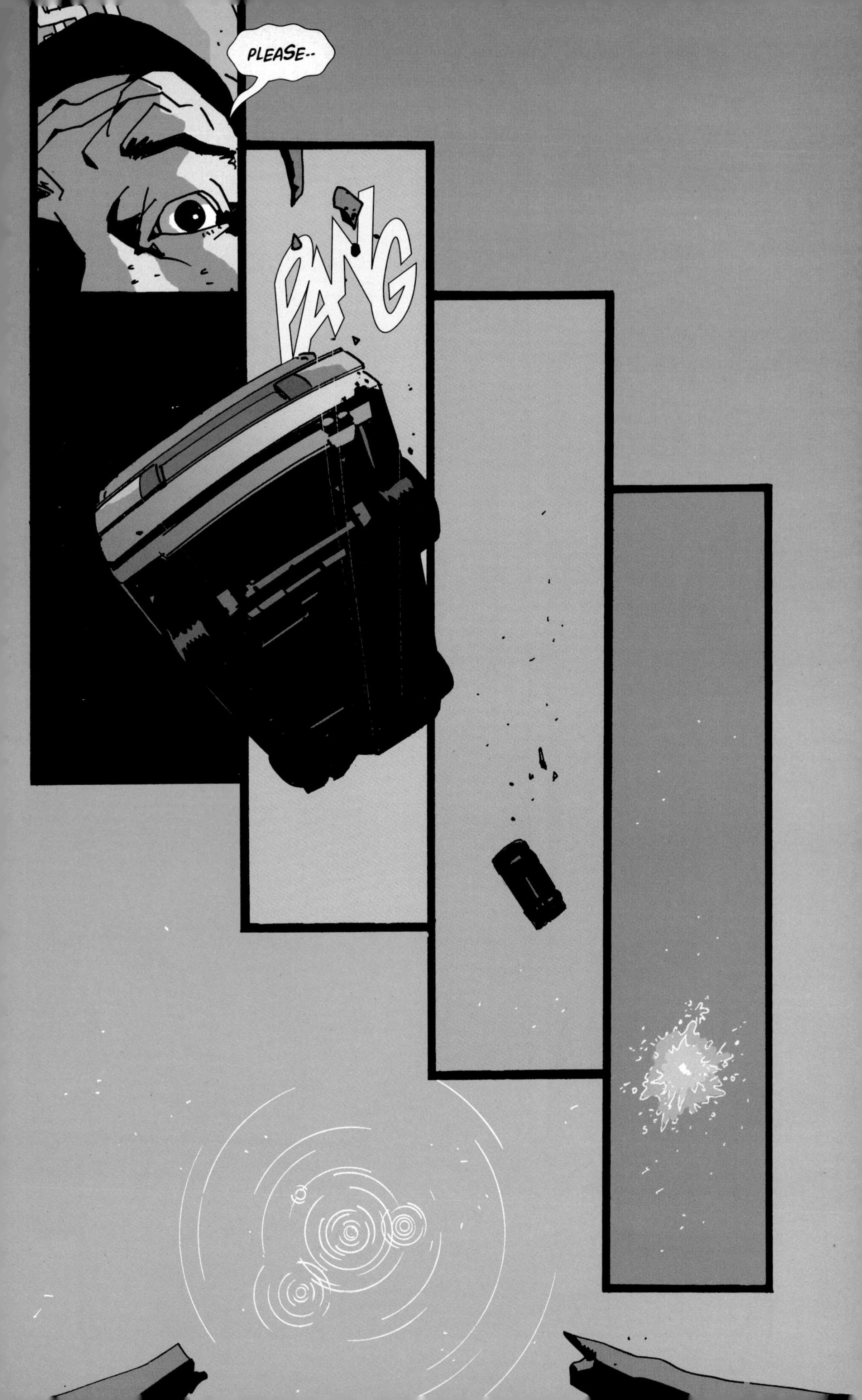
PLEASE--
PANG

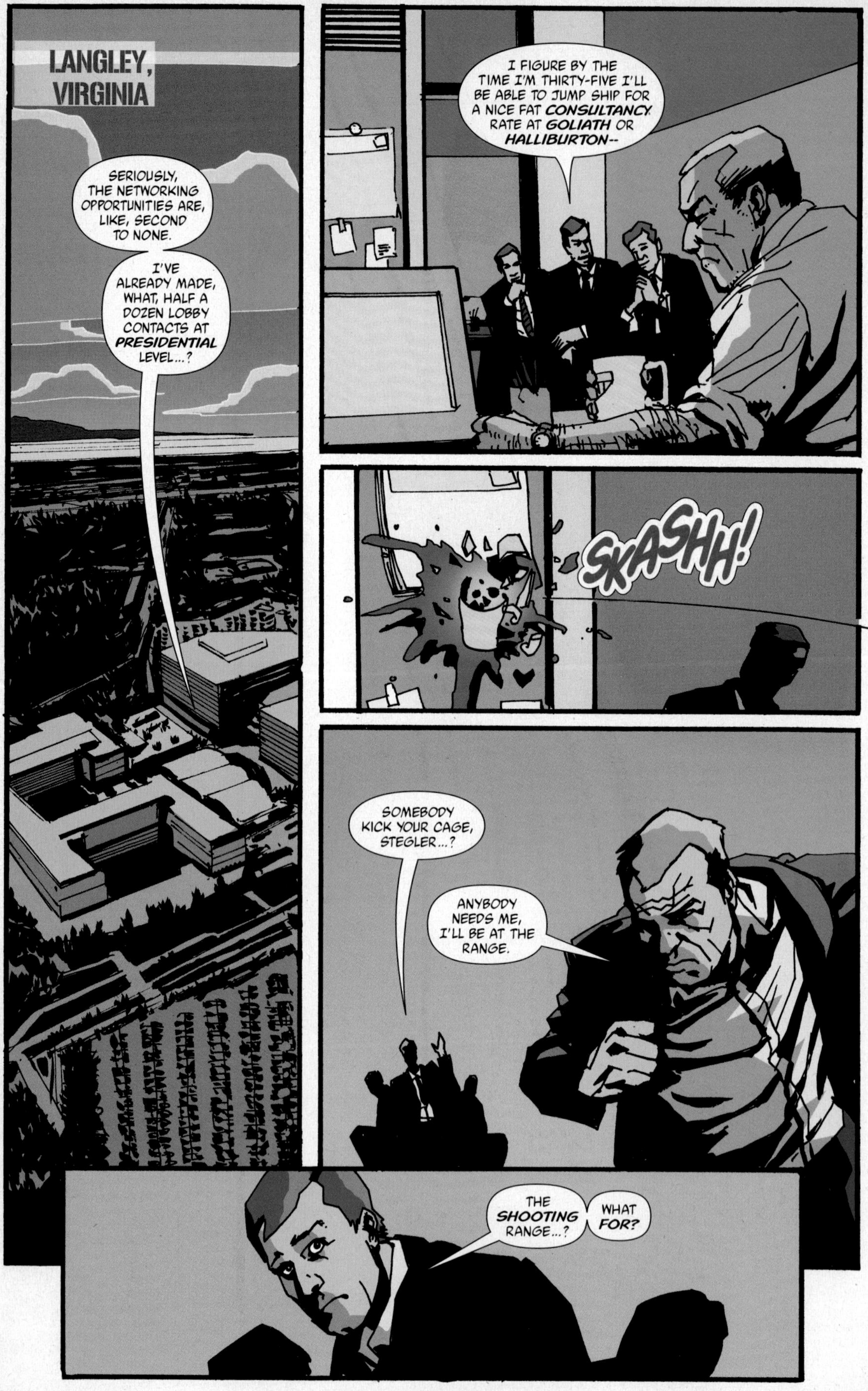
LANGLEY, VIRGINIA
SERIOUSLY, THE NETWORKING OPPORTUNITIES ARE, LIKE, SECOND TO NONE.
I'VE ALREADY MADE, WHAT, HALF A DOZEN LOBBY CONTACTS AT PRESIDENTIAL LEVEL...?
I FIGURE BY THE TIME I'M THIRTY-FIVE I'LL BE ABLE TO JUMP SHIP FOR A NICE FAT CONSULTANCY RATE AT GOLIATH OR HALLIBURTON--
SKASHH!
SOMEBODY KICK YOUR CAGE, STEGLER...?
ANYBODY NEEDS ME, I'LL BE AT THE RANGE.
THE SHOOTING RANGE...?
WHAT FOR?

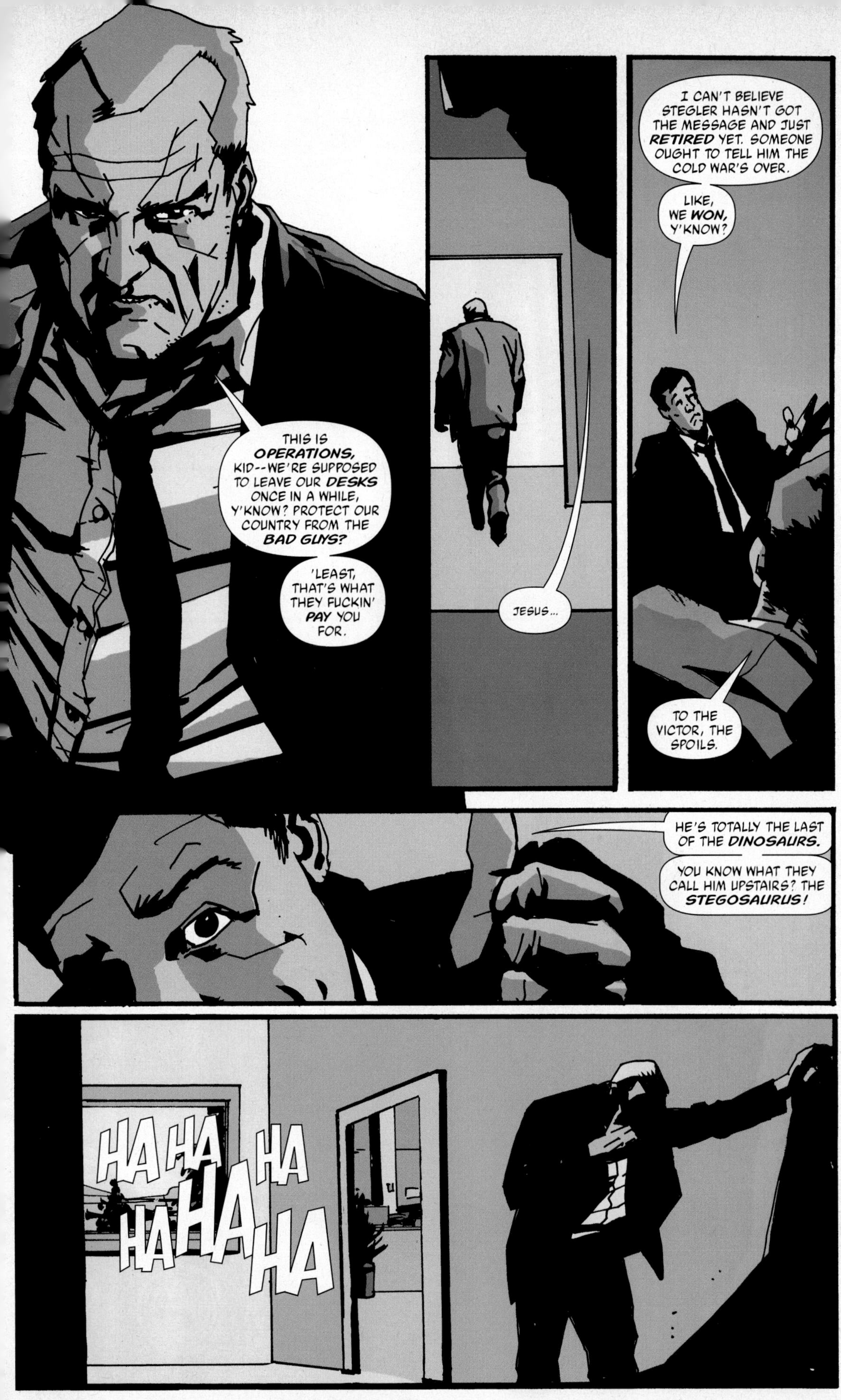
THIS IS OPERATIONS, KID--WE'RE SUPPOSED TO LEAVE OUR DESKS ONCE IN A WHILE, Y'KNOW? PROTECT OUR COUNTRY FROM THE BAD GUYS?
'LEAST, THAT'S WHAT THEY FUCKIN' PAY YOU FOR.
JESUS...
I CAN'T BELIEVE STEGLER HASN'T GOT THE MESSAGE AND JUST RETIRED YET. SOMEONE OUGHT TO TELL HIM THE COLD WAR'S OVER.
LIKE, WE WON, Y'KNOW?
TO THE VICTOR, THE SPOILS.
HE'S TOTALLY THE LAST OF THE DINOSAURS.
YOU KNOW WHAT THEY CALL HIM UPSTAIRS? THE STEGOSAURUS!
HA HA HA HA
HA HA HA HA HA

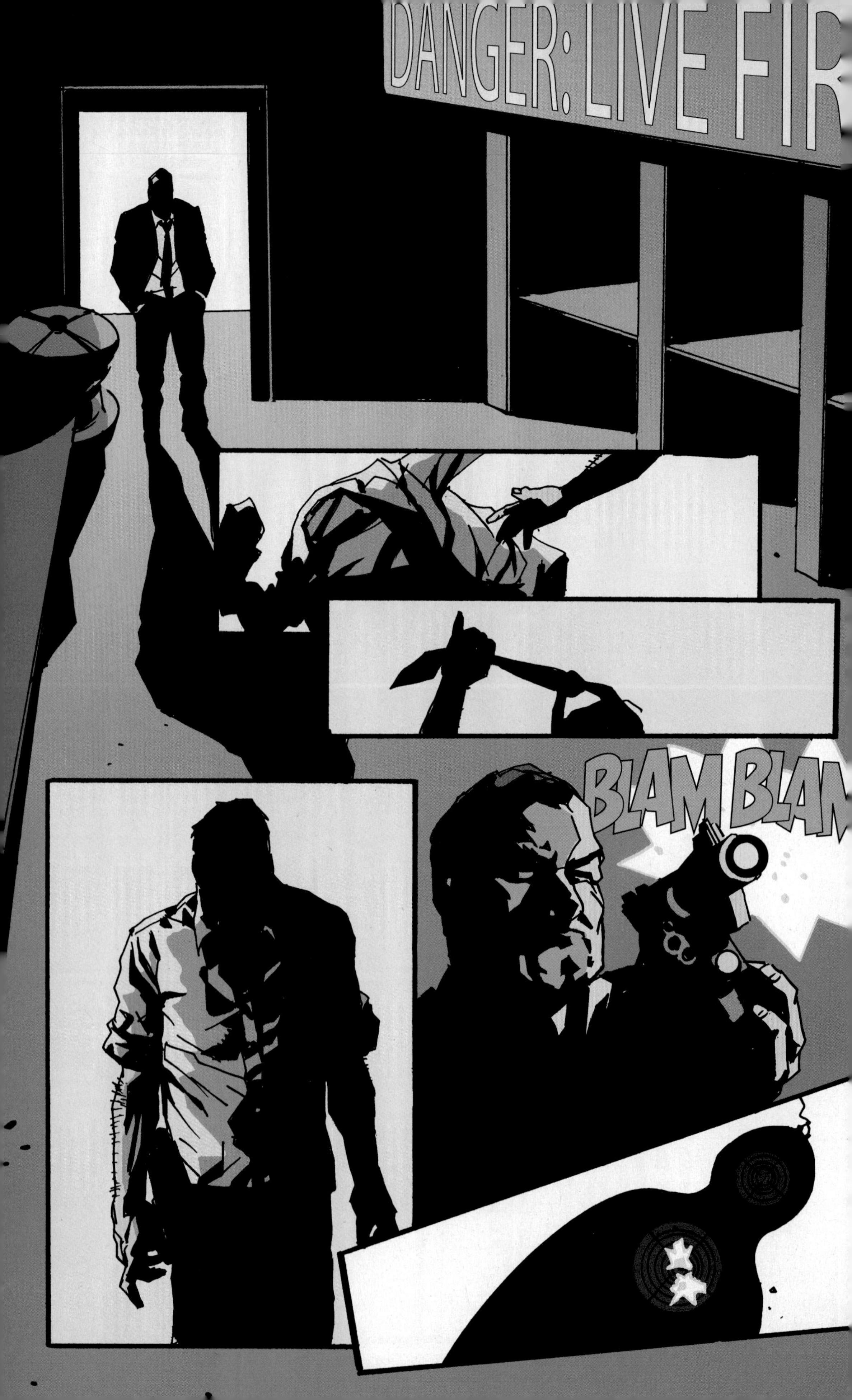
DANGER: LIVE FIR
BLAM BLAM

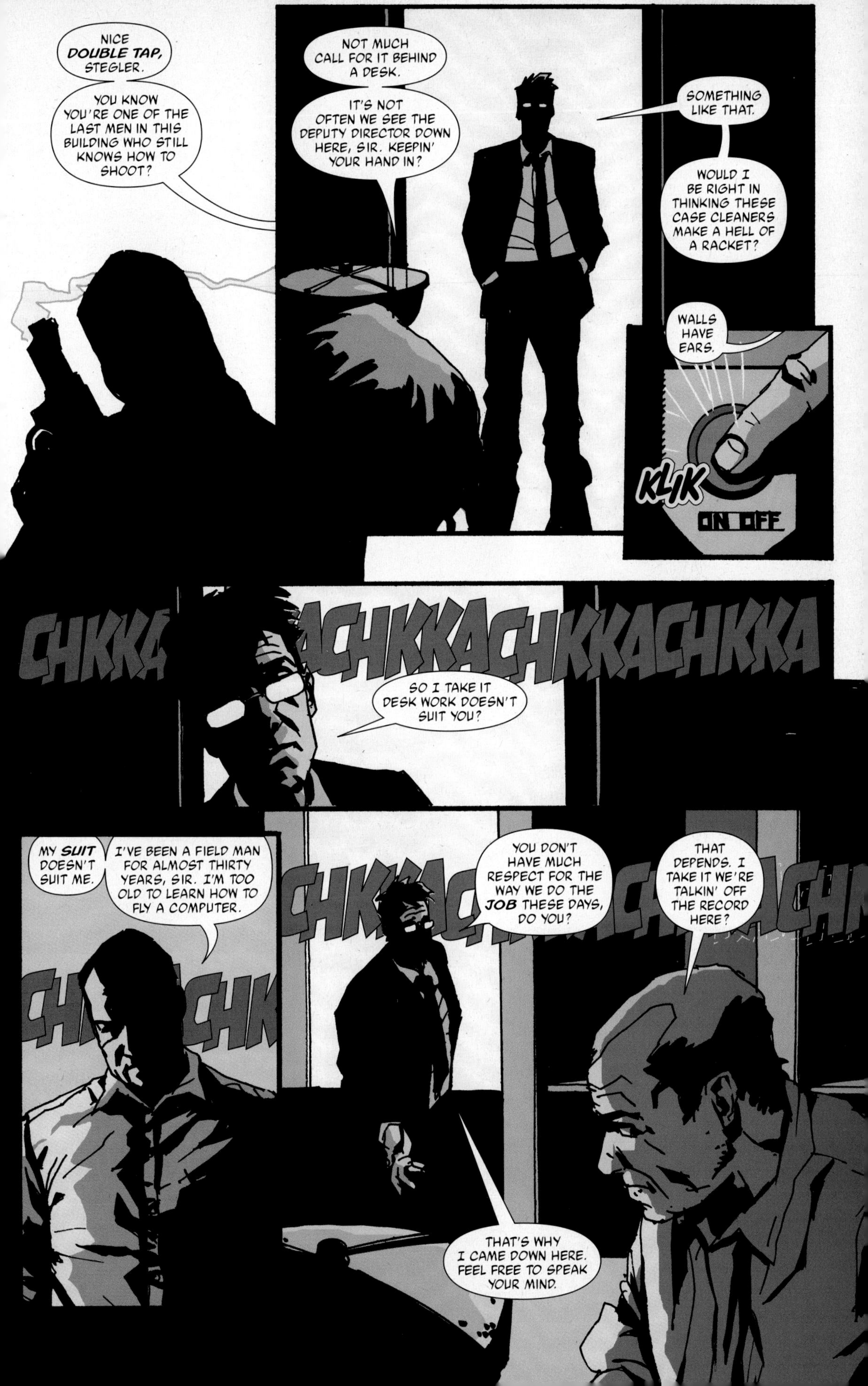

NICE DOUBLE TAP, STEGLER.
YOU KNOW YOU'RE ONE OF THE LAST MEN IN THIS BUILDING WHO STILL KNOWS HOW TO SHOOT?
NOT MUCH CALL FOR IT BEHIND A DESK.
IT'S NOT OFTEN WE SEE THE DEPUTY DIRECTOR DOWN HERE, SIR. KEEPIN' YOUR HAND IN?
SOMETHING LIKE THAT.
WOULD I BE RIGHT IN THINKING THESE CASE CLEANERS MAKE A HELL OF A RACKET?
WALLS HAVE EARS.
KLIK
ON OFF
CHKKACHKKACHKKACHKKACHKKA
SO I TAKE IT DESK WORK DOESN'T SUIT YOU?
MY SUIT DOESN'T SUIT ME.
I'VE BEEN A FIELD MAN FOR ALMOST THIRTY YEARS, SIR. I'M TOO OLD TO LEARN HOW TO FLY A COMPUTER.
YOU DON'T HAVE MUCH RESPECT FOR THE WAY WE DO THE JOB THESE DAYS, DO YOU?
THAT DEPENDS. I TAKE IT WE'RE TALKIN' OFF THE RECORD HERE?
THAT'S WHY I CAME DOWN HERE. FEEL FREE TO SPEAK YOUR MIND.

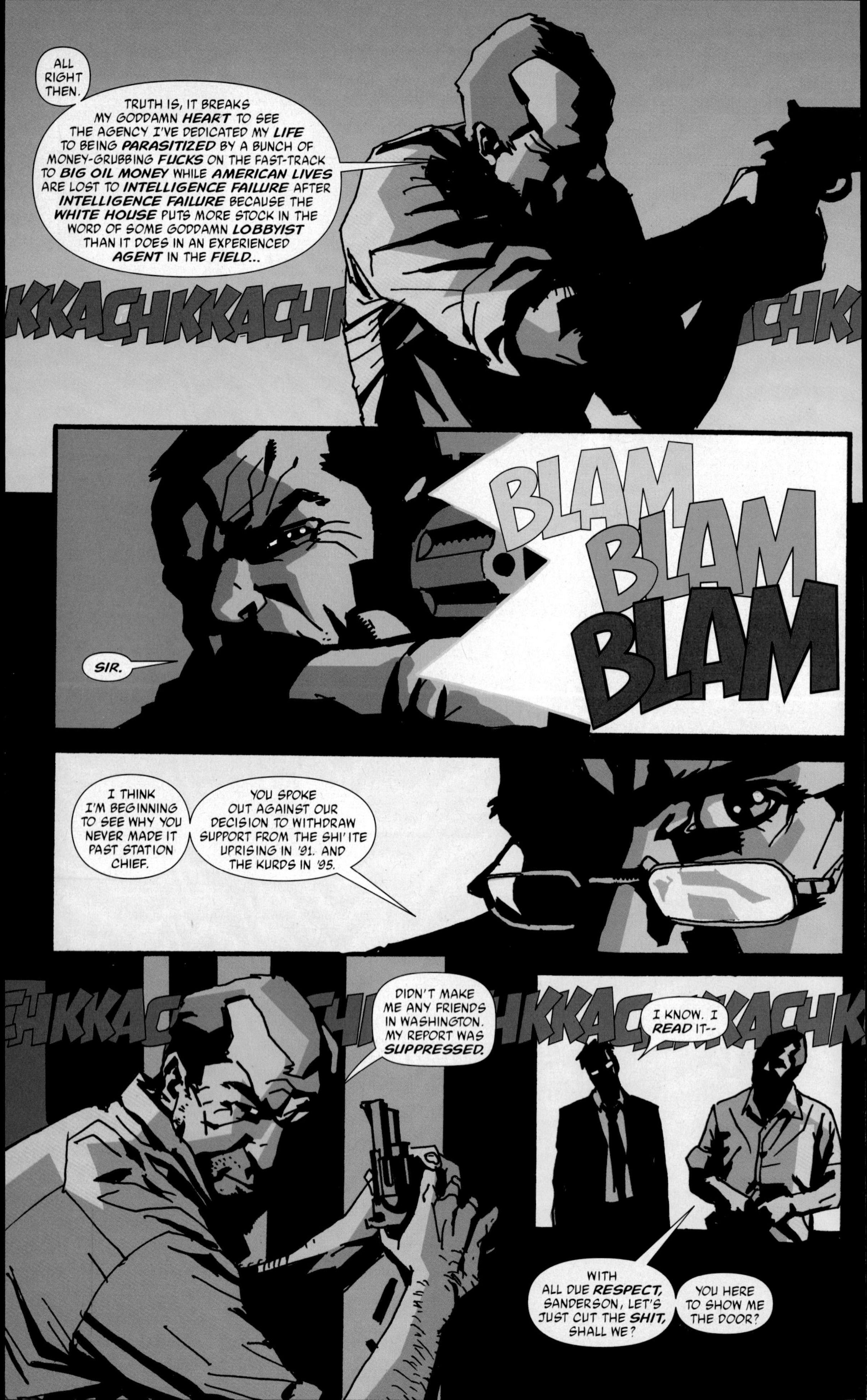
ALL RIGHT THEN.
TRUTH IS, IT BREAKS MY GODDAMN HEART TO SEE THE AGENCY I'VE DEDICATED MY LIFE TO BEING PARASITIZED BY A BUNCH OF MONEY-GRUBBING FUCKS ON THE FAST-TRACK TO BIG OIL MONEY WHILE AMERICAN LIVES ARE LOST TO INTELLIGENCE FAILURE AFTER INTELLIGENCE FAILURE BECAUSE THE WHITE HOUSE PUTS MORE STOCK IN THE WORD OF SOME GODDAMN LOBBYIST THAN IT DOES IN AN EXPERIENCED AGENT IN THE FIELD...
KKACHKKACH
ACHK
BLAM BLAM BLAM
SIR.
I THINK I'M BEGINNING TO SEE WHY YOU NEVER MADE IT PAST STATION CHIEF.
YOU SPOKE OUT AGAINST OUR DECISION TO WITHDRAW SUPPORT FROM THE SHI'ITE UPRISING IN '91. AND THE KURDS IN '95.
HKKAC
DIDN'T MAKE ME ANY FRIENDS IN WASHINGTON. MY REPORT WAS SUPPRESSED.
HKKAC KACHK
I KNOW. I READ IT--
WITH ALL DUE RESPECT, SANDERSON, LET'S JUST CUT THE SHIT, SHALL WE?
YOU HERE TO SHOW ME THE DOOR?

CHKKACHK

NO. I'M HERE TO OFFER YOU A *JOB.*

...I'M LISTENING.

I NEED SOMEONE WHO KNOWS HOW TO HANDLE HIMSELF. SOMEONE I KNOW I CAN *TRUST.*

WHY ME? WHY NOT GO THROUGH PROPER CHANNELS?

BECAUSE IT'S NOT THAT SIMPLE.

KKAC KKACHM

IKKACHKKACHKKACHKKACHKKACHK

I THINK SOMEONE MAY HAVE REACTIVATED THE *MAX* IDENTITY.

KACHKKACHKKACHKKACHKKACHKK

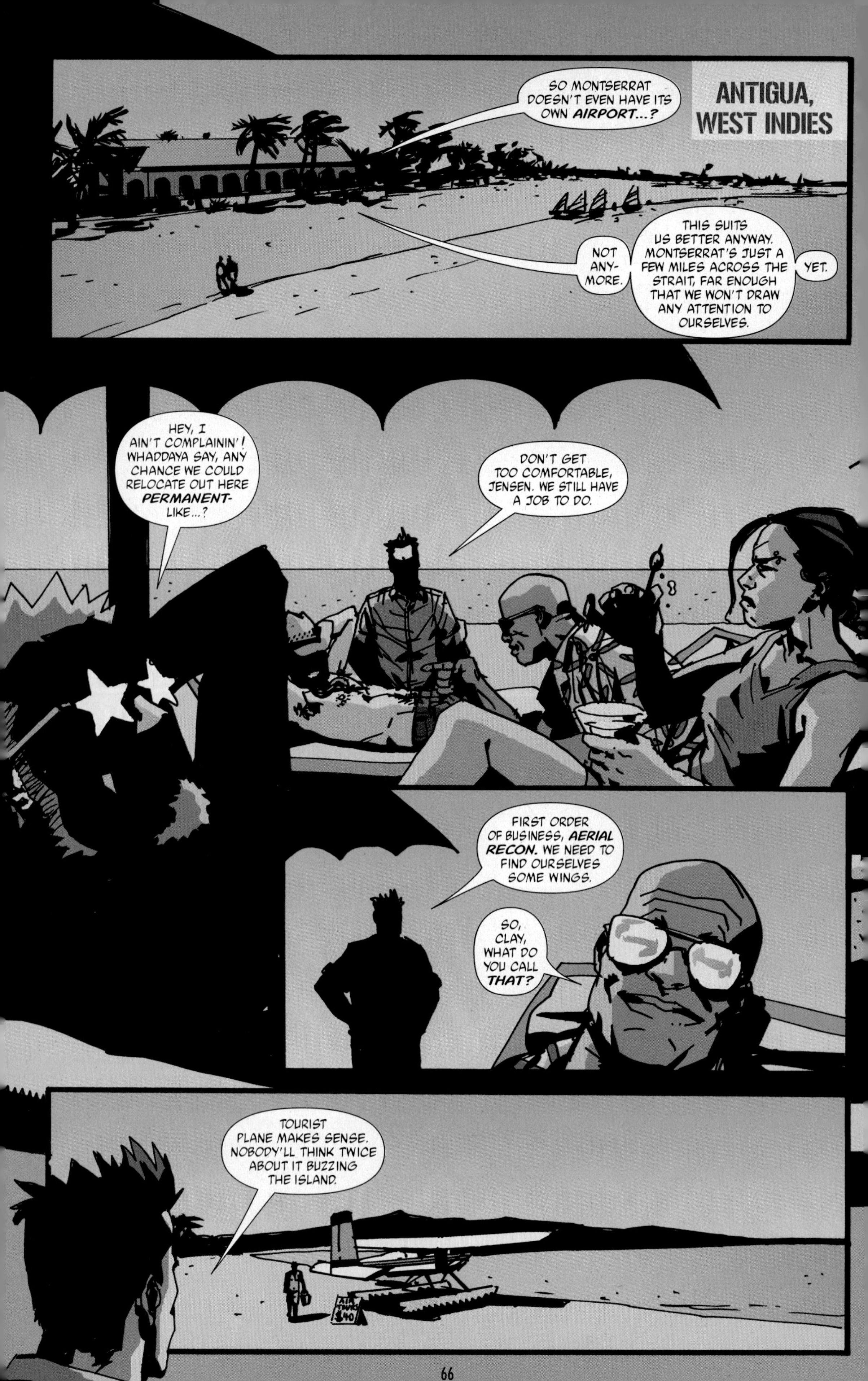
ANTIGUA, WEST INDIES
SO MONTSERRAT DOESN'T EVEN HAVE ITS OWN AIRPORT...?
NOT ANY-MORE.
THIS SUITS US BETTER ANYWAY. MONTSERRAT'S JUST A FEW MILES ACROSS THE STRAIT, FAR ENOUGH THAT WE WON'T DRAW ANY ATTENTION TO OURSELVES.
YET.
HEY, I AIN'T COMPLAININ'! WHADDAYA SAY, ANY CHANCE WE COULD RELOCATE OUT HERE PERMANENT-LIKE...?
DON'T GET TOO COMFORTABLE, JENSEN. WE STILL HAVE A JOB TO DO.
FIRST ORDER OF BUSINESS, AERIAL RECON. WE NEED TO FIND OURSELVES SOME WINGS.
SO, CLAY, WHAT DO YOU CALL THAT?
TOURIST PLANE MAKES SENSE. NOBODY'LL THINK TWICE ABOUT IT BUZZING THE ISLAND.
AIR TOURS $40

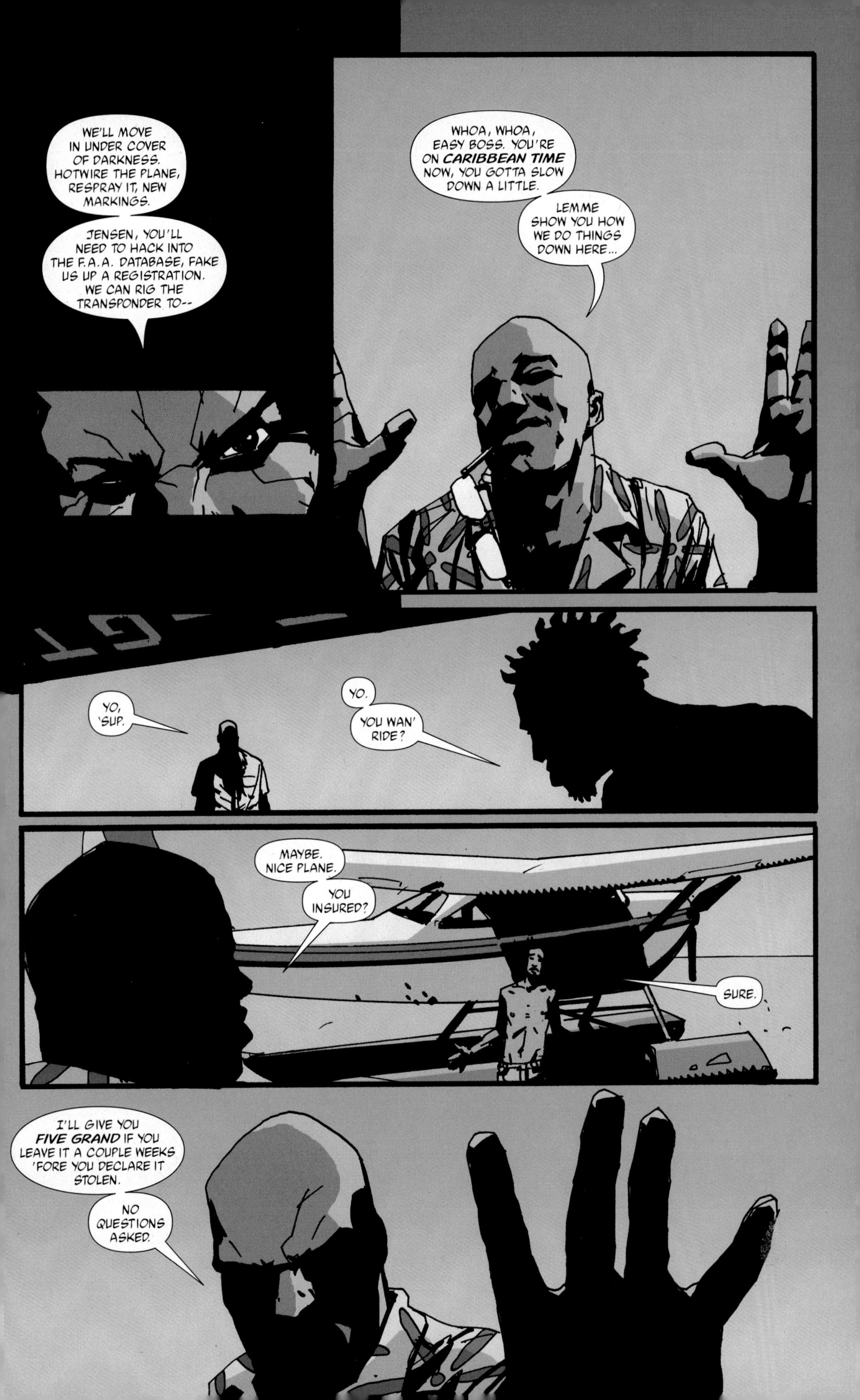

WE'LL MOVE IN UNDER COVER OF DARKNESS. HOTWIRE THE PLANE, RESPRAY IT, NEW MARKINGS.
JENSEN, YOU'LL NEED TO HACK INTO THE F.A.A. DATABASE, FAKE US UP A REGISTRATION. WE CAN RIG THE TRANSPONDER TO--
WHOA, WHOA, EASY BOSS. YOU'RE ON **CARIBBEAN TIME** NOW, YOU GOTTA SLOW DOWN A LITTLE.
LEMME SHOW YOU HOW WE DO THINGS DOWN HERE...
YO, 'SUP.
YO.
YOU WAN' RIDE?
MAYBE. NICE PLANE.
YOU INSURED?
SURE.
I'LL GIVE YOU **FIVE GRAND** IF YOU LEAVE IT A COUPLE WEEKS 'FORE YOU DECLARE IT STOLEN.
NO QUESTIONS ASKED.

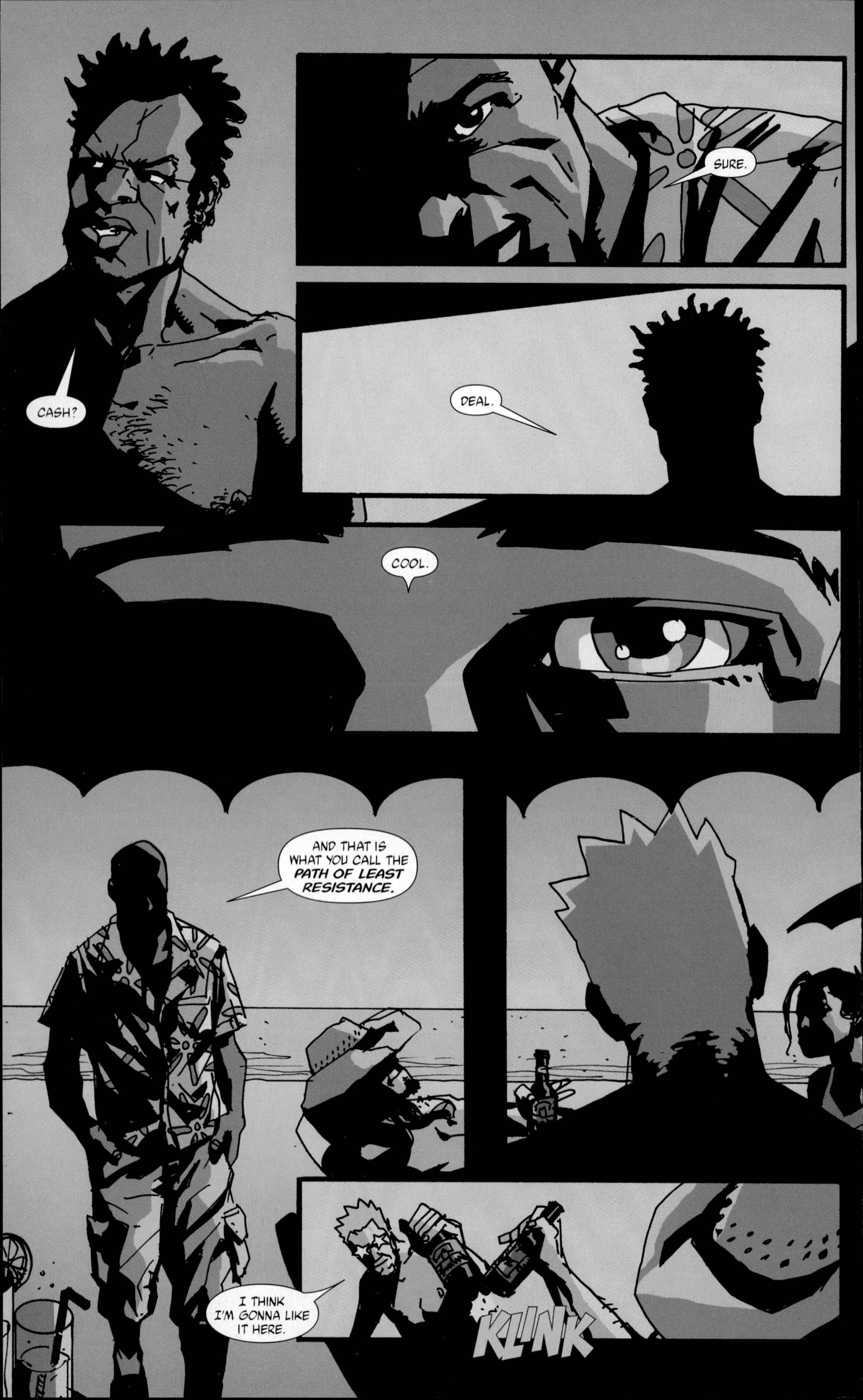
CASH?
SURE.
DEAL.
COOL.
AND THAT IS WHAT YOU CALL THE *PATH OF LEAST RESISTANCE.*
I THINK I'M GONNA LIKE IT HERE.
KLINK

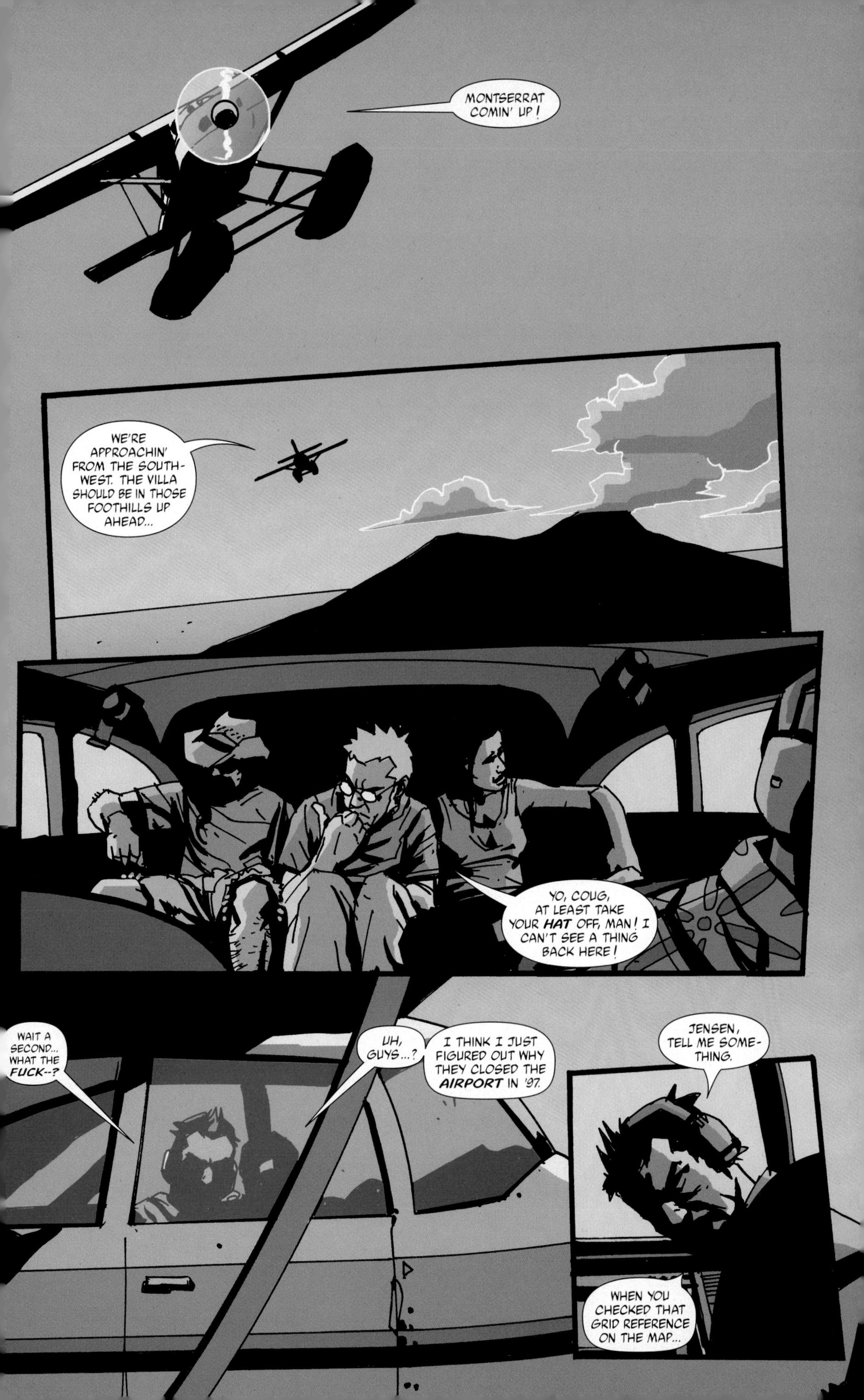

MONTSERRAT COMIN' UP!
WE'RE APPROACHIN' FROM THE SOUTH-WEST. THE VILLA SHOULD BE IN THOSE FOOTHILLS UP AHEAD...
YO, COUG, AT LEAST TAKE YOUR **HAT** OFF, MAN! I CAN'T SEE A THING BACK HERE!
WAIT A SECOND... WHAT THE **FUCK**--?
UH, GUYS...?
I THINK I JUST FIGURED OUT WHY THEY CLOSED THE **AIRPORT** IN '97.
JENSEN, TELL ME SOME-THING.
WHEN YOU CHECKED THAT GRID REFERENCE ON THE MAP...

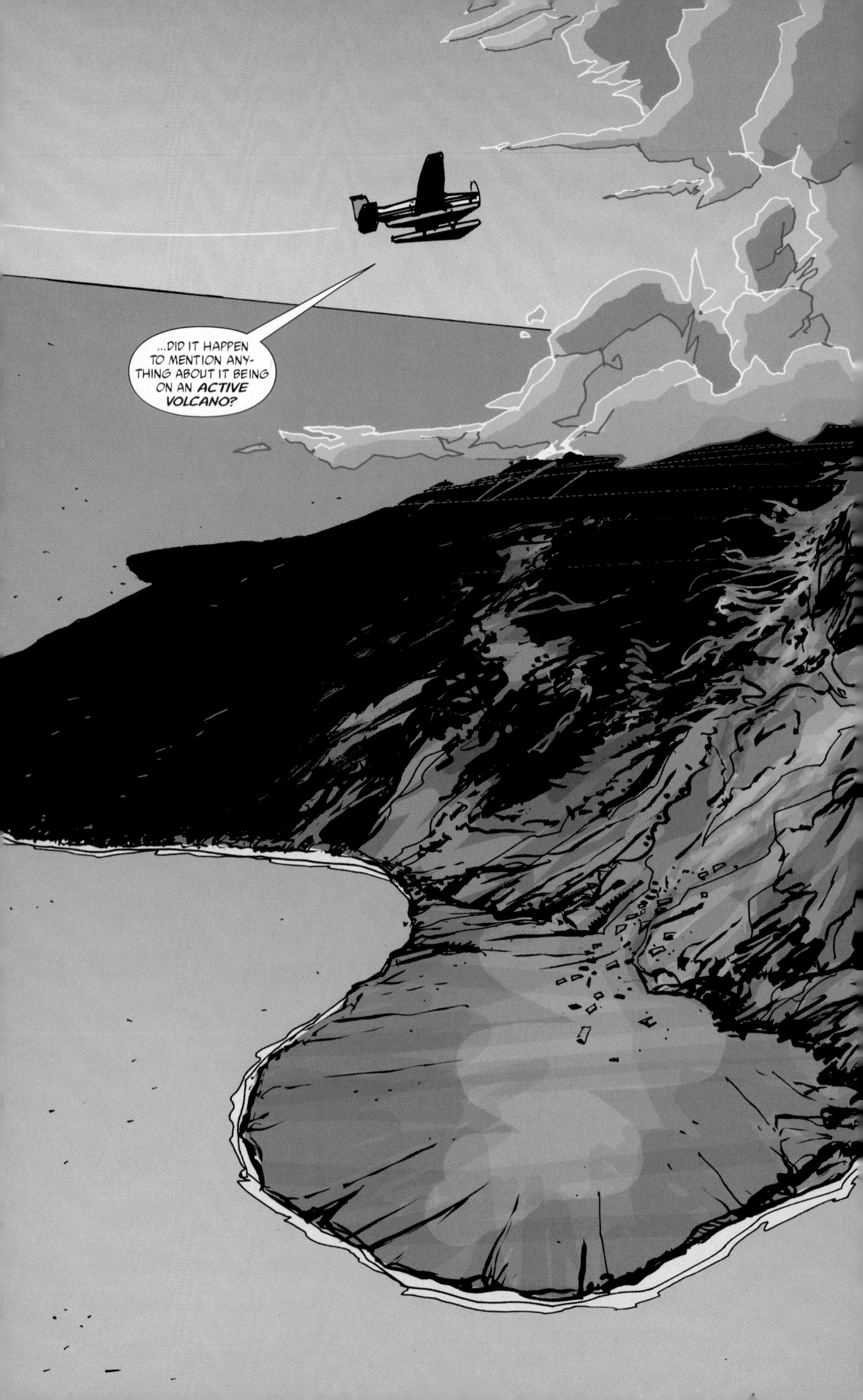
...DID IT HAPPEN TO MENTION ANY-THING ABOUT IT BEING ON AN ACTIVE VOLCANO?

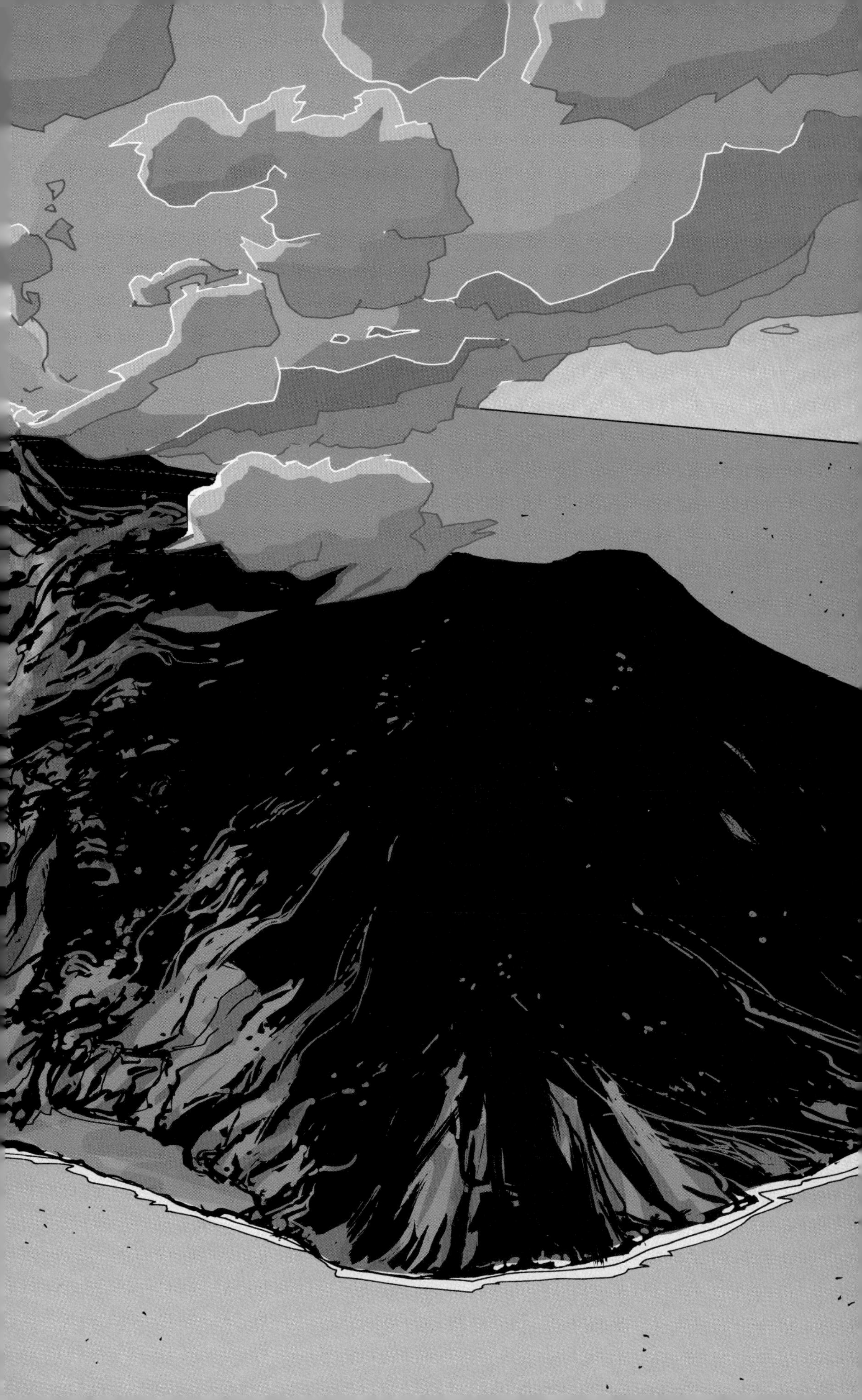

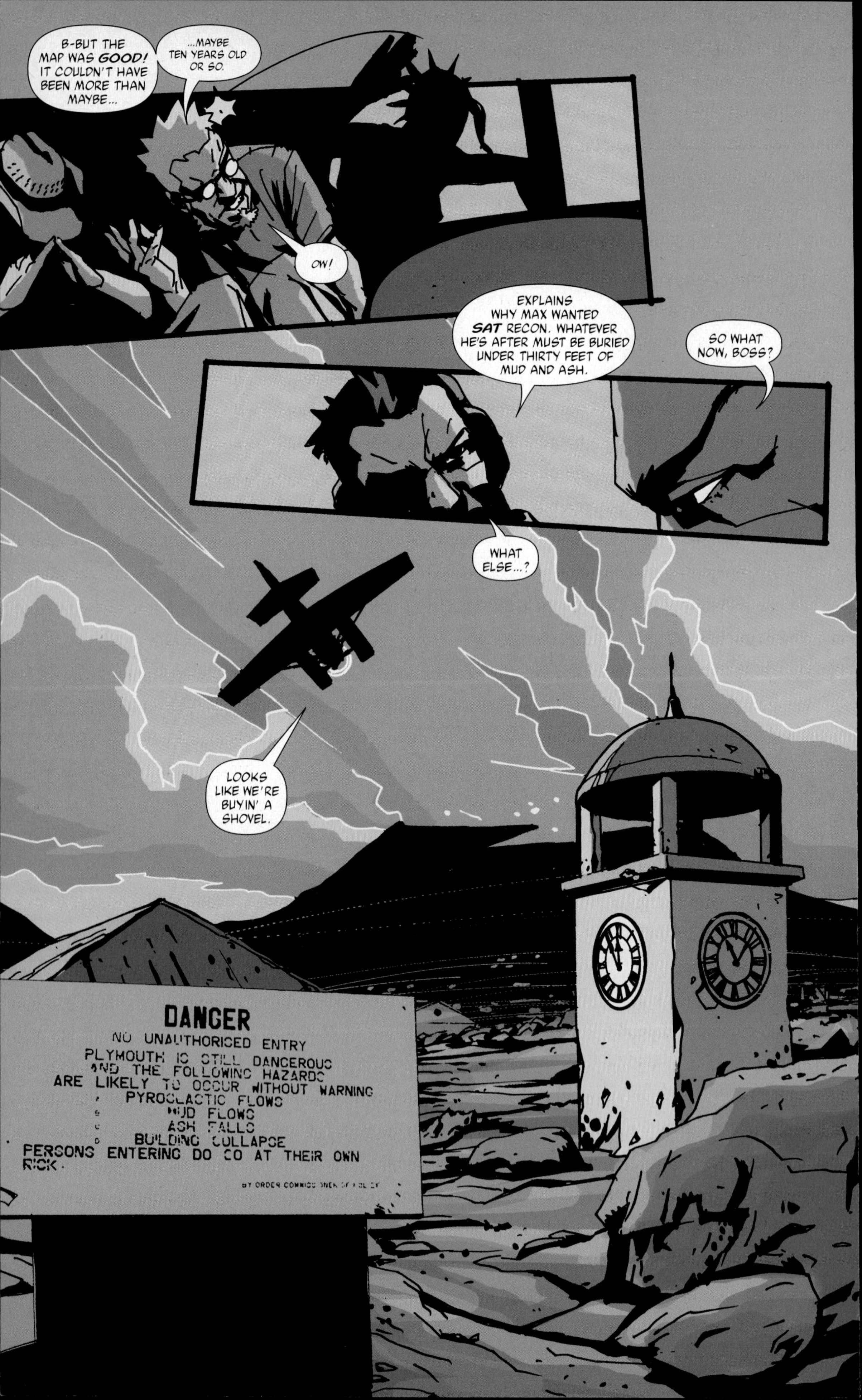
B-BUT THE MAP WAS **GOOD!** IT COULDN'T HAVE BEEN MORE THAN MAYBE...
...MAYBE TEN YEARS OLD OR SO.
OW!
EXPLAINS WHY MAX WANTED **SAT** RECON. WHATEVER HE'S AFTER MUST BE BURIED UNDER THIRTY FEET OF MUD AND ASH.
SO WHAT NOW, BOSS?
WHAT ELSE...?
LOOKS LIKE WE'RE BUYIN' A SHOVEL.
DANGER
NO UNAUTHORICED ENTRY
PLYMOUTH IC STILL DANCEROUC
AND THE FOLLOWINC HAZARDC
ARE LIKELY TO OCCUR WITHOUT WARNING
PYROCLACTIC FLOWC
MUD FLOWC
ASH FALLC
BUILDINC COLLAPCE
PERSONS ENTERINC DO CO AT THEIR OWN RICK.

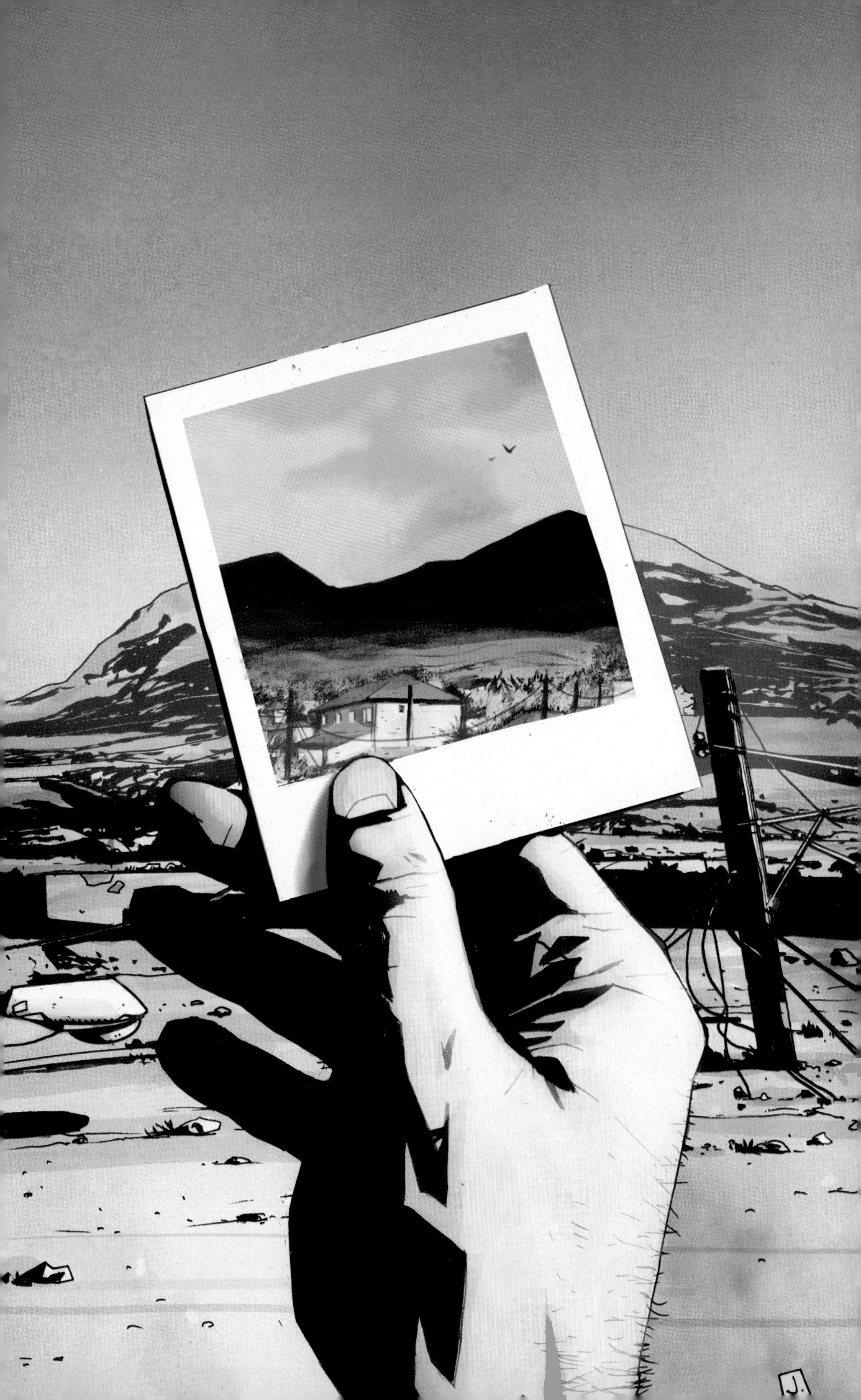
J.

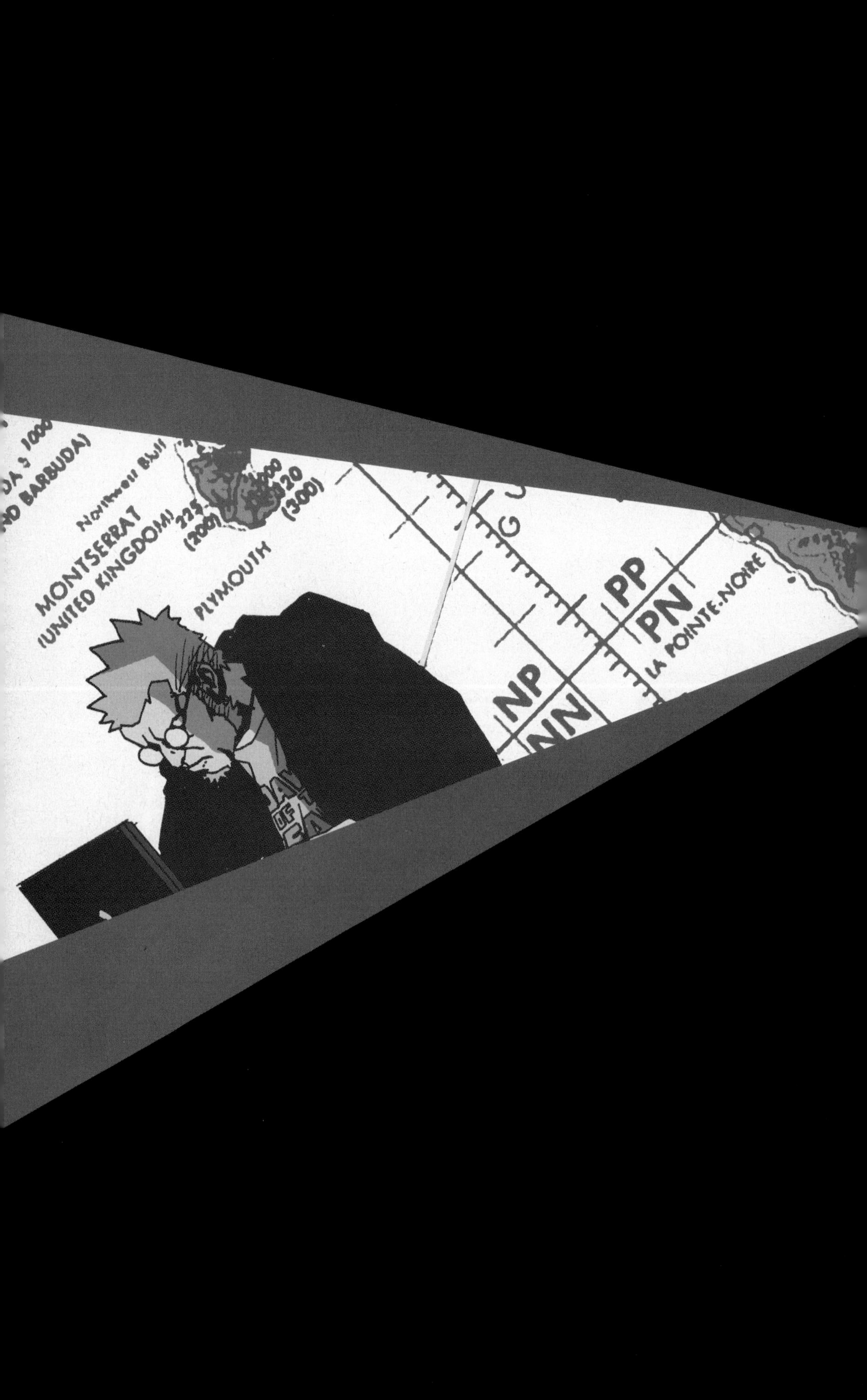
MONTSERRAT
(UNITED KINGDOM)
PLYMOUTH
PP
PN
NP
LA POINTE-NOIRE

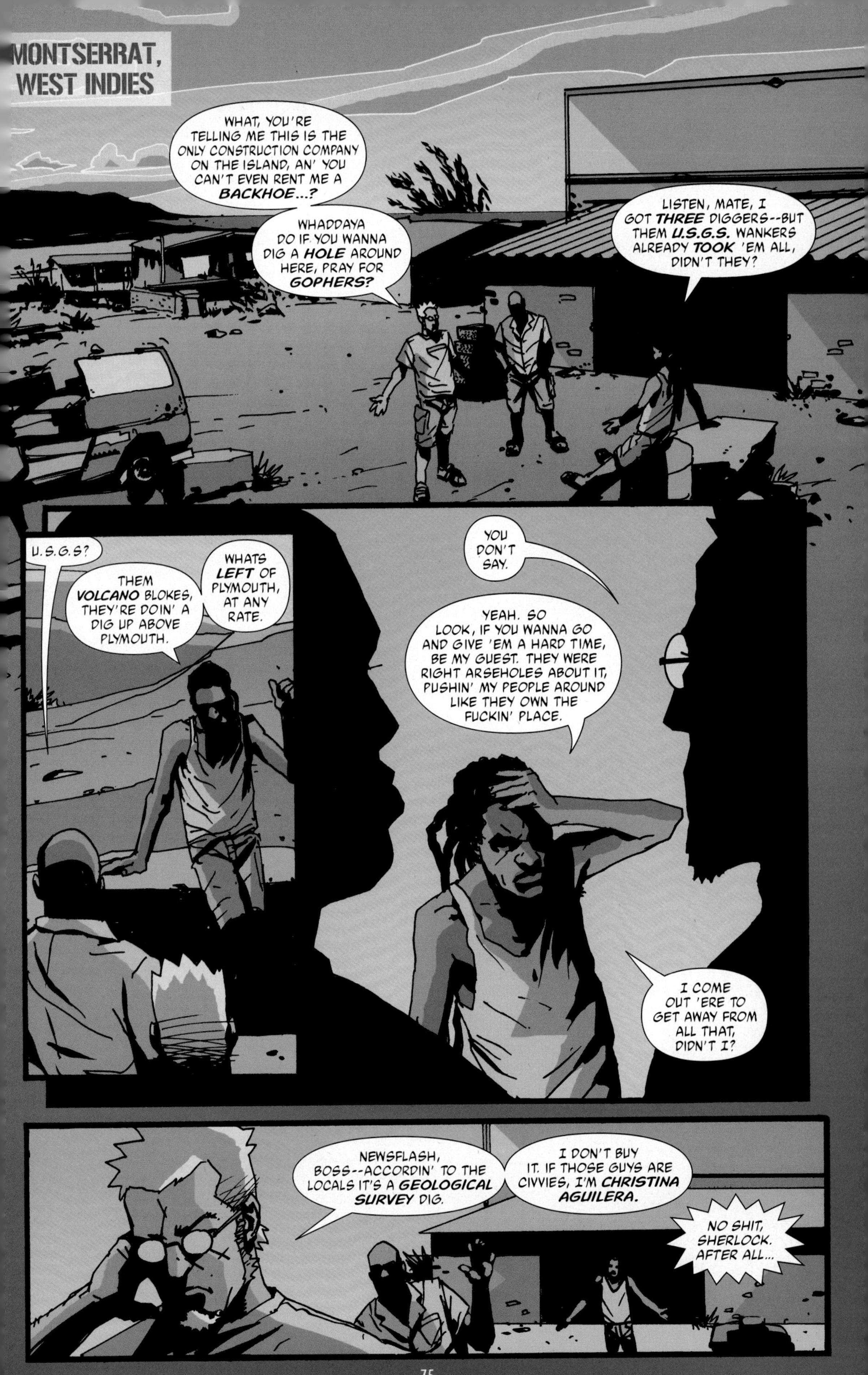
MONTSERRAT, WEST INDIES
WHAT, YOU'RE TELLING ME THIS IS THE ONLY CONSTRUCTION COMPANY ON THE ISLAND, AN' YOU CAN'T EVEN RENT ME A BACKHOE...?
WHADDAYA DO IF YOU WANNA DIG A HOLE AROUND HERE, PRAY FOR GOPHERS?
LISTEN, MATE, I GOT THREE DIGGERS--BUT THEM U.S.G.S. WANKERS ALREADY TOOK 'EM ALL, DIDN'T THEY?
U.S.G.S?
THEM VOLCANO BLOKES, THEY'RE DOIN' A DIG UP ABOVE PLYMOUTH.
WHATS LEFT OF PLYMOUTH, AT ANY RATE.
YOU DON'T SAY.
YEAH. SO LOOK, IF YOU WANNA GO AND GIVE 'EM A HARD TIME, BE MY GUEST. THEY WERE RIGHT ARSEHOLES ABOUT IT, PUSHIN' MY PEOPLE AROUND LIKE THEY OWN THE FUCKIN' PLACE.
I COME OUT 'ERE TO GET AWAY FROM ALL THAT, DIDN'T I?
NEWSFLASH, BOSS--ACCORDIN' TO THE LOCALS IT'S A GEOLOGICAL SURVEY DIG.
I DON'T BUY IT. IF THOSE GUYS ARE CIVVIES, I'M CHRISTINA AGUILERA.
NO SHIT, SHERLOCK. AFTER ALL...

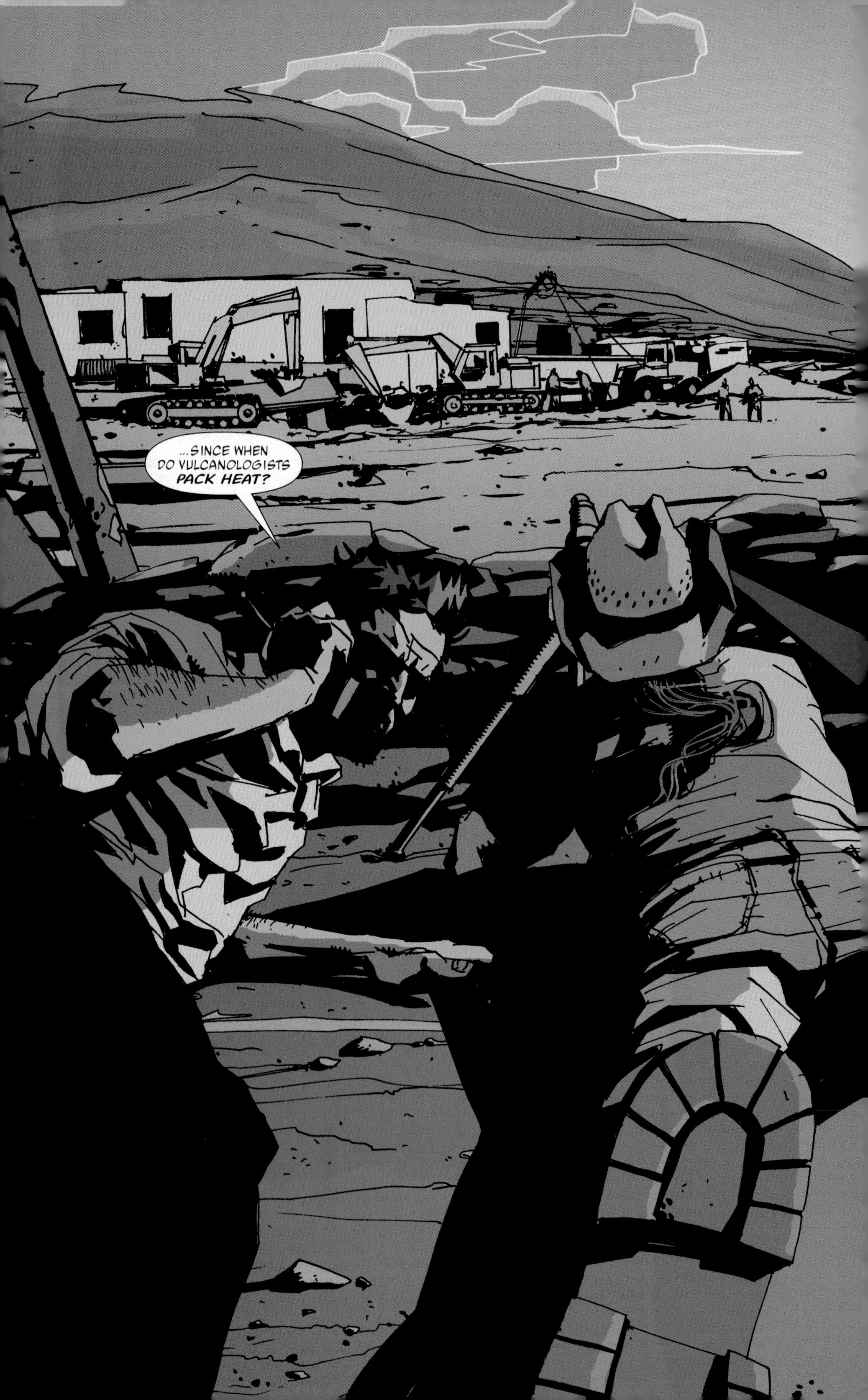
...SINCE WHEN DO VULCANOLOGISTS PACK HEAT?

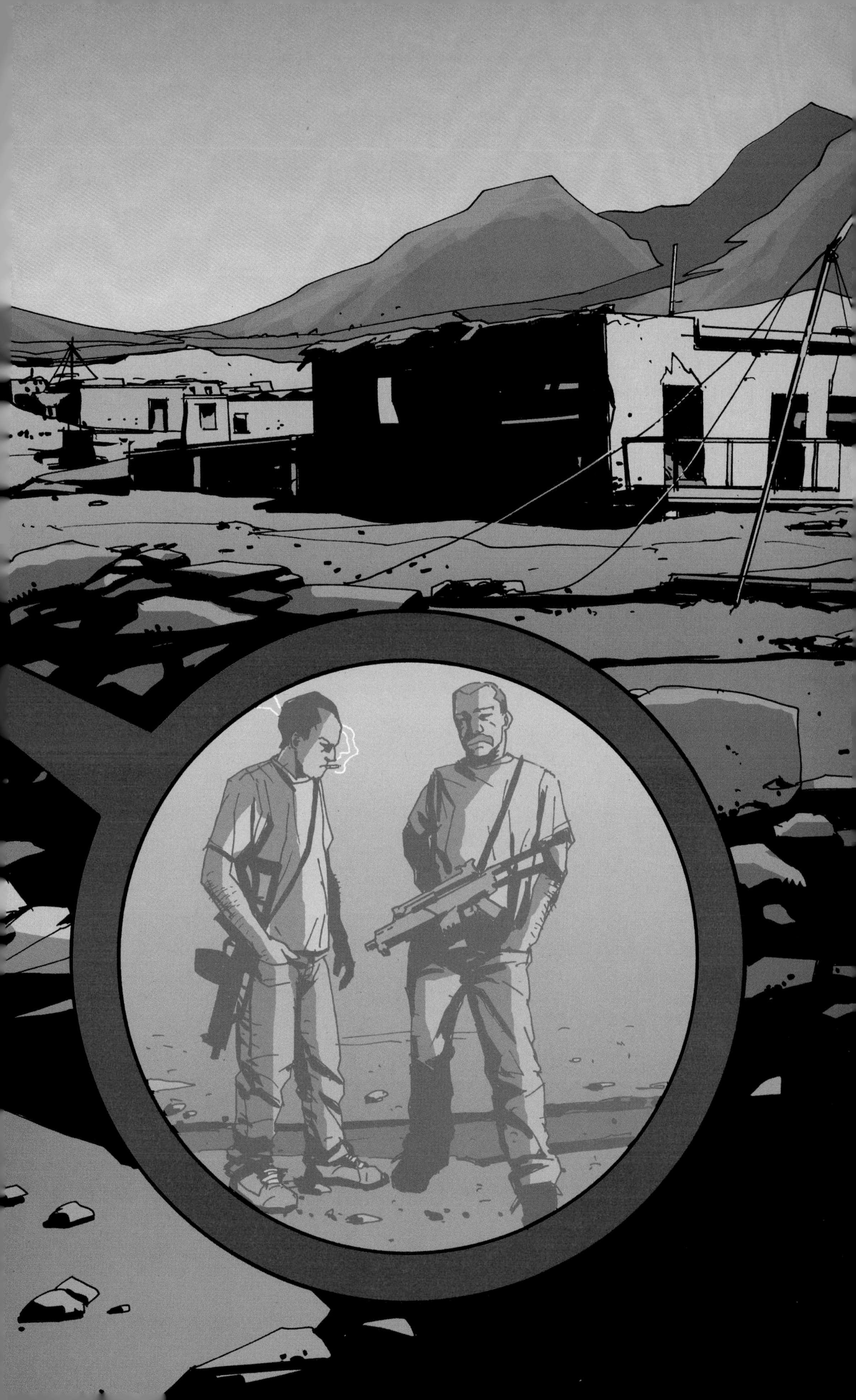

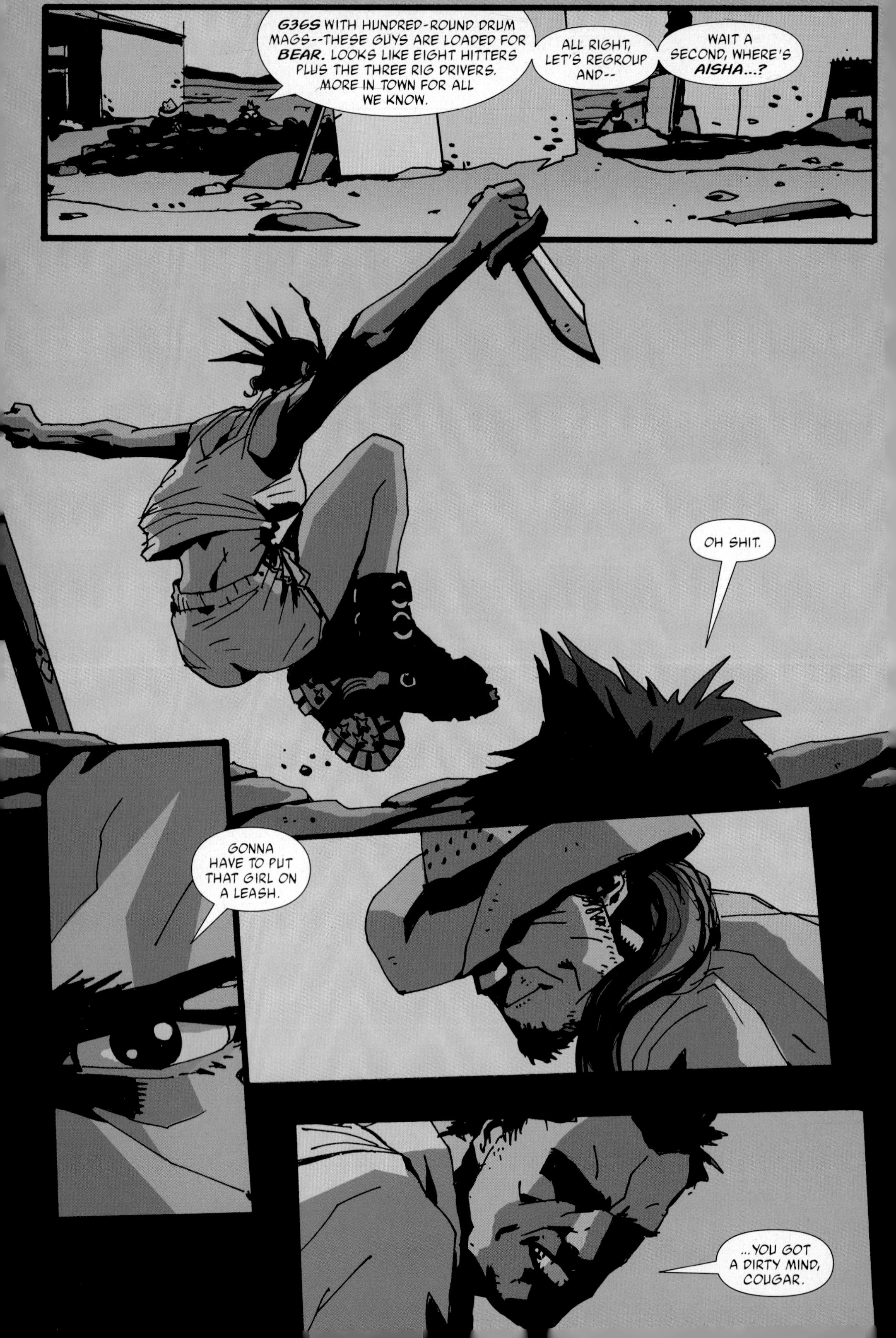
G36S WITH HUNDRED-ROUND DRUM MAGS--THESE GUYS ARE LOADED FOR BEAR. LOOKS LIKE EIGHT HITTERS PLUS THE THREE RIG DRIVERS. MORE IN TOWN FOR ALL WE KNOW.
ALL RIGHT, LET'S REGROUP AND--
WAIT A SECOND, WHERE'S AISHA...?
OH SHIT.
GONNA HAVE TO PUT THAT GIRL ON A LEASH.
...YOU GOT A DIRTY MIND, COUGAR.

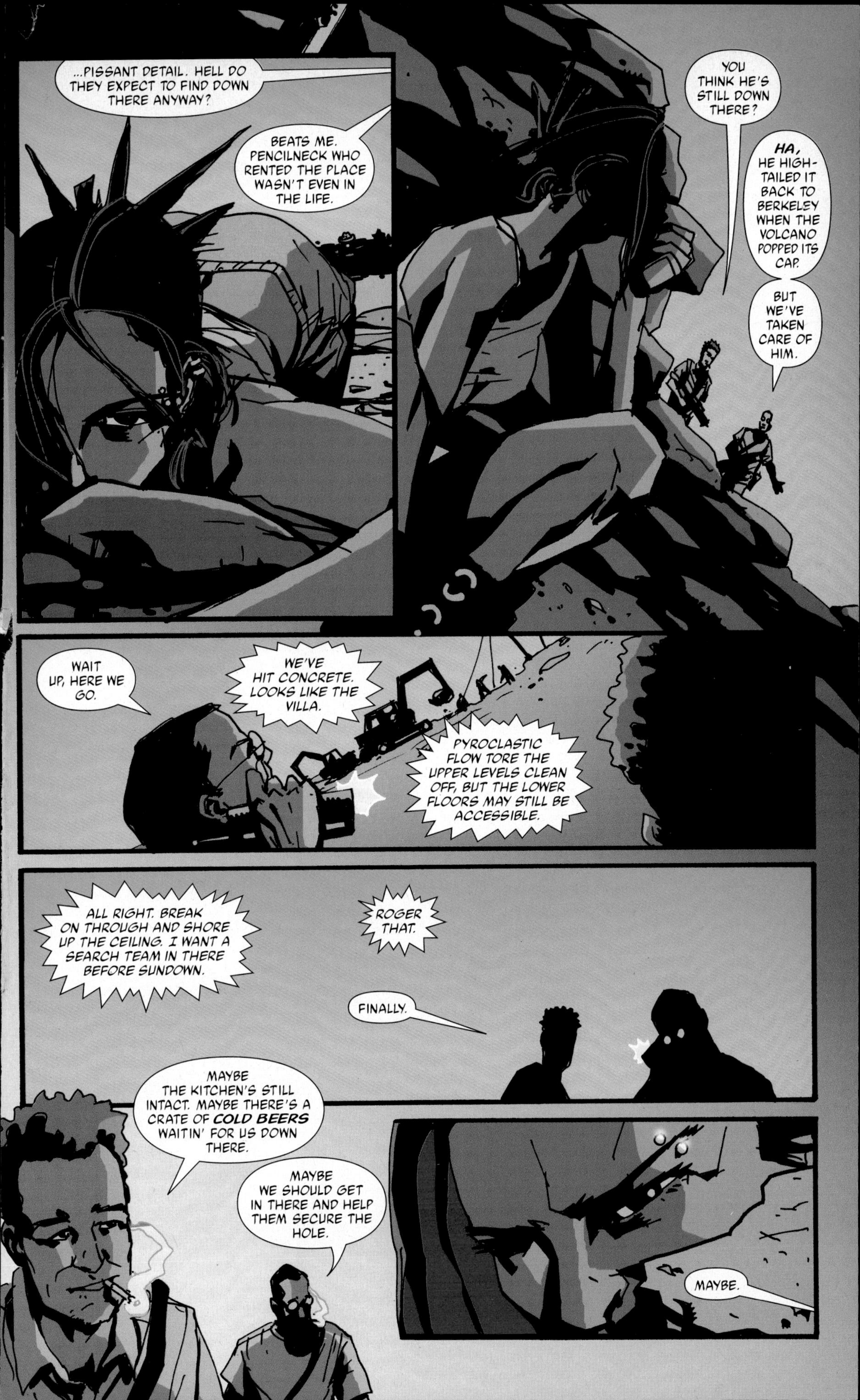
...PISSANT DETAIL. HELL DO THEY EXPECT TO FIND DOWN THERE ANYWAY?
BEATS ME. PENCILNECK WHO RENTED THE PLACE WASN'T EVEN IN THE LIFE.
YOU THINK HE'S STILL DOWN THERE?
HA, HE HIGH-TAILED IT BACK TO BERKELEY WHEN THE VOLCANO POPPED ITS CAP.
BUT WE'VE TAKEN CARE OF HIM.
WAIT UP, HERE WE GO.
WE'VE HIT CONCRETE. LOOKS LIKE THE VILLA.
PYROCLASTIC FLOW TORE THE UPPER LEVELS CLEAN OFF, BUT THE LOWER FLOORS MAY STILL BE ACCESSIBLE.
ALL RIGHT. BREAK ON THROUGH AND SHORE UP THE CEILING. I WANT A SEARCH TEAM IN THERE BEFORE SUNDOWN.
ROGER THAT.
FINALLY.
MAYBE THE KITCHEN'S STILL INTACT. MAYBE THERE'S A CRATE OF COLD BEERS WAITIN' FOR US DOWN THERE.
MAYBE WE SHOULD GET IN THERE AND HELP THEM SECURE THE HOLE.
MAYBE.

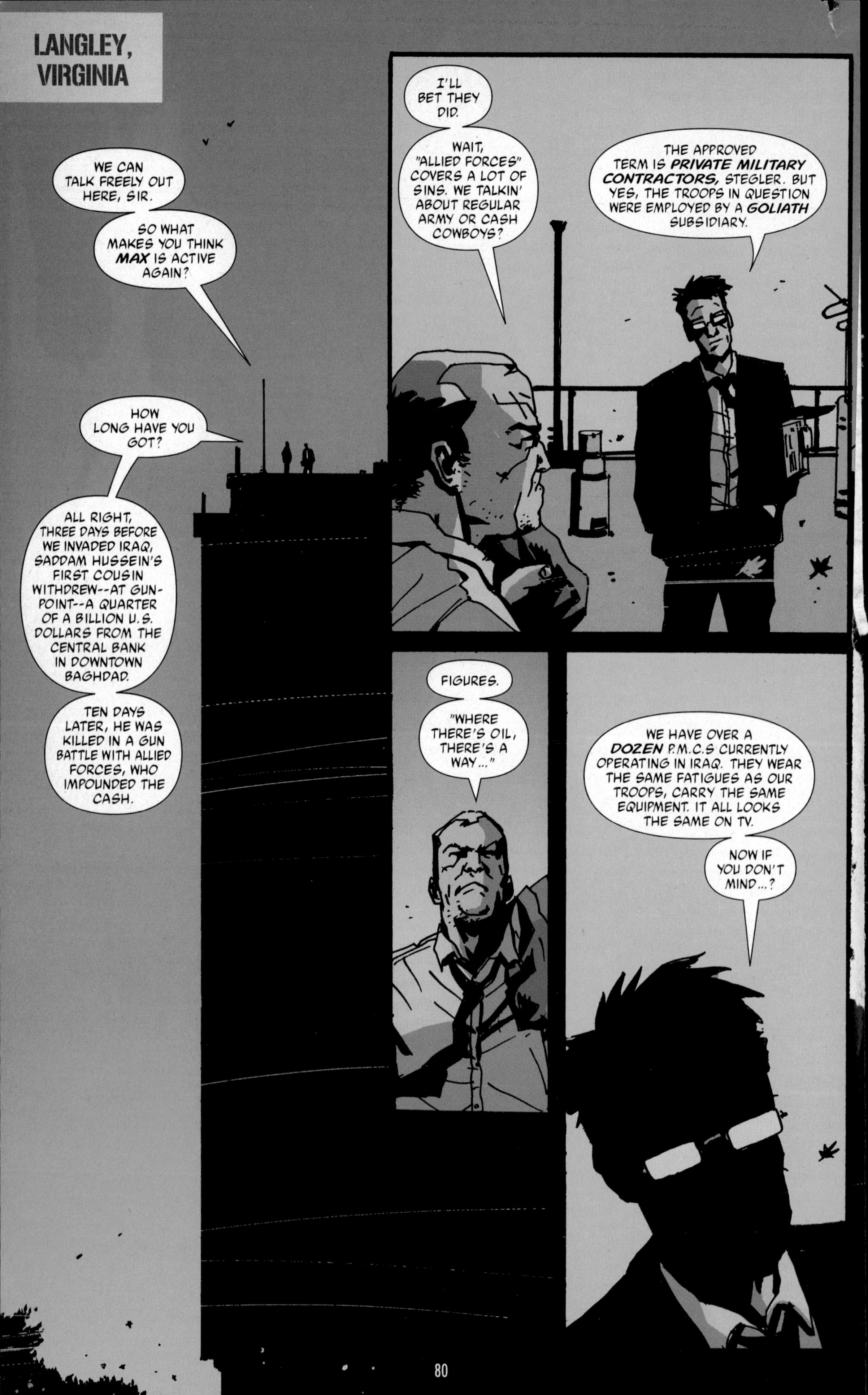
LANGLEY, VIRGINIA
WE CAN TALK FREELY OUT HERE, SIR.
SO WHAT MAKES YOU THINK MAX IS ACTIVE AGAIN?
HOW LONG HAVE YOU GOT?
ALL RIGHT, THREE DAYS BEFORE WE INVADED IRAQ, SADDAM HUSSEIN'S FIRST COUSIN WITHDREW--AT GUN-POINT--A QUARTER OF A BILLION U.S. DOLLARS FROM THE CENTRAL BANK IN DOWNTOWN BAGHDAD.
TEN DAYS LATER, HE WAS KILLED IN A GUN BATTLE WITH ALLIED FORCES, WHO IMPOUNDED THE CASH.
I'LL BET THEY DID.
WAIT, "ALLIED FORCES" COVERS A LOT OF SINS. WE TALKIN' ABOUT REGULAR ARMY OR CASH COWBOYS?
THE APPROVED TERM IS PRIVATE MILITARY CONTRACTORS, STEGLER. BUT YES, THE TROOPS IN QUESTION WERE EMPLOYED BY A GOLIATH SUBSIDIARY.
FIGURES.
"WHERE THERE'S OIL, THERE'S A WAY..."
WE HAVE OVER A DOZEN P.M.C.S CURRENTLY OPERATING IN IRAQ. THEY WEAR THE SAME FATIGUES AS OUR TROOPS, CARRY THE SAME EQUIPMENT. IT ALL LOOKS THE SAME ON TV.
NOW IF YOU DON'T MIND...?

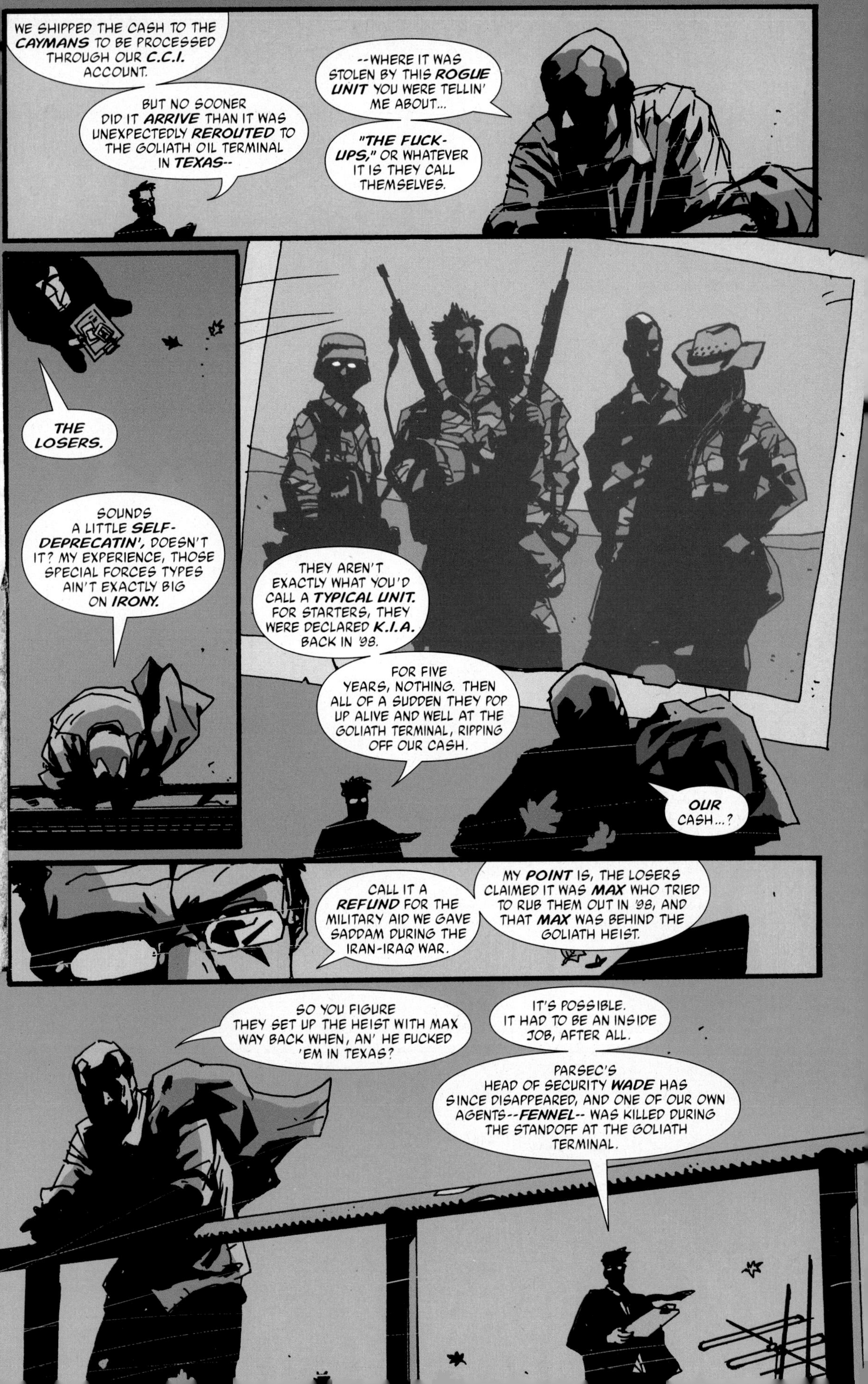
WE SHIPPED THE CASH TO THE CAYMANS TO BE PROCESSED THROUGH OUR C.C.I. ACCOUNT.
BUT NO SOONER DID IT ARRIVE THAN IT WAS UNEXPECTEDLY REROUTED TO THE GOLIATH OIL TERMINAL IN TEXAS--
--WHERE IT WAS STOLEN BY THIS ROGUE UNIT YOU WERE TELLIN' ME ABOUT...
"THE FUCK-UPS," OR WHATEVER IT IS THEY CALL THEMSELVES.
THE LOSERS.
SOUNDS A LITTLE SELF-DEPRECATIN', DOESN'T IT? MY EXPERIENCE, THOSE SPECIAL FORCES TYPES AIN'T EXACTLY BIG ON IRONY.
THEY AREN'T EXACTLY WHAT YOU'D CALL A TYPICAL UNIT. FOR STARTERS, THEY WERE DECLARED K.I.A. BACK IN '98.
FOR FIVE YEARS, NOTHING. THEN ALL OF A SUDDEN THEY POP UP ALIVE AND WELL AT THE GOLIATH TERMINAL, RIPPING OFF OUR CASH.
OUR CASH...?
CALL IT A REFUND FOR THE MILITARY AID WE GAVE SADDAM DURING THE IRAN-IRAQ WAR.
MY POINT IS, THE LOSERS CLAIMED IT WAS MAX WHO TRIED TO RUB THEM OUT IN '98, AND THAT MAX WAS BEHIND THE GOLIATH HEIST.
SO YOU FIGURE THEY SET UP THE HEIST WITH MAX WAY BACK WHEN, AN' HE FUCKED 'EM IN TEXAS?
IT'S POSSIBLE. IT HAD TO BE AN INSIDE JOB, AFTER ALL.
PARSEC'S HEAD OF SECURITY WADE HAS SINCE DISAPPEARED, AND ONE OF OUR OWN AGENTS--FENNEL-- WAS KILLED DURING THE STANDOFF AT THE GOLIATH TERMINAL.

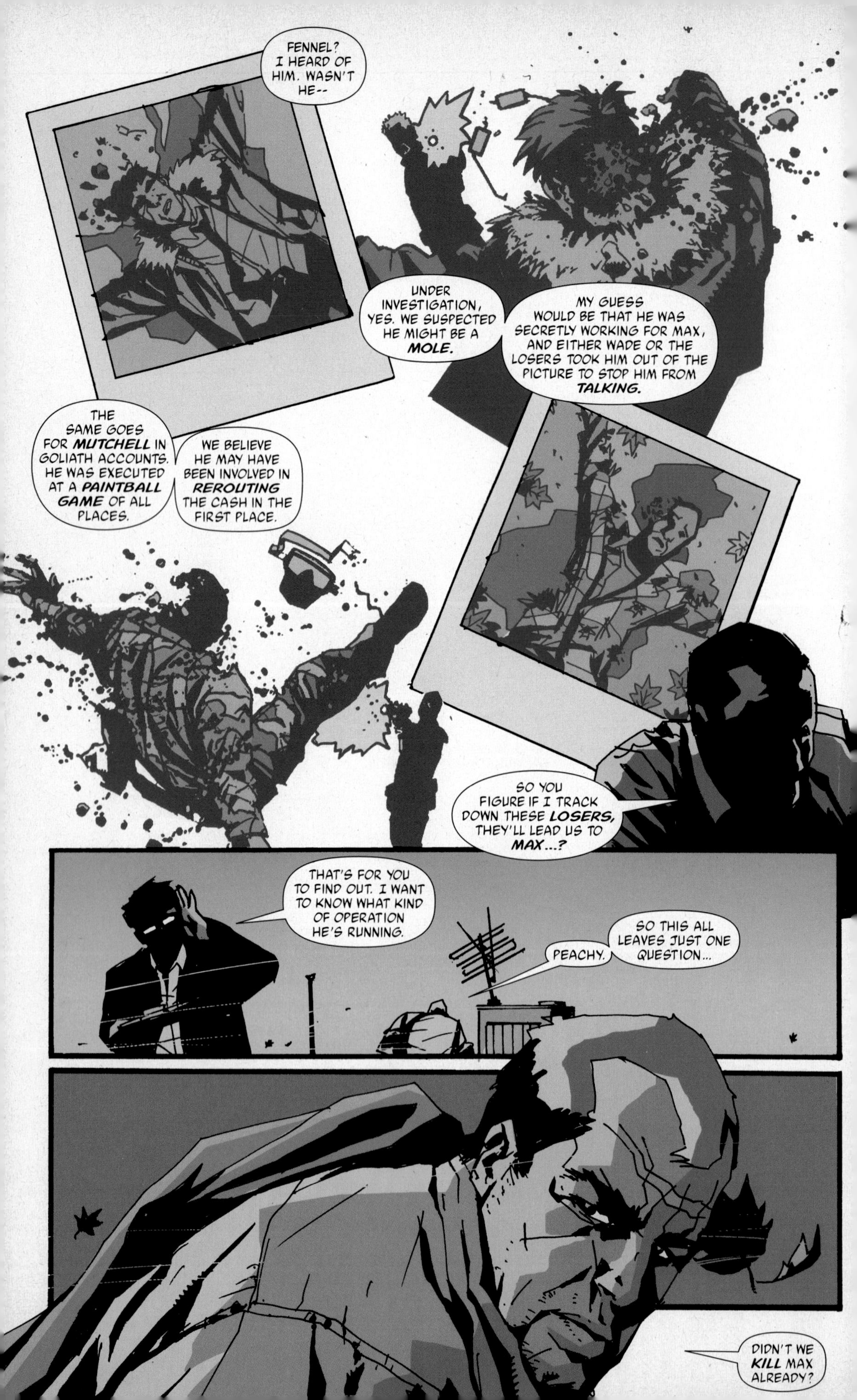
FENNEL? I HEARD OF HIM. WASN'T HE--
UNDER INVESTIGATION, YES. WE SUSPECTED HE MIGHT BE A MOLE.
MY GUESS WOULD BE THAT HE WAS SECRETLY WORKING FOR MAX, AND EITHER WADE OR THE LOSERS TOOK HIM OUT OF THE PICTURE TO STOP HIM FROM TALKING.
THE SAME GOES FOR MUTCHELL IN GOLIATH ACCOUNTS. HE WAS EXECUTED AT A PAINTBALL GAME OF ALL PLACES.
WE BELIEVE HE MAY HAVE BEEN INVOLVED IN REROUTING THE CASH IN THE FIRST PLACE.
SO YOU FIGURE IF I TRACK DOWN THESE LOSERS, THEY'LL LEAD US TO MAX...?
THAT'S FOR YOU TO FIND OUT. I WANT TO KNOW WHAT KIND OF OPERATION HE'S RUNNING.
PEACHY.
SO THIS ALL LEAVES JUST ONE QUESTION...
DIDN'T WE KILL MAX ALREADY?

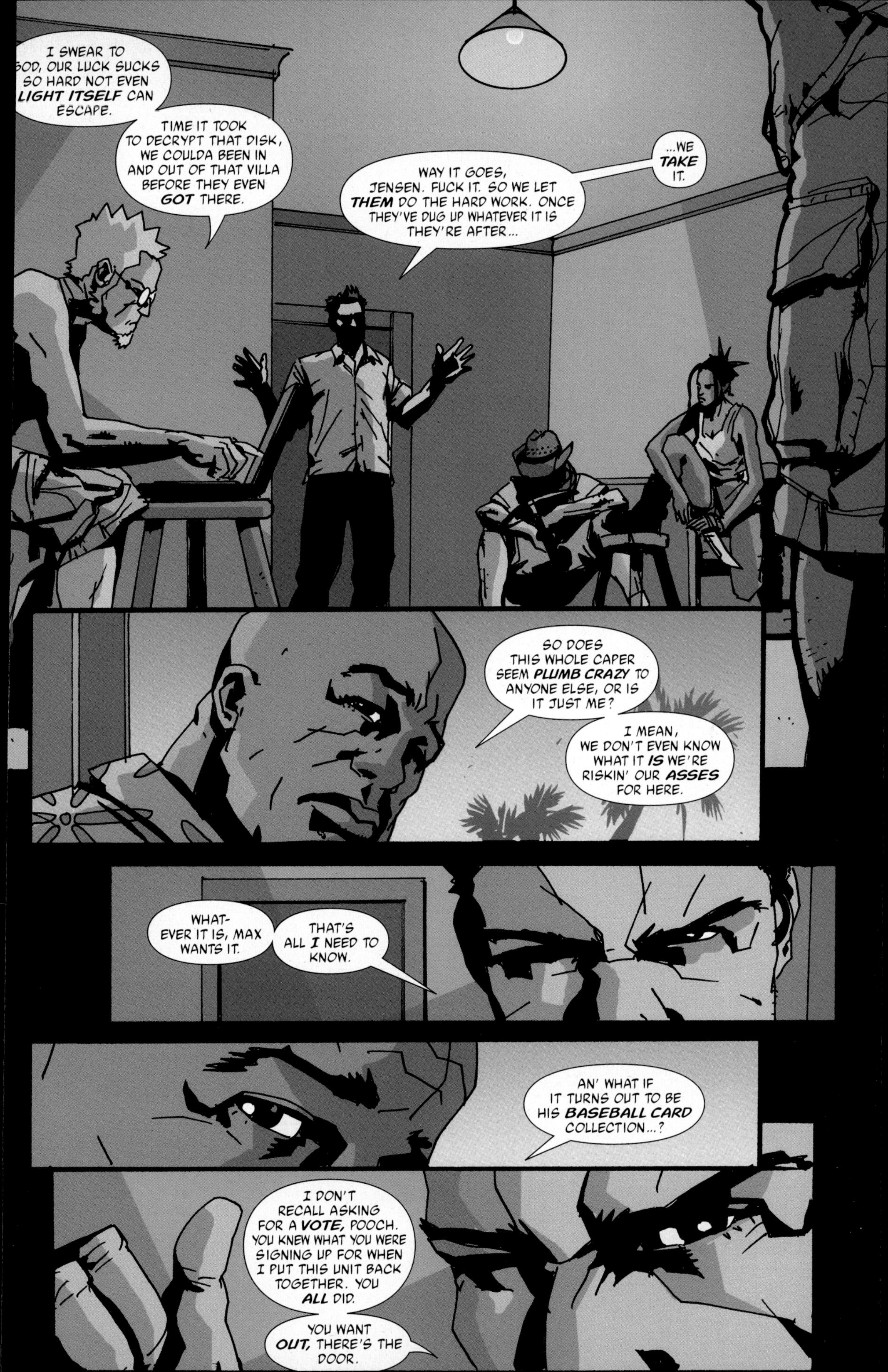
I SWEAR TO GOD, OUR LUCK SUCKS SO HARD NOT EVEN LIGHT ITSELF CAN ESCAPE.
TIME IT TOOK TO DECRYPT THAT DISK, WE COULDA BEEN IN AND OUT OF THAT VILLA BEFORE THEY EVEN GOT THERE.
WAY IT GOES, JENSEN. FUCK IT. SO WE LET THEM DO THE HARD WORK. ONCE THEY'VE DUG UP WHATEVER IT IS THEY'RE AFTER...
...WE TAKE IT.
SO DOES THIS WHOLE CAPER SEEM PLUMB CRAZY TO ANYONE ELSE, OR IS IT JUST ME?
I MEAN, WE DON'T EVEN KNOW WHAT IT IS WE'RE RISKIN' OUR ASSES FOR HERE.
WHAT-EVER IT IS, MAX WANTS IT.
THAT'S ALL I NEED TO KNOW.
AN' WHAT IF IT TURNS OUT TO BE HIS BASEBALL CARD COLLECTION...?
I DON'T RECALL ASKING FOR A VOTE, POOCH. YOU KNEW WHAT YOU WERE SIGNING UP FOR WHEN I PUT THIS UNIT BACK TOGETHER. YOU ALL DID.
YOU WANT OUT, THERE'S THE DOOR.

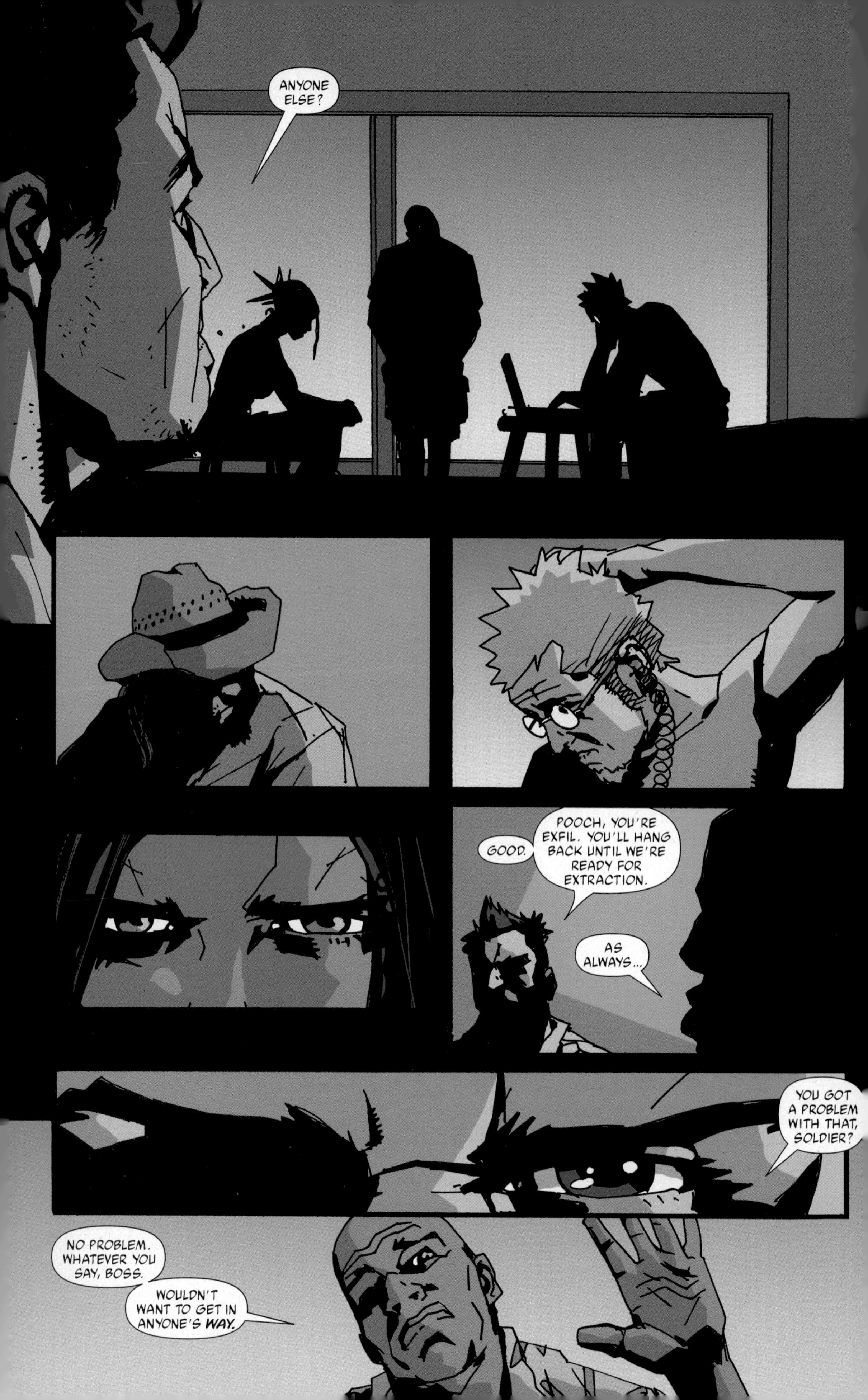
ANYONE ELSE?
GOOD.
POOCH, YOU'RE EXFIL. YOU'LL HANG BACK UNTIL WE'RE READY FOR EXTRACTION.
AS ALWAYS...
YOU GOT A PROBLEM WITH THAT, SOLDIER?
NO PROBLEM. WHATEVER YOU SAY, BOSS.
WOULDN'T WANT TO GET IN ANYONE'S **WAY.**

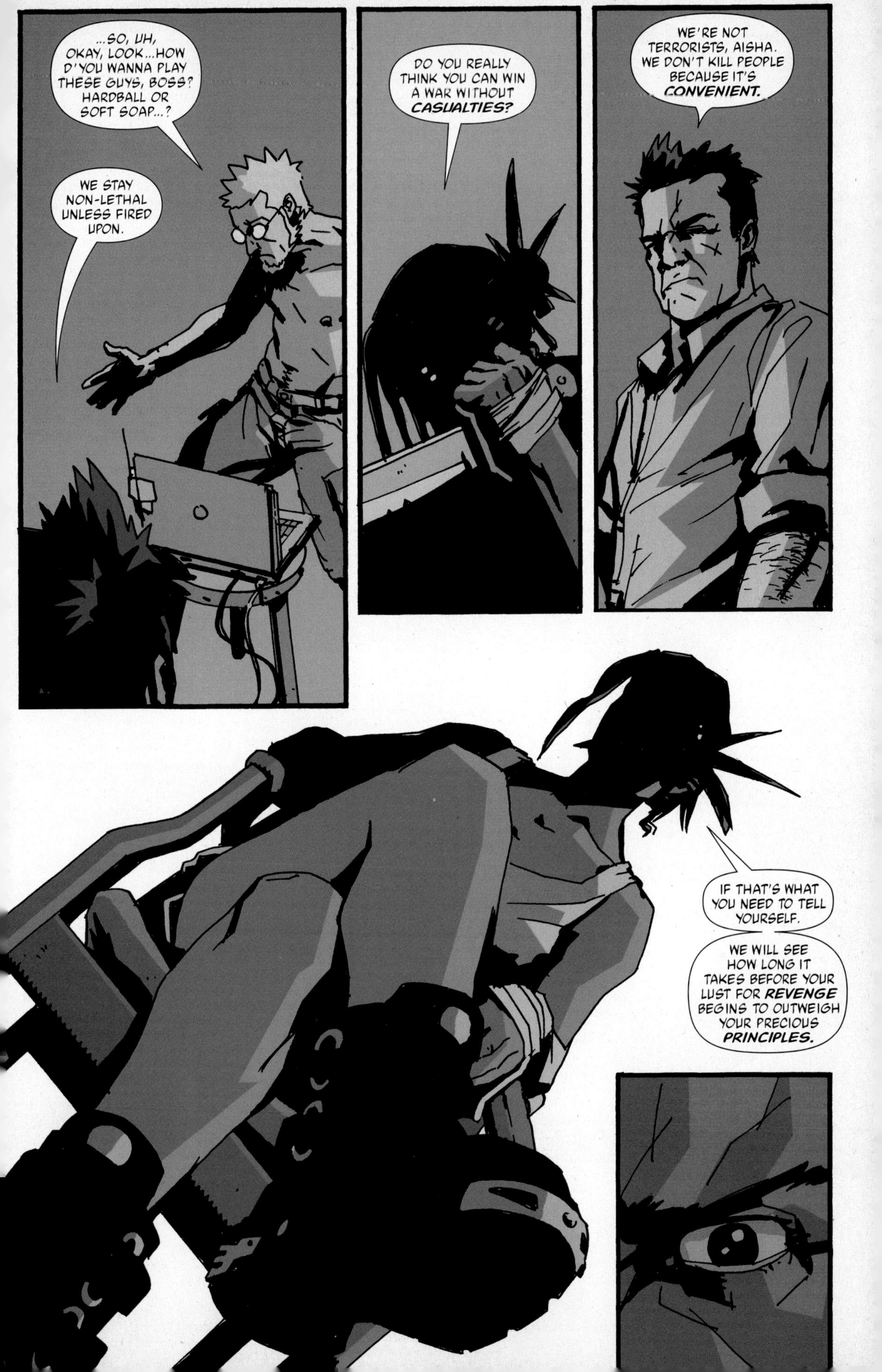
...SO, UH, OKAY, LOOK...HOW D'YOU WANNA PLAY THESE GUYS, BOSS? HARDBALL OR SOFT SOAP...?
WE STAY NON-LETHAL UNLESS FIRED UPON.
DO YOU REALLY THINK YOU CAN WIN A WAR WITHOUT CASUALTIES?
WE'RE NOT TERRORISTS, AISHA. WE DON'T KILL PEOPLE BECAUSE IT'S CONVENIENT.
IF THAT'S WHAT YOU NEED TO TELL YOURSELF.
WE WILL SEE HOW LONG IT TAKES BEFORE YOUR LUST FOR REVENGE BEGINS TO OUTWEIGH YOUR PRECIOUS PRINCIPLES.

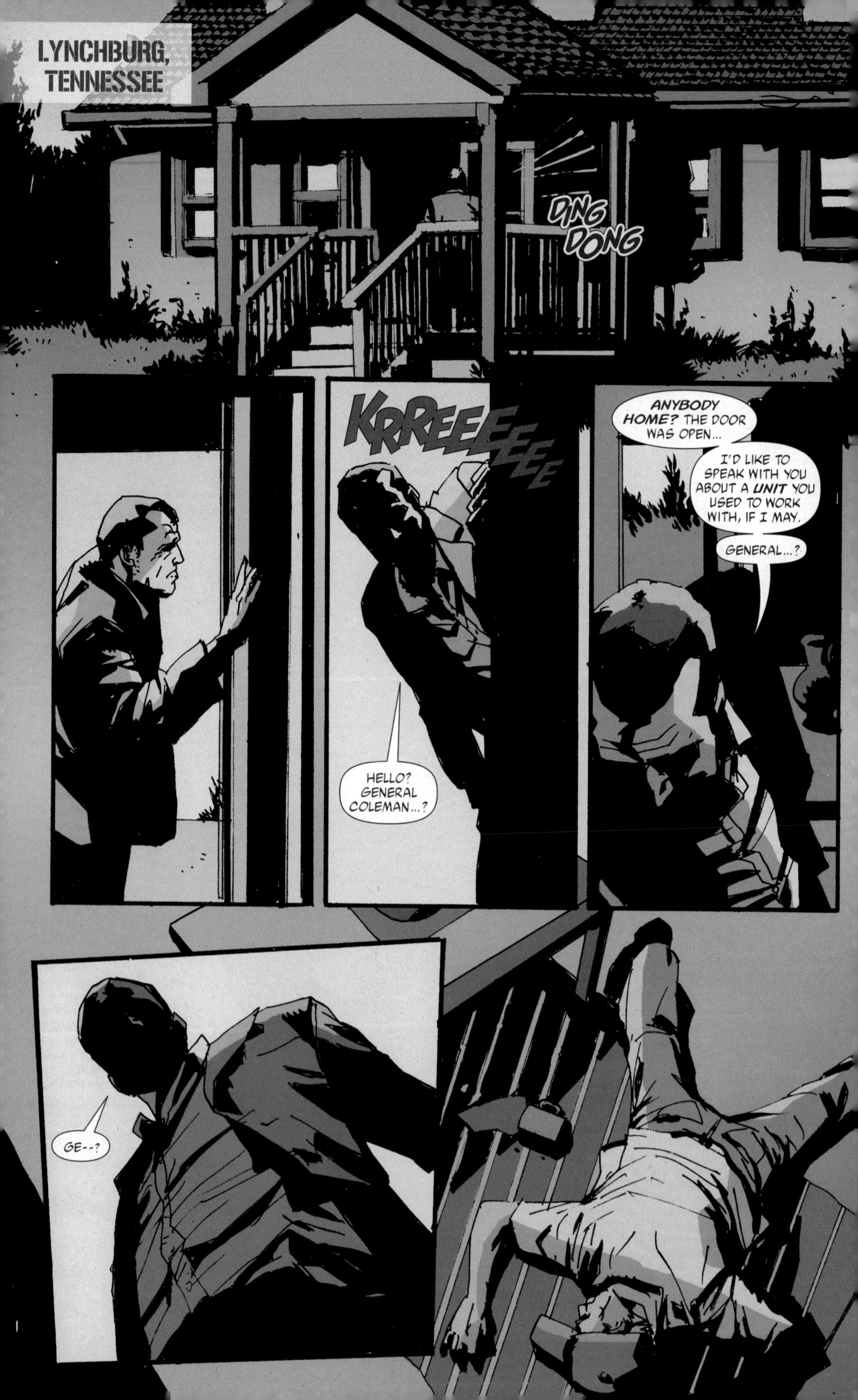
LYNCHBURG, TENNESSEE
DING DONG
KRREEEEEEE
HELLO? GENERAL COLEMAN...?
ANYBODY HOME? THE DOOR WAS OPEN...
I'D LIKE TO SPEAK WITH YOU ABOUT A UNIT YOU USED TO WORK WITH, IF I MAY.
GENERAL...?
GE--?

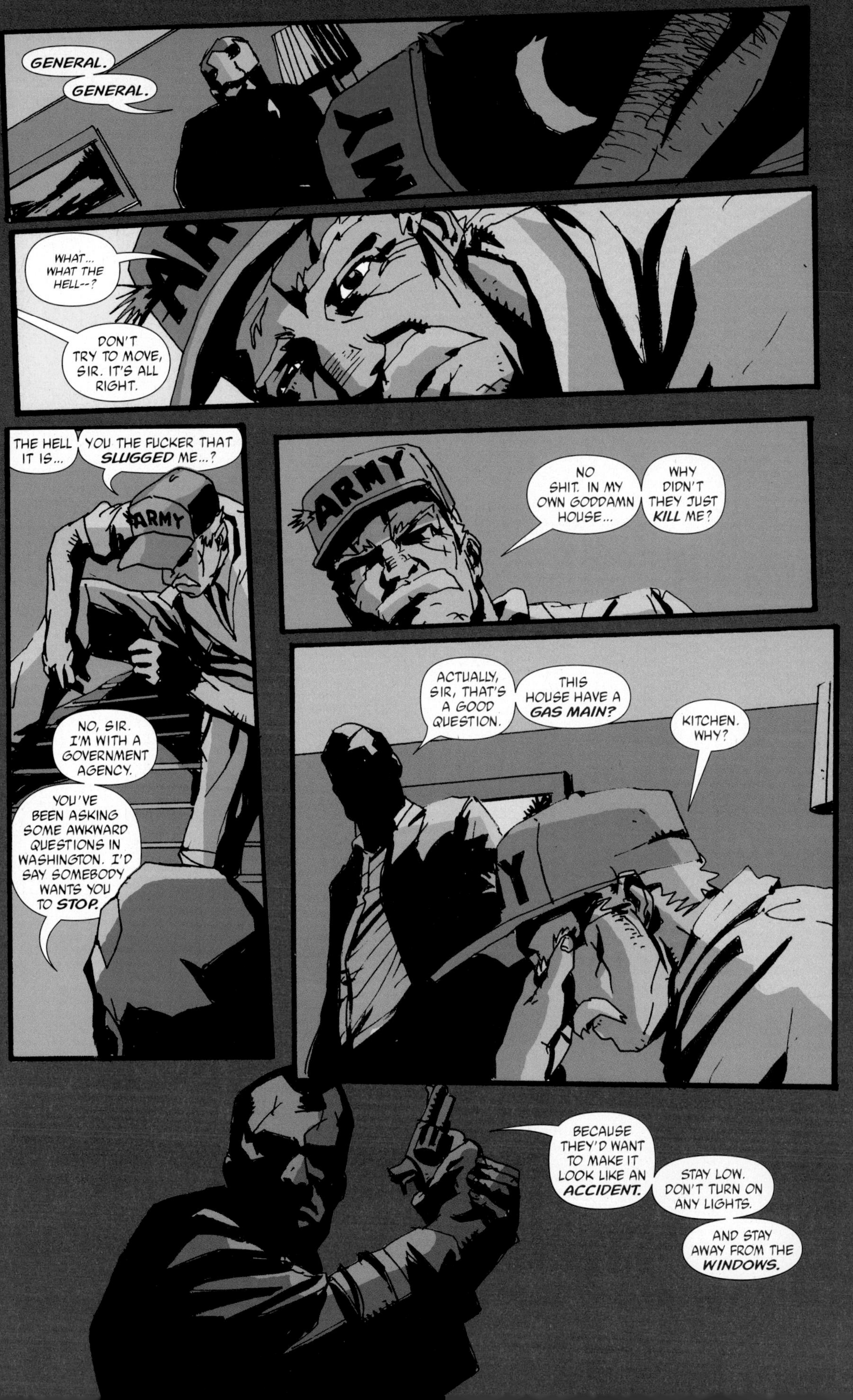
GENERAL.
GENERAL.
WHAT... WHAT THE HELL--?
DON'T TRY TO MOVE, SIR. IT'S ALL RIGHT.
THE HELL IT IS...
YOU THE FUCKER THAT SLUGGED ME...?
NO, SIR. I'M WITH A GOVERNMENT AGENCY.
YOU'VE BEEN ASKING SOME AWKWARD QUESTIONS IN WASHINGTON. I'D SAY SOMEBODY WANTS YOU TO STOP.
NO SHIT. IN MY OWN GODDAMN HOUSE...
WHY DIDN'T THEY JUST KILL ME?
ACTUALLY, SIR, THAT'S A GOOD QUESTION.
THIS HOUSE HAVE A GAS MAIN?
KITCHEN. WHY?
BECAUSE THEY'D WANT TO MAKE IT LOOK LIKE AN ACCIDENT.
STAY LOW. DON'T TURN ON ANY LIGHTS.
AND STAY AWAY FROM THE WINDOWS.

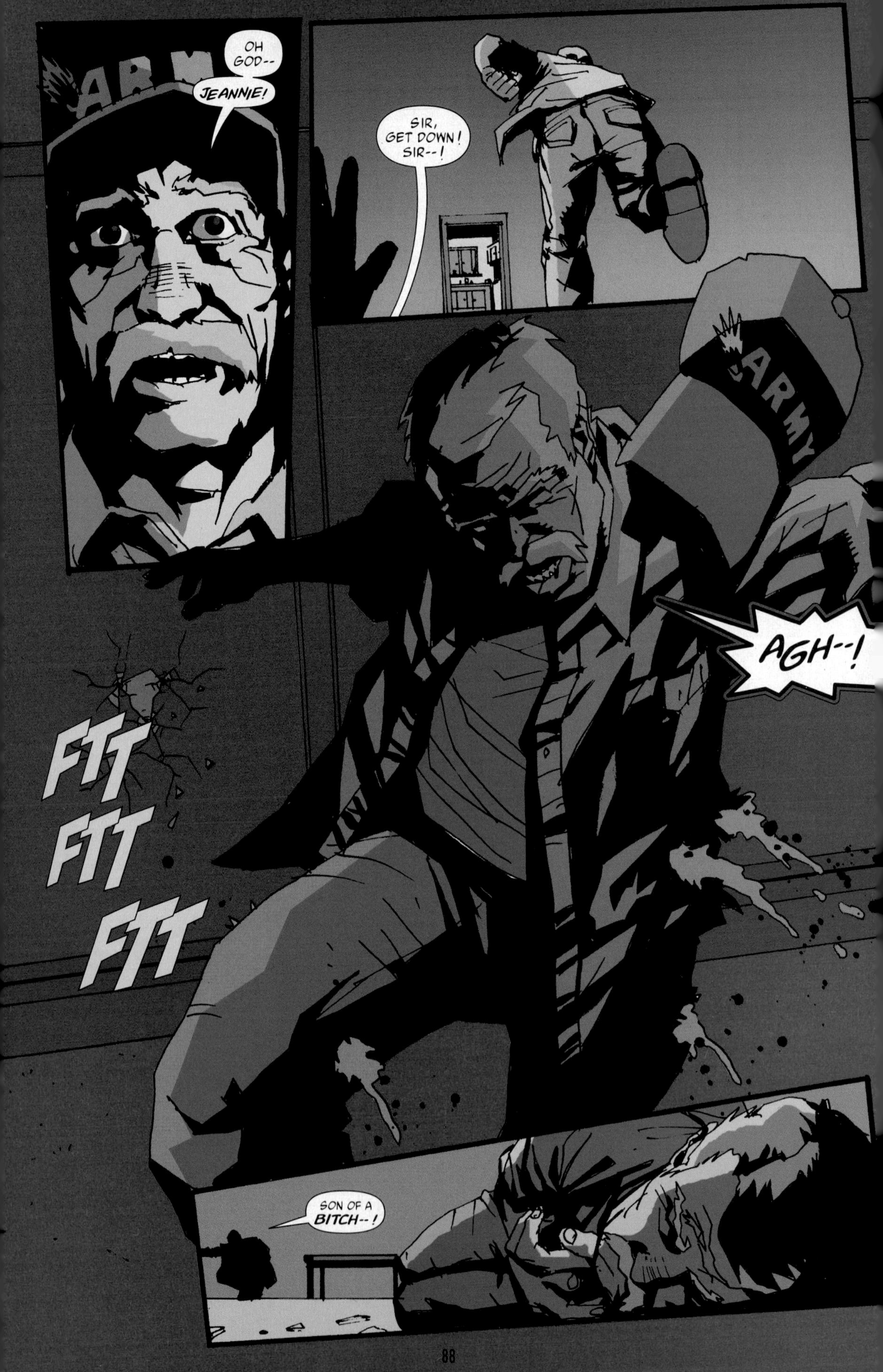

OH GOD--
JEANNIE!
SIR, GET DOWN! SIR--!
AGH--!
FTT FTT FTT
SON OF A BITCH--!

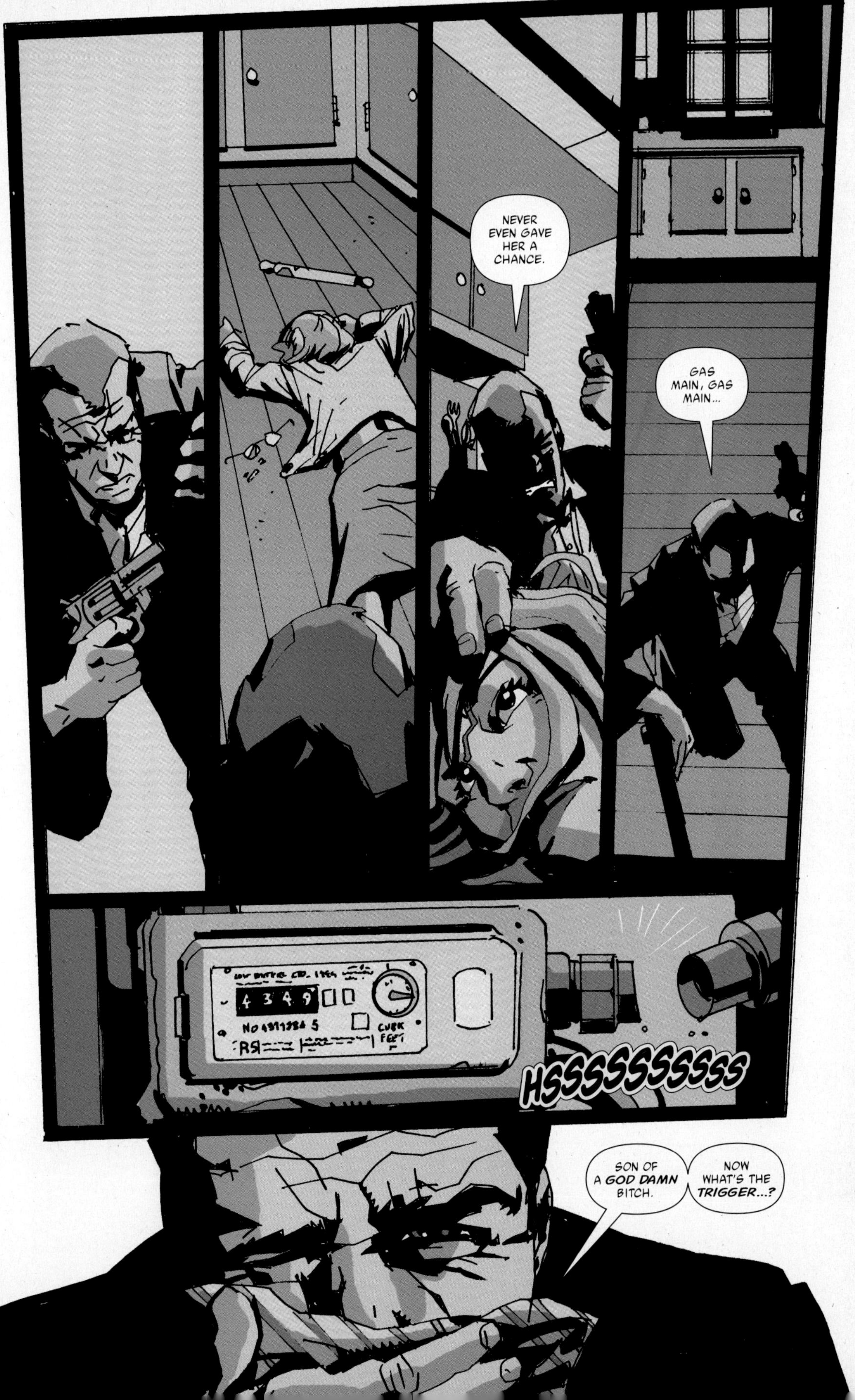
NEVER EVEN GAVE HER A CHANCE.
GAS MAIN, GAS MAIN...
HSSSSSSSSSSS
SON OF A GOD DAMN BITCH.
NOW WHAT'S THE TRIGGER...?

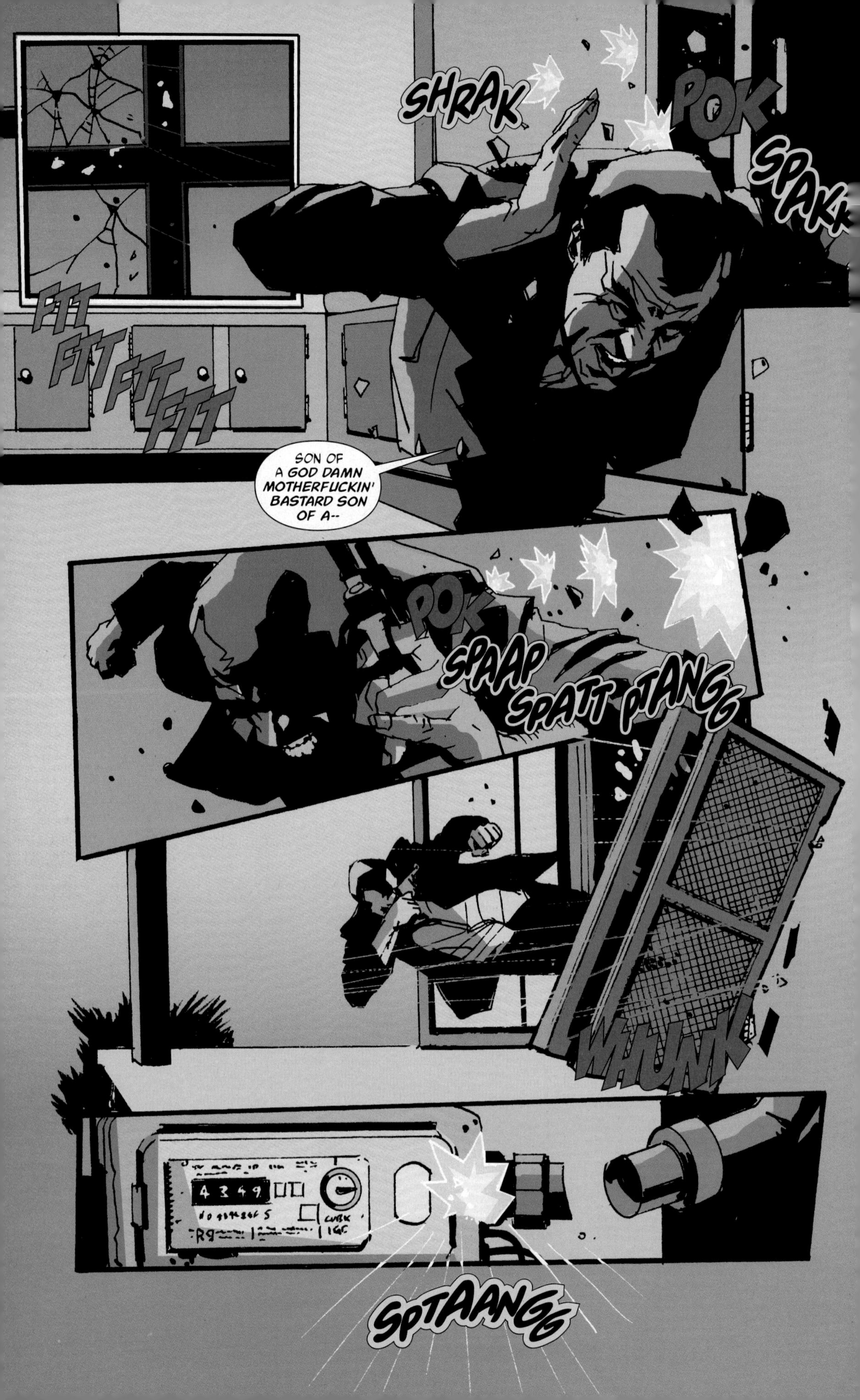
SHRAK
POK
SPAKK
FTT FTT FTT FTT
SON OF A GOD DAMN MOTHERFUCKIN' BASTARD SON OF A--
POK
SPAAP
SPATT PTANGG
WHUNK
SPTAANGG

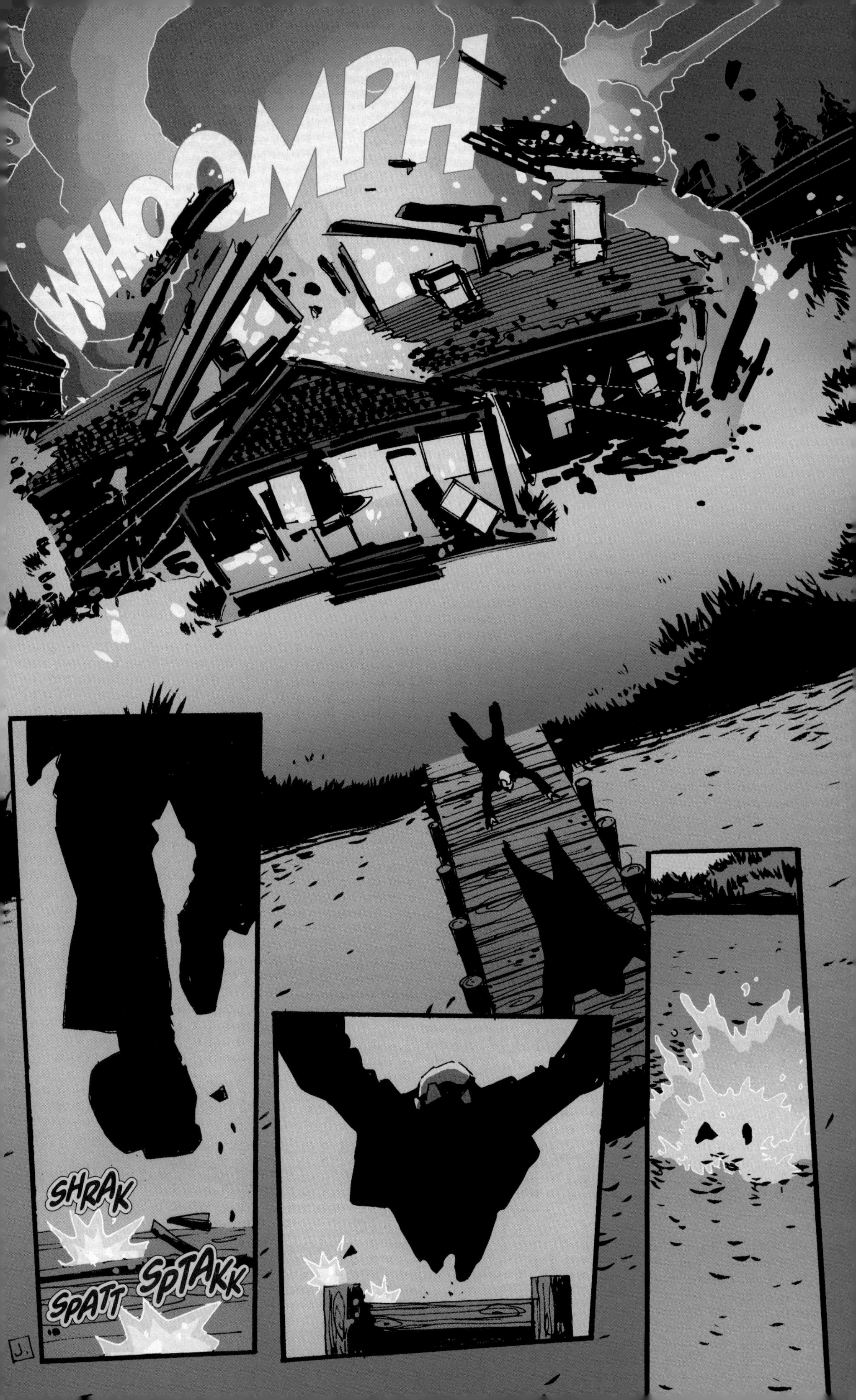
WHOOOMPH
SHRAK
SPTAKK
SPATT
J.

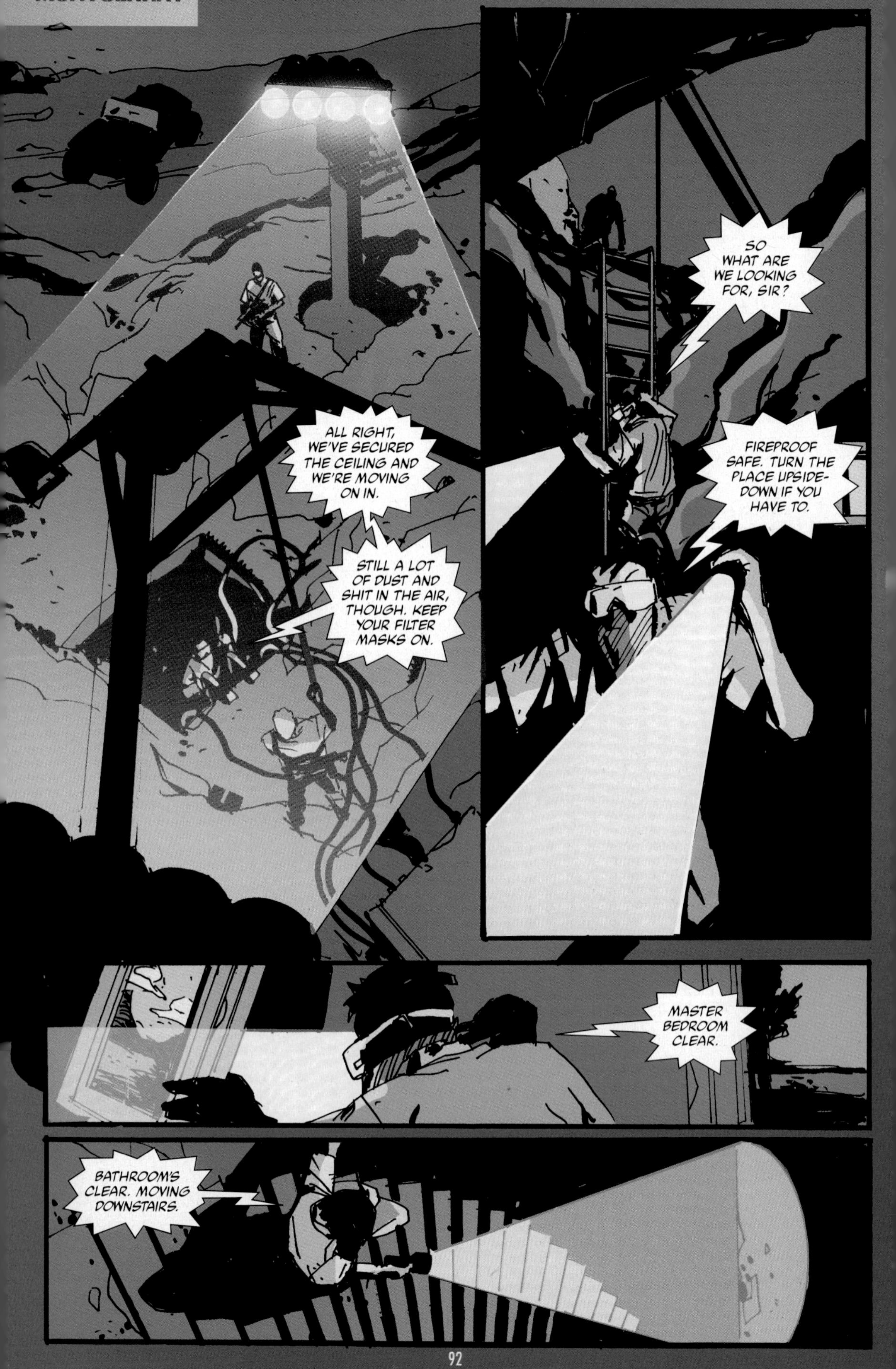
ALL RIGHT, WE'VE SECURED THE CEILING AND WE'RE MOVING ON IN.
STILL A LOT OF DUST AND SHIT IN THE AIR, THOUGH. KEEP YOUR FILTER MASKS ON.
SO WHAT ARE WE LOOKING FOR, SIR?
FIREPROOF SAFE. TURN THE PLACE UPSIDE-DOWN IF YOU HAVE TO.
MASTER BEDROOM CLEAR.
BATHROOM'S CLEAR. MOVING DOWNSTAIRS.

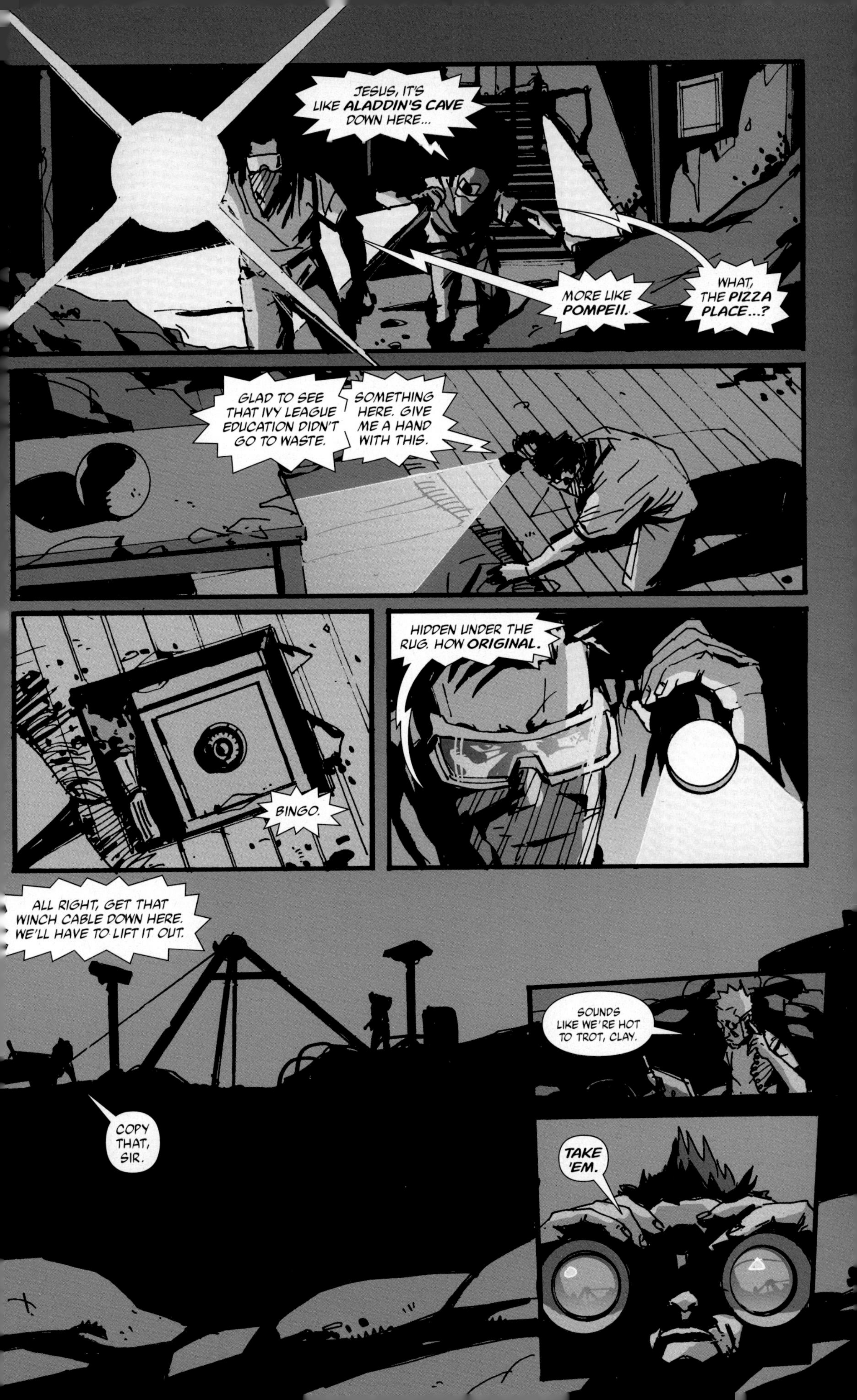
JESUS, IT'S LIKE ALADDIN'S CAVE DOWN HERE...
MORE LIKE POMPEII.
WHAT, THE PIZZA PLACE...?
GLAD TO SEE THAT IVY LEAGUE EDUCATION DIDN'T GO TO WASTE.
SOMETHING HERE. GIVE ME A HAND WITH THIS.
BINGO.
HIDDEN UNDER THE RUG. HOW ORIGINAL.
ALL RIGHT, GET THAT WINCH CABLE DOWN HERE. WE'LL HAVE TO LIFT IT OUT.
COPY THAT, SIR.
SOUNDS LIKE WE'RE HOT TO TROT, CLAY.
TAKE 'EM.

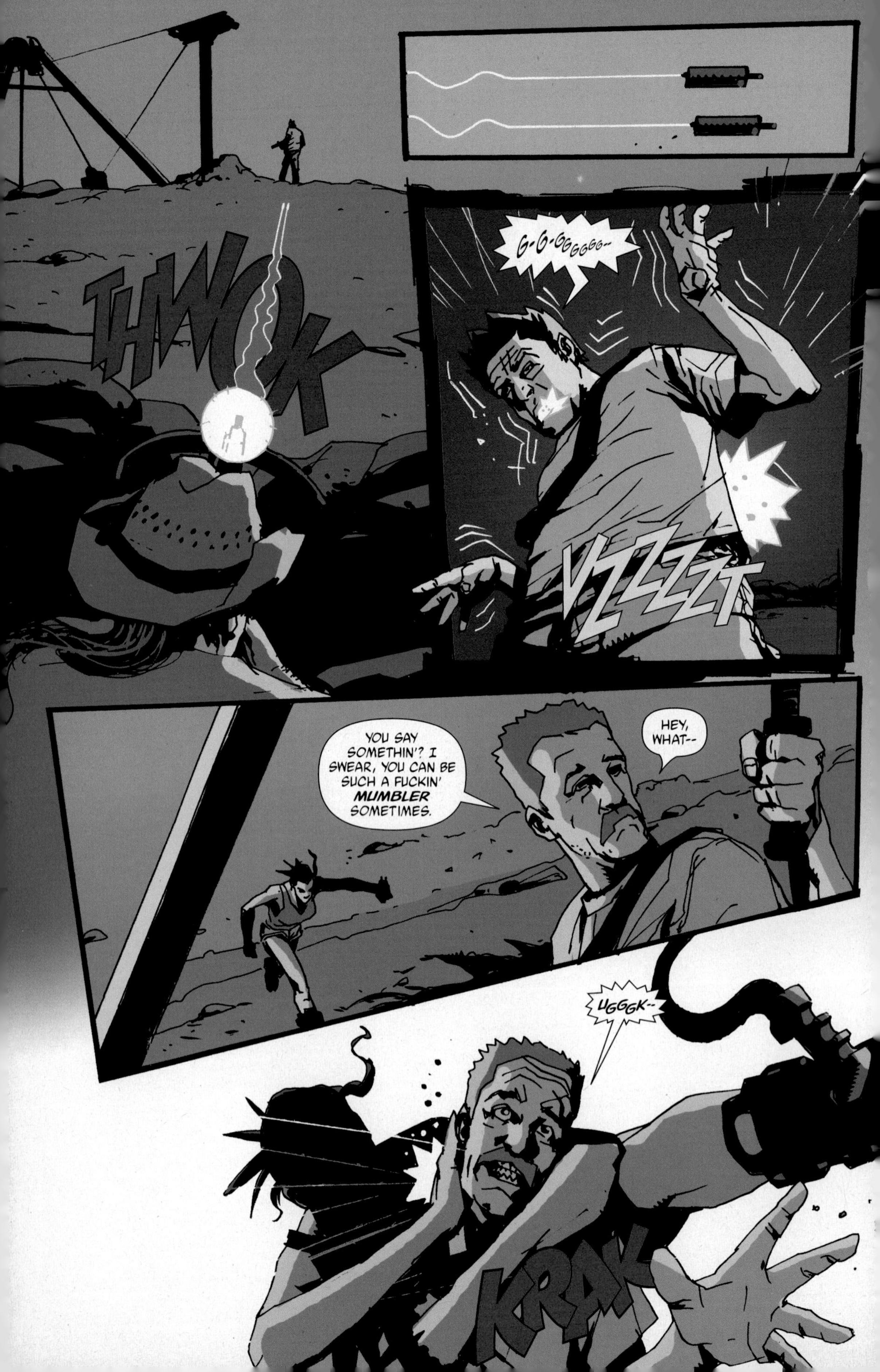
THWOK
G-G-GGGGGGG--
VZZZZZT
YOU SAY SOMETHIN'? I SWEAR, YOU CAN BE SUCH A FUCKIN' **MUMBLER** SOMETIMES.
HEY, WHAT--
UGGGK--
KRAK

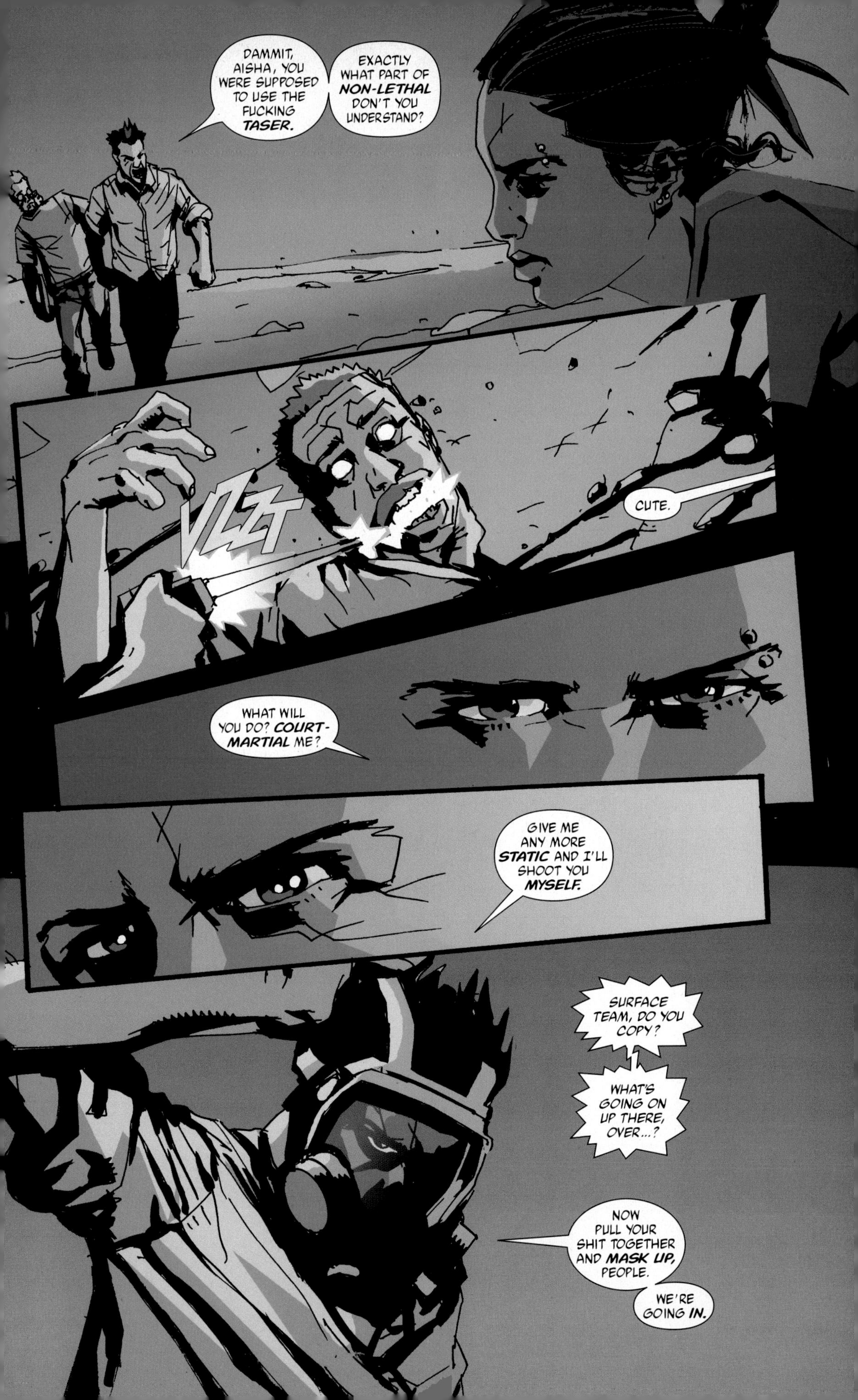

DAMMIT, AISHA, YOU WERE SUPPOSED TO USE THE FUCKING TASER.
EXACTLY WHAT PART OF NON-LETHAL DON'T YOU UNDERSTAND?
VZZT
CUTE.
WHAT WILL YOU DO? COURT-MARTIAL ME?
GIVE ME ANY MORE STATIC AND I'LL SHOOT YOU MYSELF.
SURFACE TEAM, DO YOU COPY?
WHAT'S GOING ON UP THERE, OVER...?
NOW PULL YOUR SHIT TOGETHER AND MASK UP, PEOPLE.
WE'RE GOING IN.

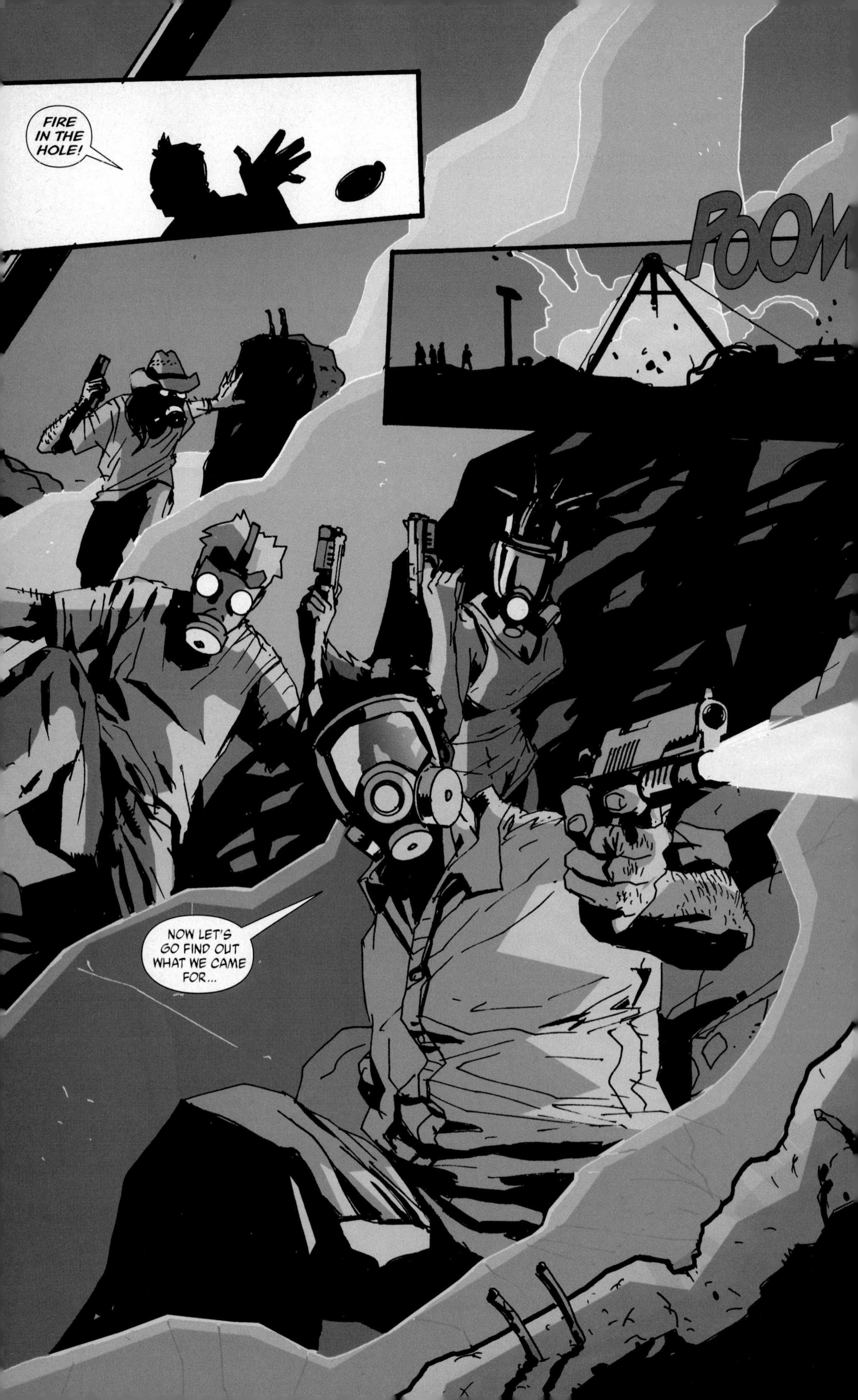
FIRE IN THE HOLE!
POOM
NOW LET'S GO FIND OUT WHAT WE CAME FOR...

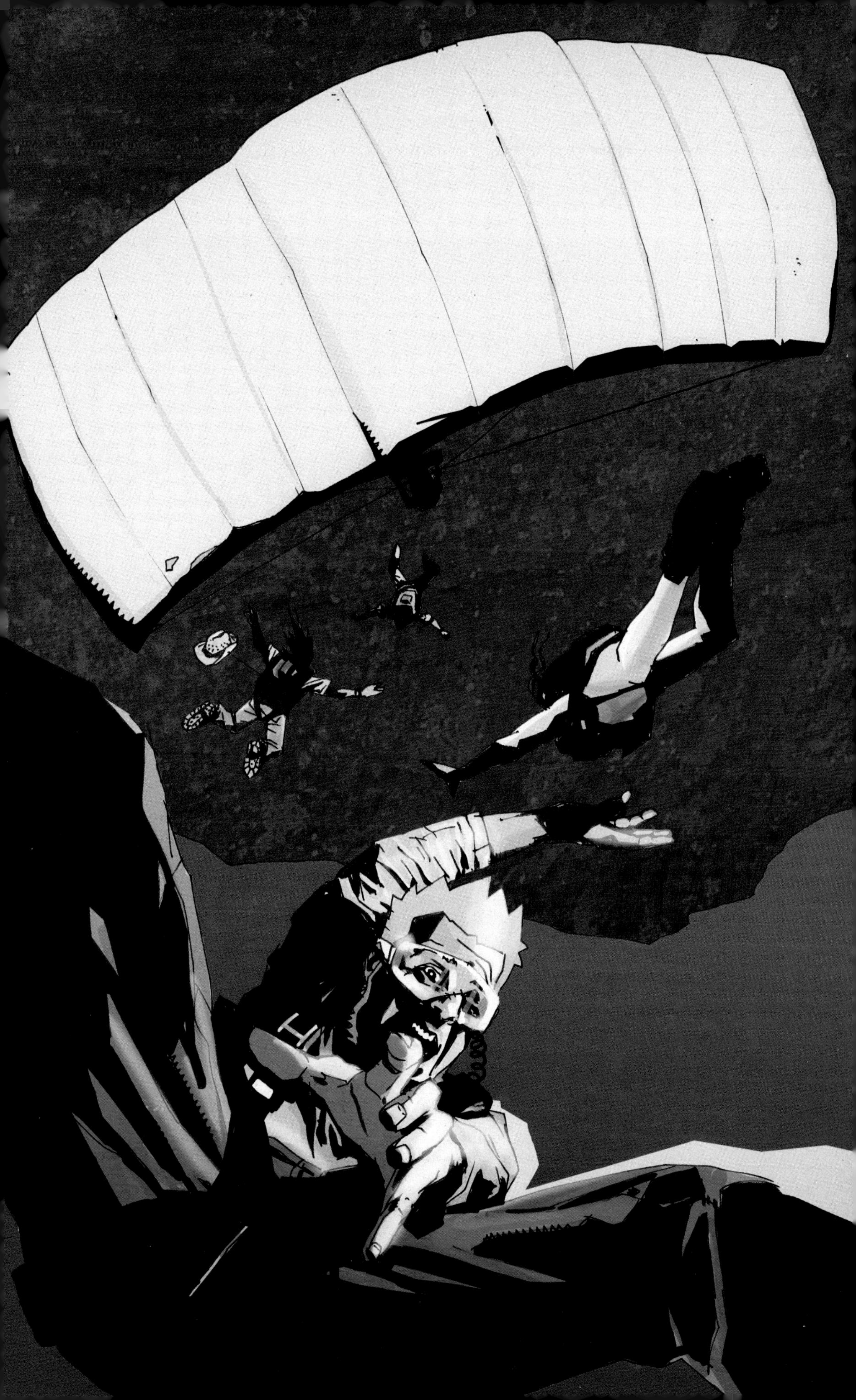

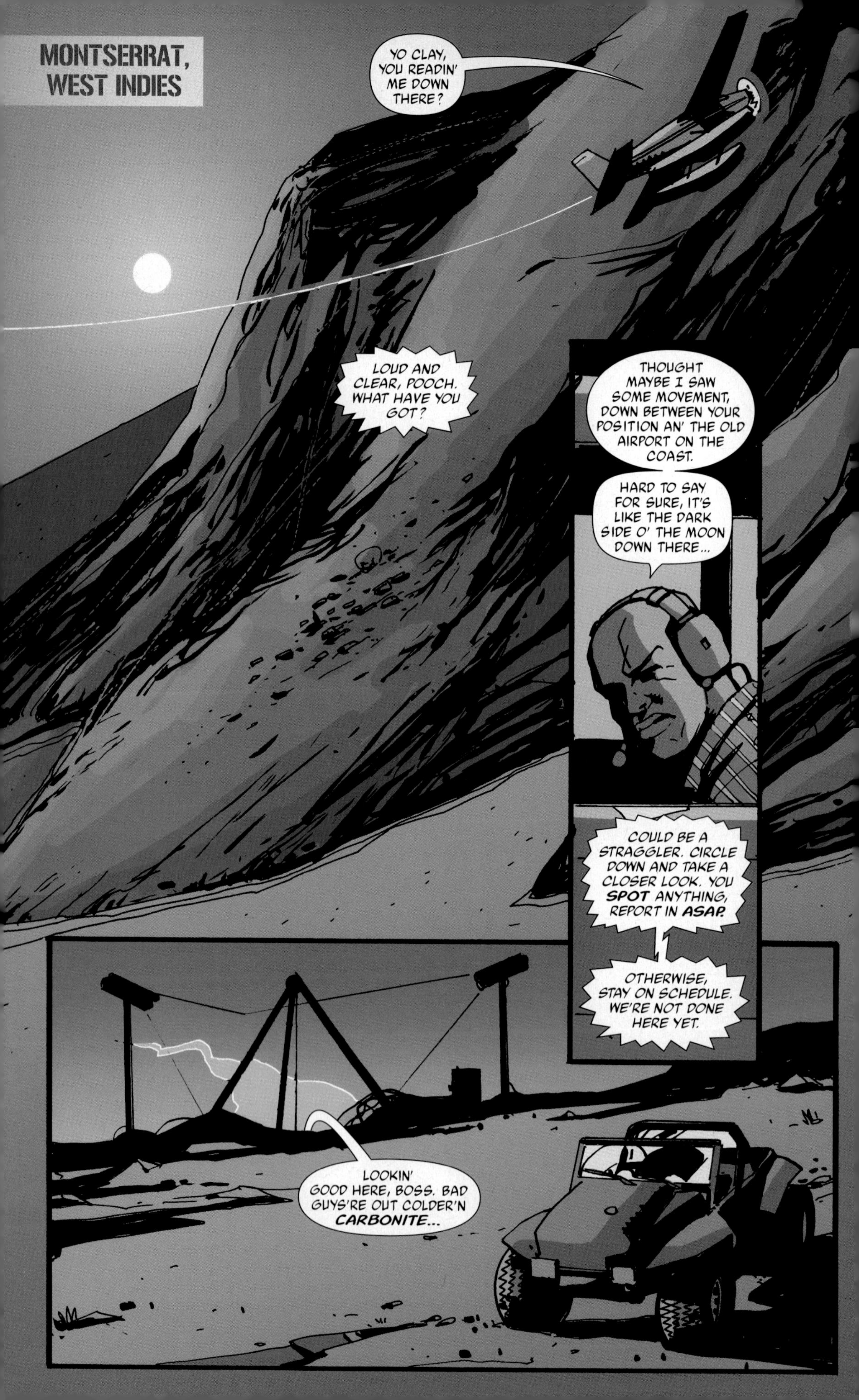
MONTSERRAT, WEST INDIES
YO CLAY, YOU READIN' ME DOWN THERE?
LOUD AND CLEAR, POOCH. WHAT HAVE YOU GOT?
THOUGHT MAYBE I SAW SOME MOVEMENT, DOWN BETWEEN YOUR POSITION AN' THE OLD AIRPORT ON THE COAST.
HARD TO SAY FOR SURE, IT'S LIKE THE DARK SIDE O' THE MOON DOWN THERE...
COULD BE A STRAGGLER. CIRCLE DOWN AND TAKE A CLOSER LOOK. YOU SPOT ANYTHING, REPORT IN ASAP.
OTHERWISE, STAY ON SCHEDULE. WE'RE NOT DONE HERE YET.
LOOKIN' GOOD HERE, BOSS. BAD GUYS'RE OUT COLDER'N CARBONITE...

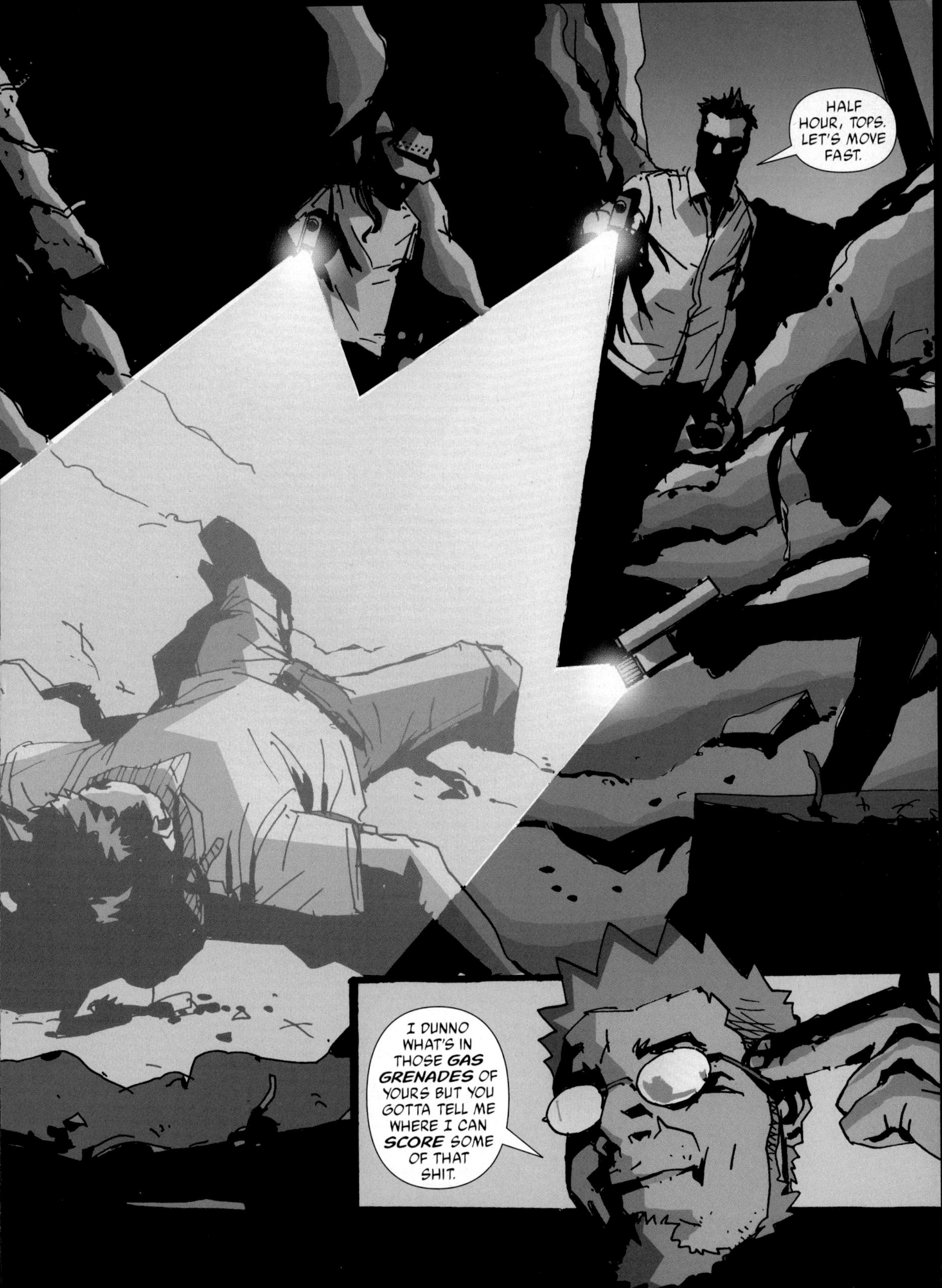
HALF HOUR, TOPS. LET'S MOVE FAST.
I DUNNO WHAT'S IN THOSE GAS GRENADES OF YOURS BUT YOU GOTTA TELL ME WHERE I CAN SCORE SOME OF THAT SHIT.

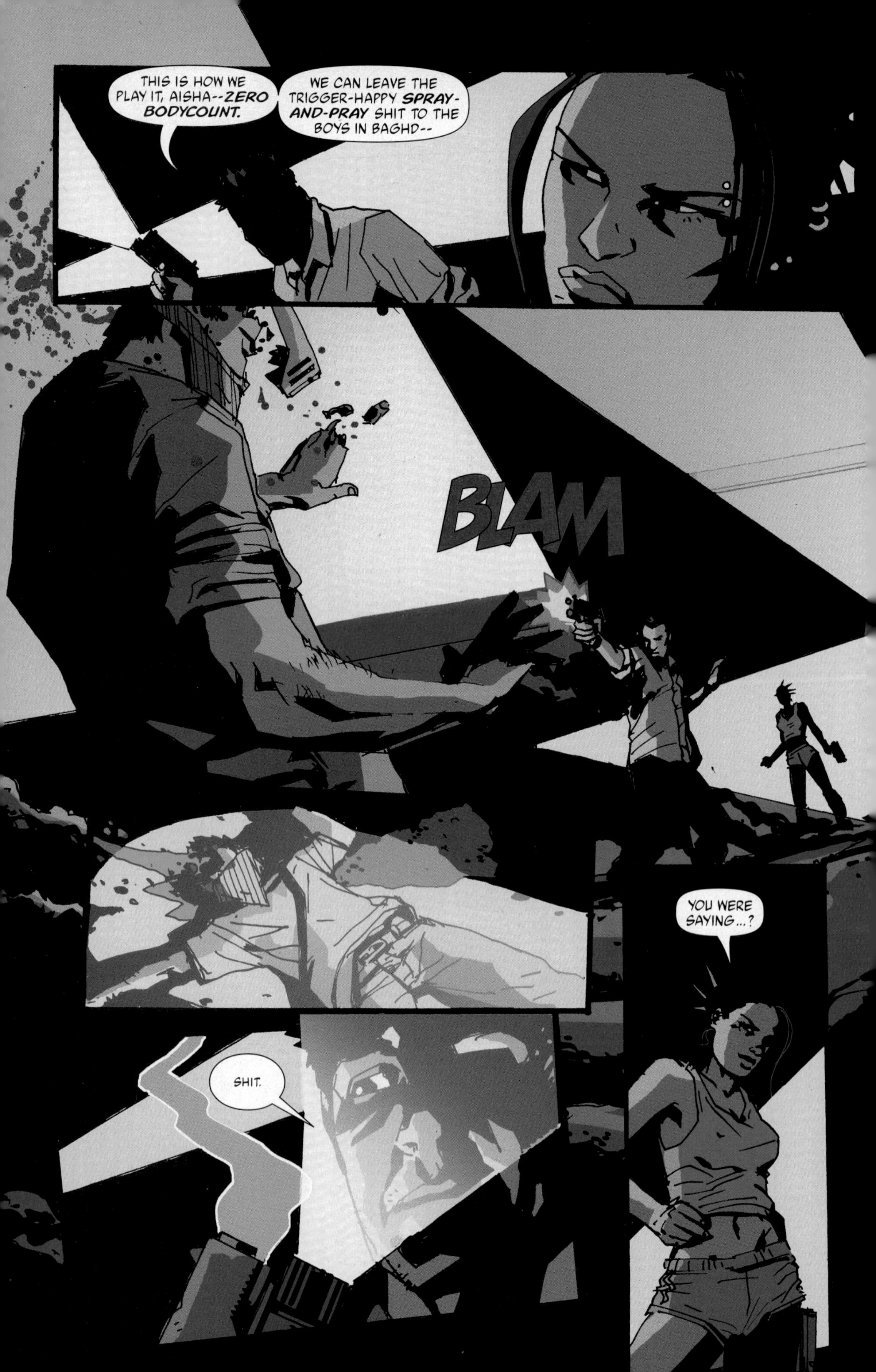
THIS IS HOW WE PLAY IT, AISHA--ZERO BODYCOUNT.
WE CAN LEAVE THE TRIGGER-HAPPY SPRAY-AND-PRAY SHIT TO THE BOYS IN BAGHD--
BLAM
YOU WERE SAYING...?
SHIT.

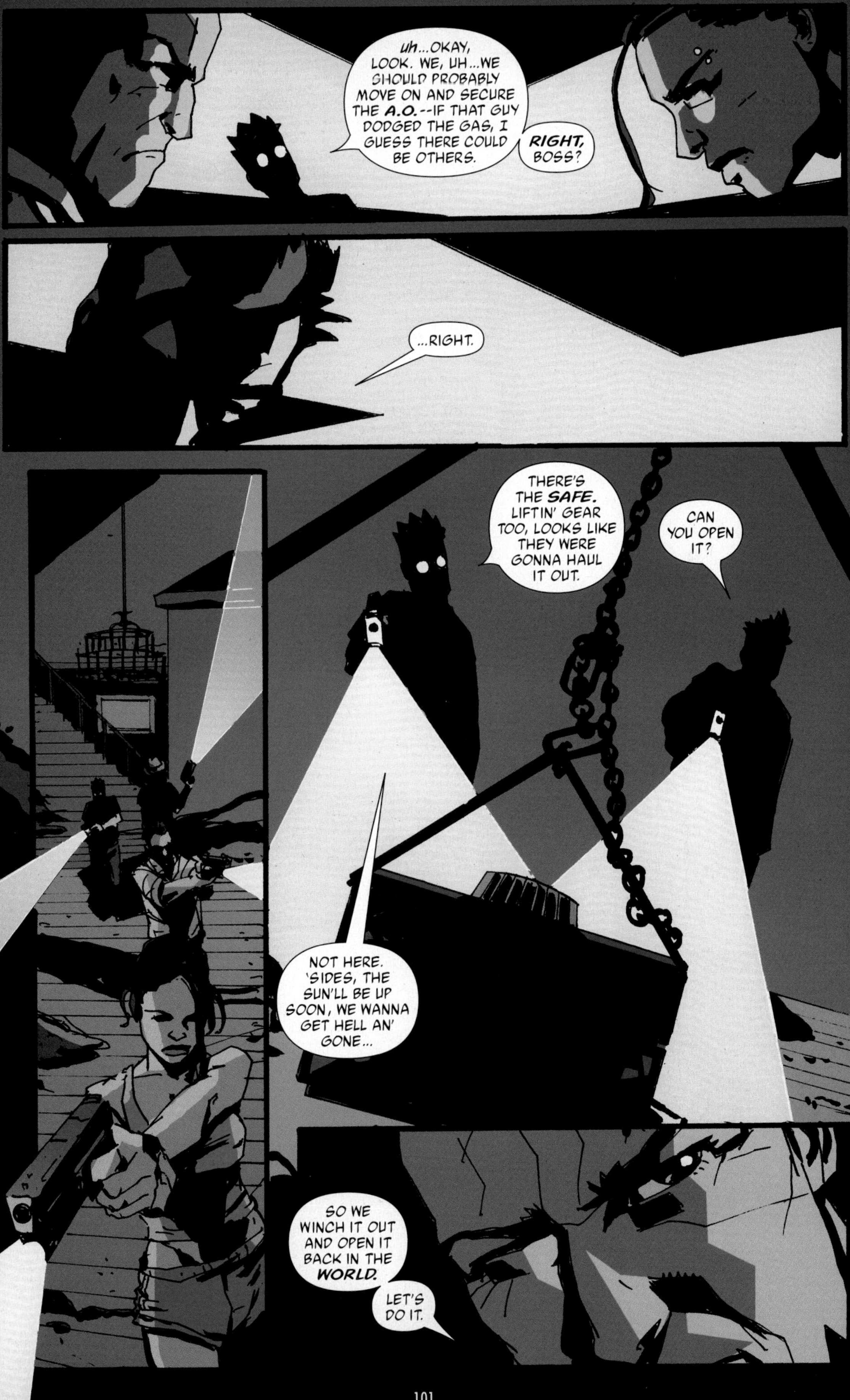

UH...OKAY, LOOK. WE, UH...WE SHOULD PROBABLY MOVE ON AND SECURE THE A.O.--IF THAT GUY DODGED THE GAS, I GUESS THERE COULD BE OTHERS.
RIGHT, BOSS?
...RIGHT.
THERE'S THE SAFE. LIFTIN' GEAR TOO, LOOKS LIKE THEY WERE GONNA HAUL IT OUT.
CAN YOU OPEN IT?
NOT HERE. 'SIDES, THE SUN'LL BE UP SOON, WE WANNA GET HELL AN' GONE...
SO WE WINCH IT OUT AND OPEN IT BACK IN THE WORLD.
LET'S DO IT.

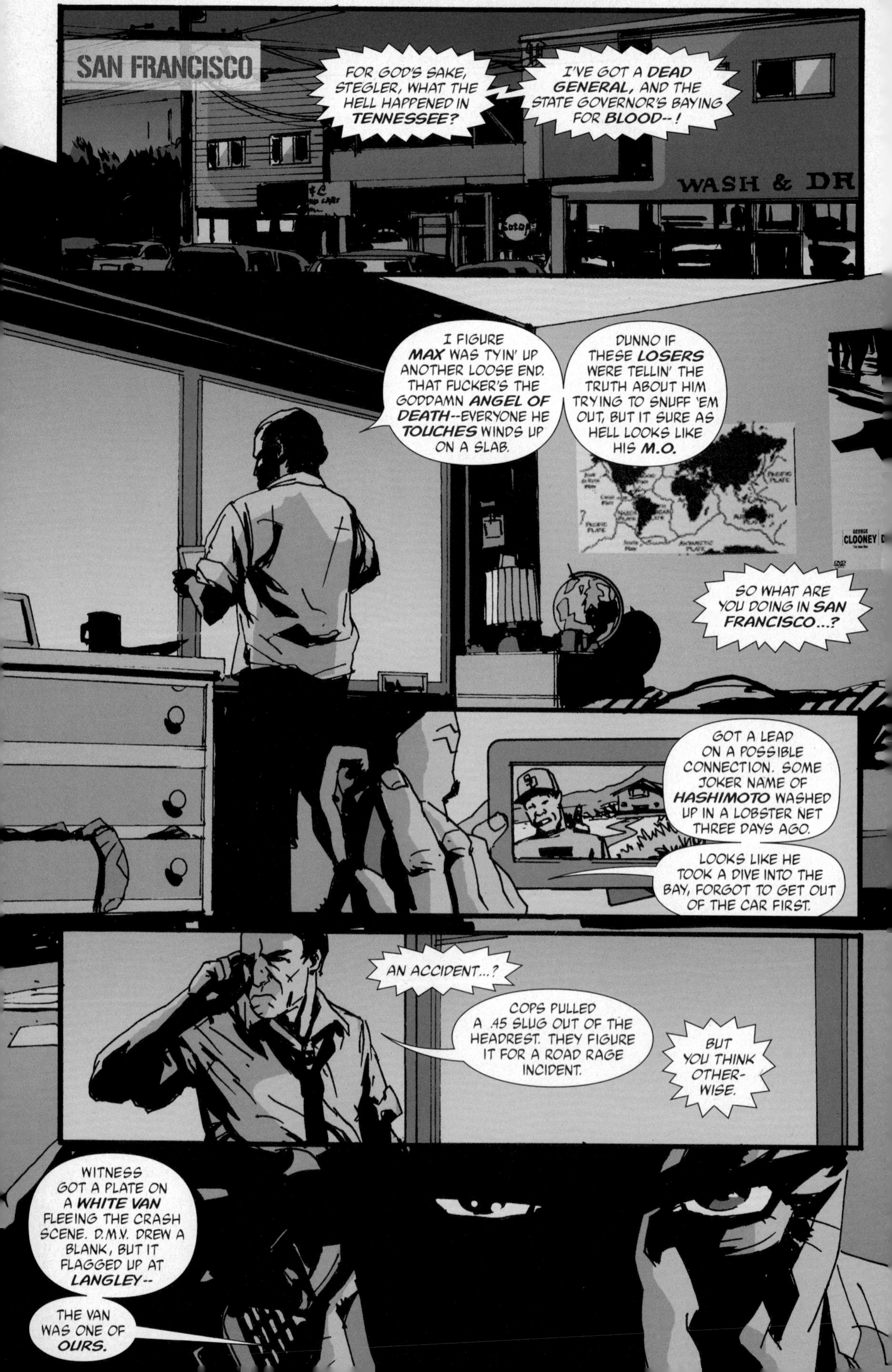
SAN FRANCISCO
FOR GOD'S SAKE, STEGLER, WHAT THE HELL HAPPENED IN TENNESSEE?
I'VE GOT A DEAD GENERAL, AND THE STATE GOVERNOR'S BAYING FOR BLOOD--!
WASH & DR
I FIGURE MAX WAS TYIN' UP ANOTHER LOOSE END. THAT FUCKER'S THE GODDAMN ANGEL OF DEATH--EVERYONE HE TOUCHES WINDS UP ON A SLAB.
DUNNO IF THESE LOSERS WERE TELLIN' THE TRUTH ABOUT HIM TRYING TO SNUFF 'EM OUT, BUT IT SURE AS HELL LOOKS LIKE HIS M.O.
CLOONEY
SO WHAT ARE YOU DOING IN SAN FRANCISCO...?
GOT A LEAD ON A POSSIBLE CONNECTION. SOME JOKER NAME OF HASHIMOTO WASHED UP IN A LOBSTER NET THREE DAYS AGO.
LOOKS LIKE HE TOOK A DIVE INTO THE BAY, FORGOT TO GET OUT OF THE CAR FIRST.
AN ACCIDENT...?
COPS PULLED A .45 SLUG OUT OF THE HEADREST. THEY FIGURE IT FOR A ROAD RAGE INCIDENT.
BUT YOU THINK OTHER-WISE.
WITNESS GOT A PLATE ON A WHITE VAN FLEEING THE CRASH SCENE. D.M.V. DREW A BLANK, BUT IT FLAGGED UP AT LANGLEY--
THE VAN WAS ONE OF OURS.

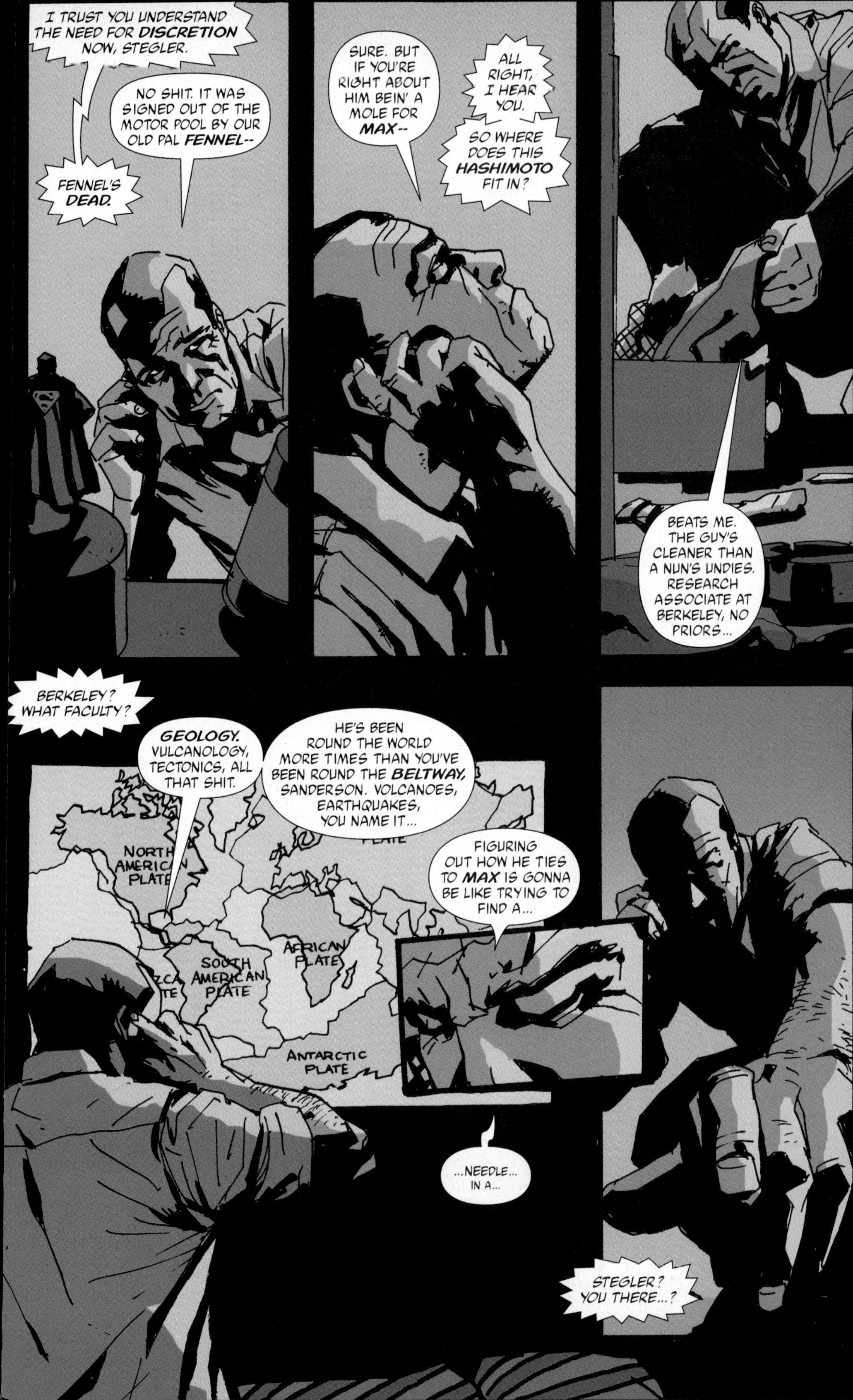
I TRUST YOU UNDERSTAND THE NEED FOR DISCRETION NOW, STEGLER.
NO SHIT. IT WAS SIGNED OUT OF THE MOTOR POOL BY OUR OLD PAL FENNEL--
FENNEL'S DEAD.
SURE. BUT IF YOU'RE RIGHT ABOUT HIM BEIN' A MOLE FOR MAX--
ALL RIGHT, I HEAR YOU.
SO WHERE DOES THIS HASHIMOTO FIT IN?
BEATS ME. THE GUY'S CLEANER THAN A NUN'S UNDIES. RESEARCH ASSOCIATE AT BERKELEY, NO PRIORS...
BERKELEY? WHAT FACULTY?
GEOLOGY. VULCANOLOGY, TECTONICS, ALL THAT SHIT.
HE'S BEEN ROUND THE WORLD MORE TIMES THAN YOU'VE BEEN ROUND THE BELTWAY, SANDERSON. VOLCANOES, EARTHQUAKES, YOU NAME IT...
NORTH AMERICAN PLATE
AFRICAN PLATE
SOUTH AMERICAN PLATE
ANTARCTIC PLATE
FIGURING OUT HOW HE TIES TO MAX IS GONNA BE LIKE TRYING TO FIND A...
...NEEDLE... IN A...
STEGLER? YOU THERE...?

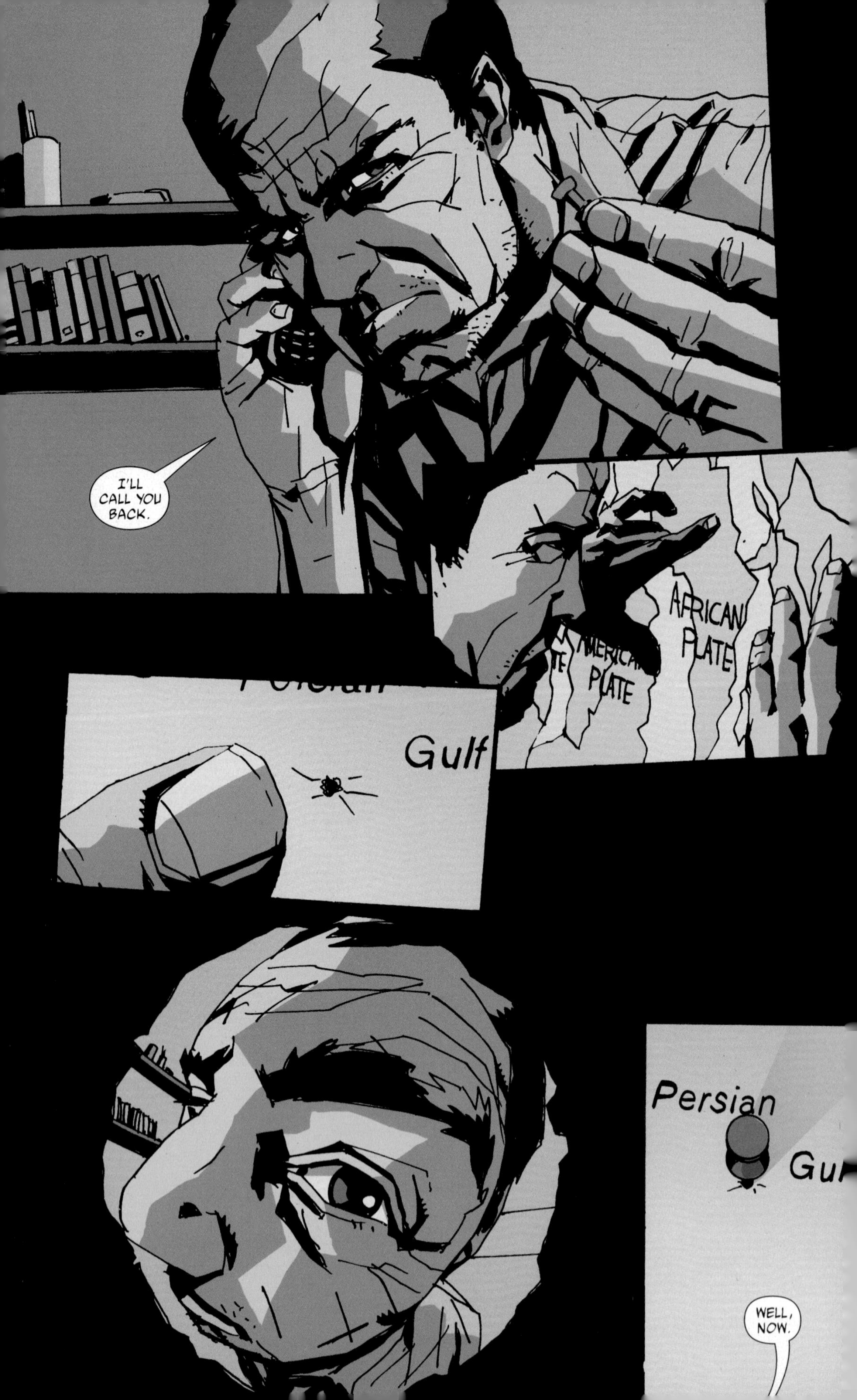
I'LL CALL YOU BACK.
AFRICAN PLATE
AMERICAN PLATE
Gulf
Persian
WELL, NOW.

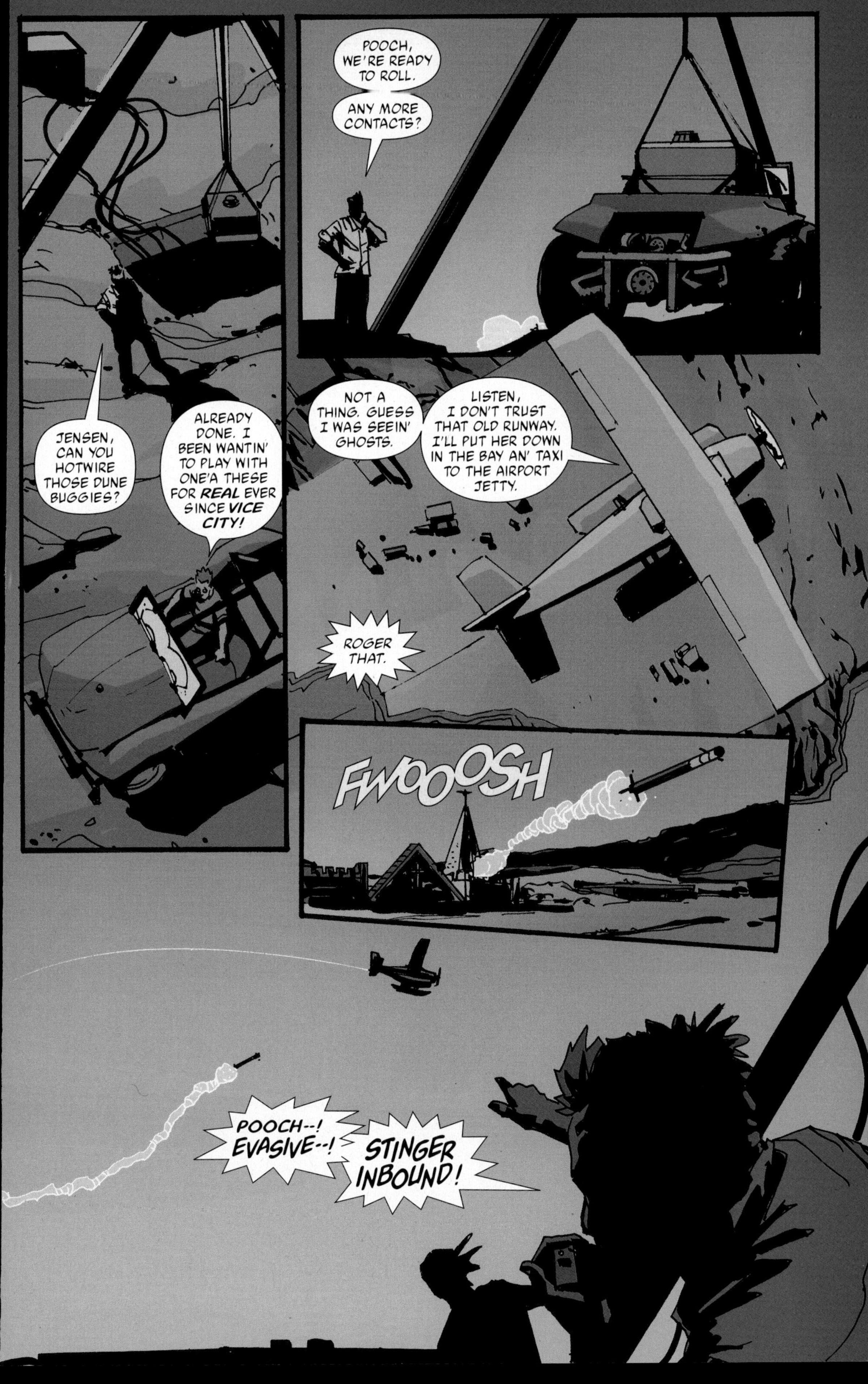
POOCH, WE'RE READY TO ROLL.
ANY MORE CONTACTS?
JENSEN, CAN YOU HOTWIRE THOSE DUNE BUGGIES?
ALREADY DONE. I BEEN WANTIN' TO PLAY WITH ONE'A THESE FOR REAL EVER SINCE VICE CITY!
NOT A THING. GUESS I WAS SEEIN' GHOSTS.
LISTEN, I DON'T TRUST THAT OLD RUNWAY. I'LL PUT HER DOWN IN THE BAY AN' TAXI TO THE AIRPORT JETTY.
ROGER THAT.
FWOOOSH
POOCH--! EVASIVE--!
STINGER INBOUND!

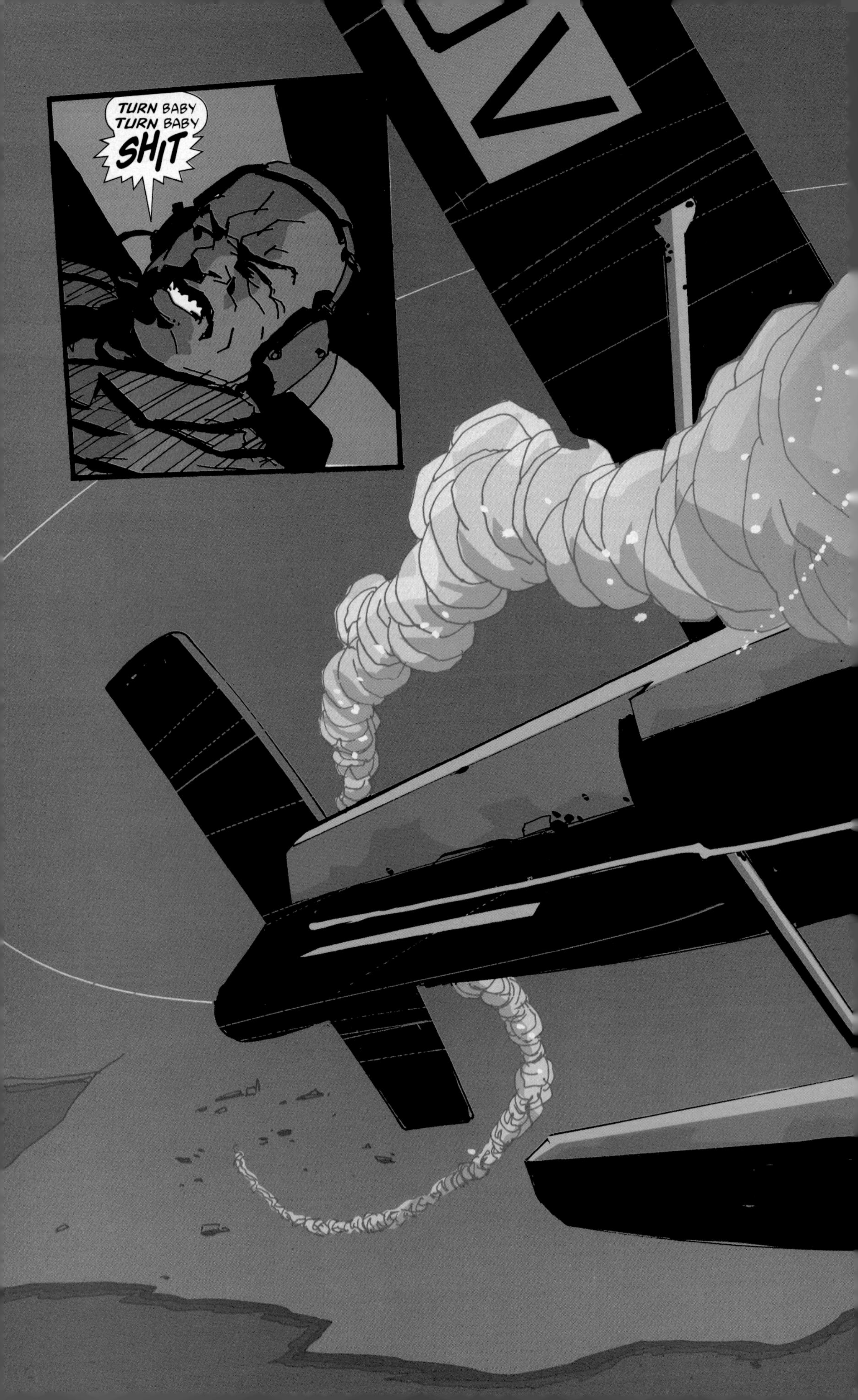
TURN BABY TURN BABY SHIT

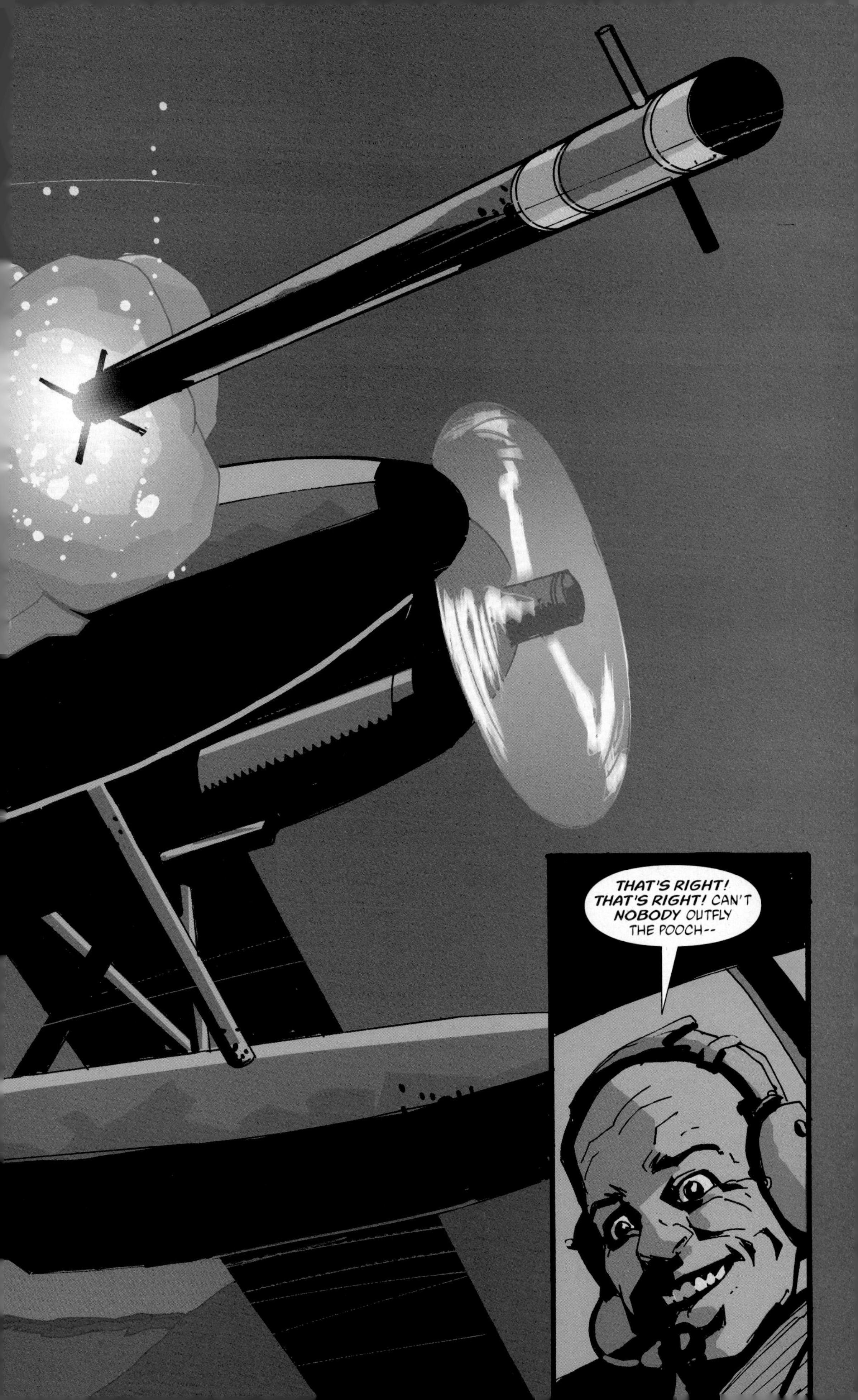
THAT'S RIGHT! THAT'S RIGHT! CAN'T NOBODY OUTFLY THE POOCH--

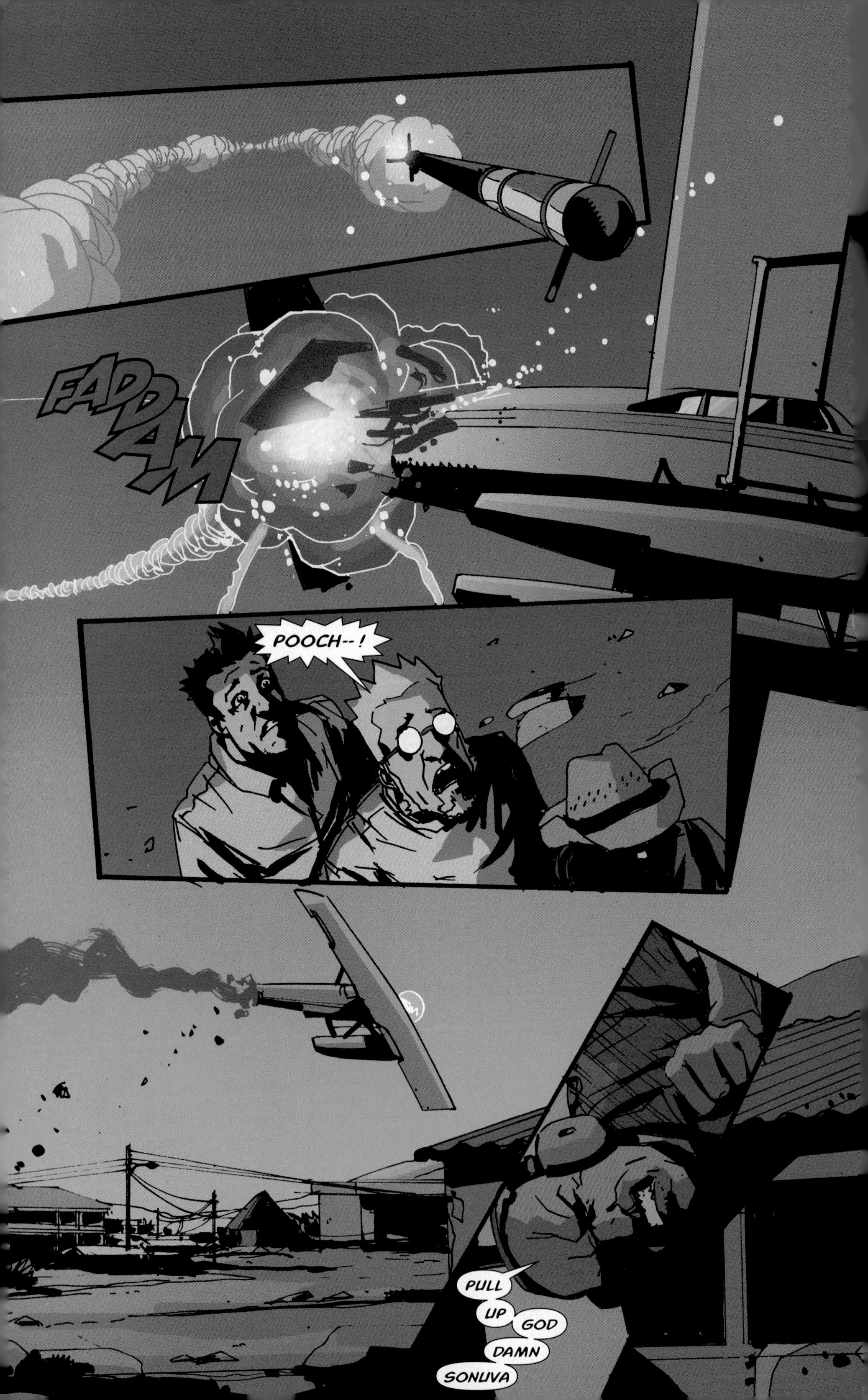
FADDAM
POOCH--!
PULL
UP
GOD
DAMN
SONUVA

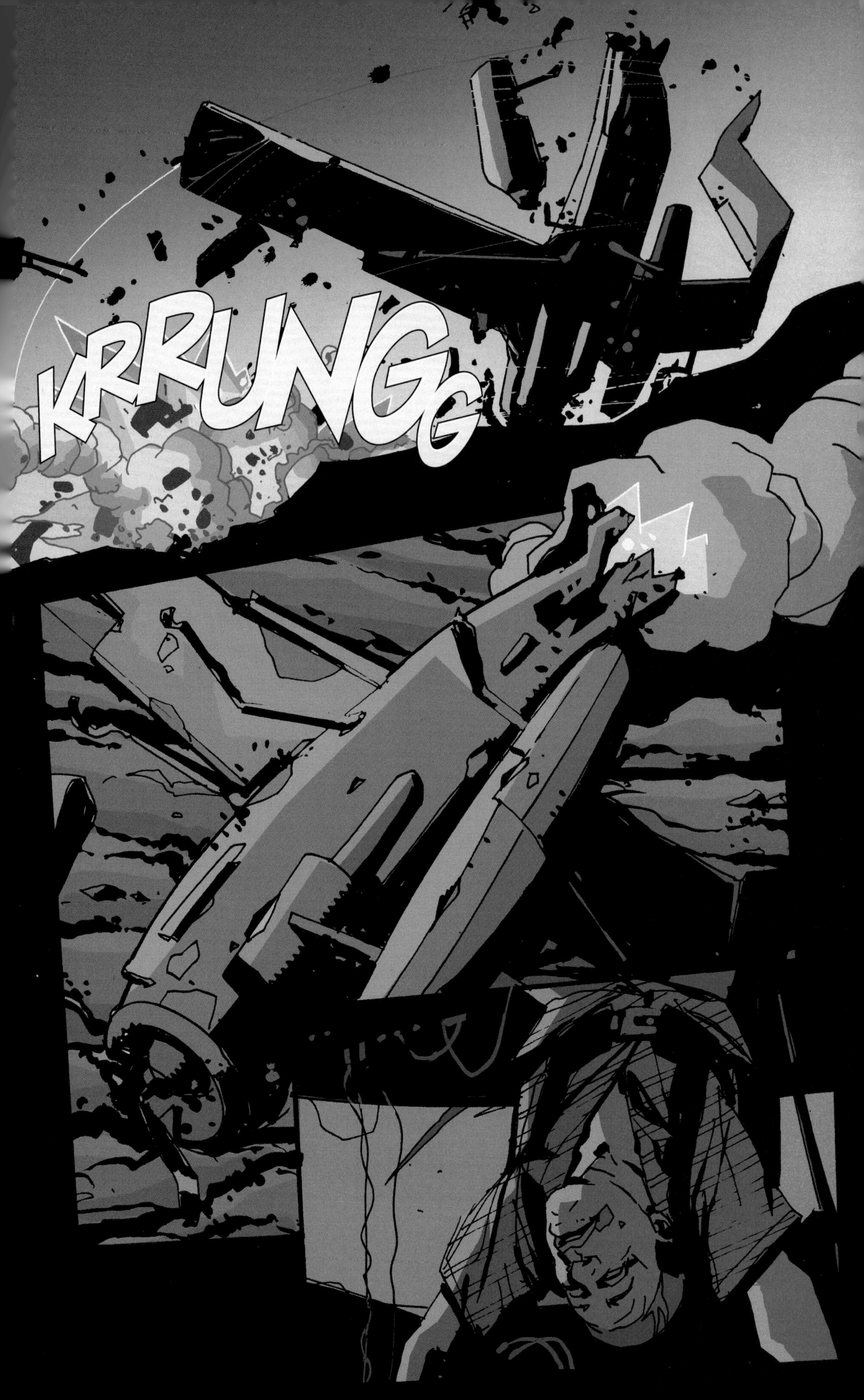
KRRUNGG

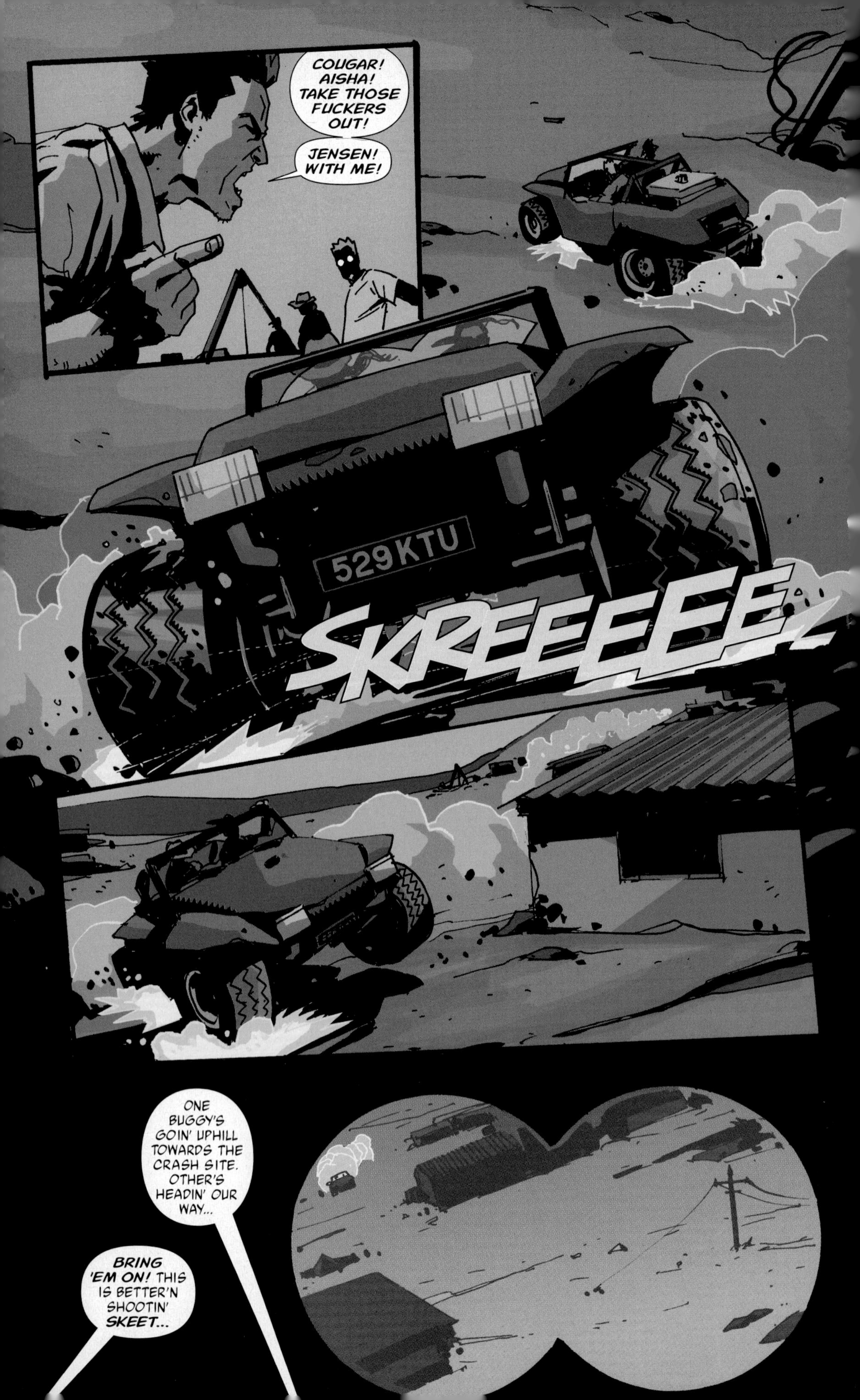
COUGAR! AISHA! TAKE THOSE FUCKERS OUT!
JENSEN! WITH ME!
529 KTU
SKREEEEEE
ONE BUGGY'S GOIN' UPHILL TOWARDS THE CRASH SITE. OTHER'S HEADIN' OUR WAY...
BRING 'EM ON! THIS IS BETTER'N SHOOTIN' SKEET...

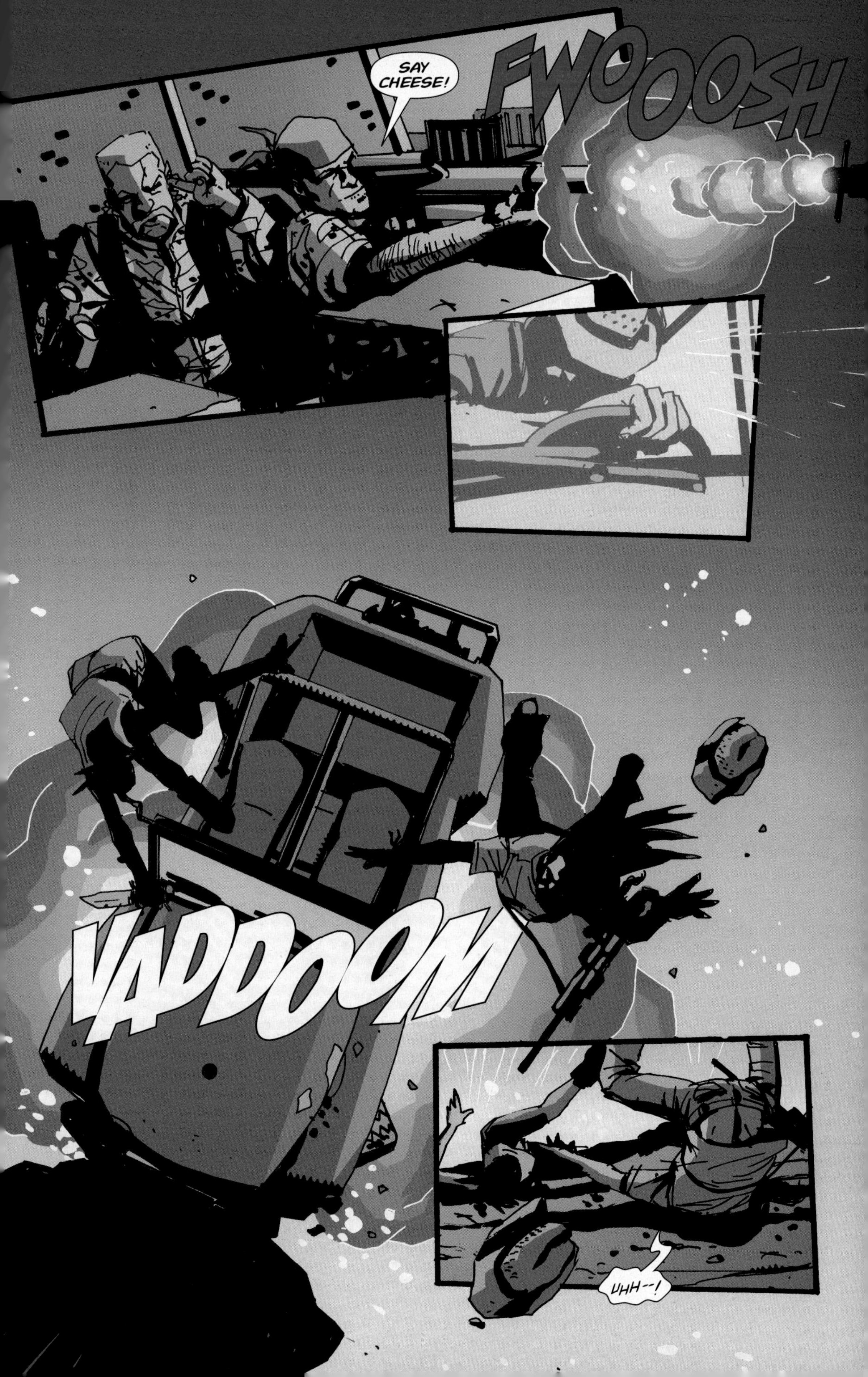
SAY CHEESE!
FWOOOSH
VADDOOM
UHH--!

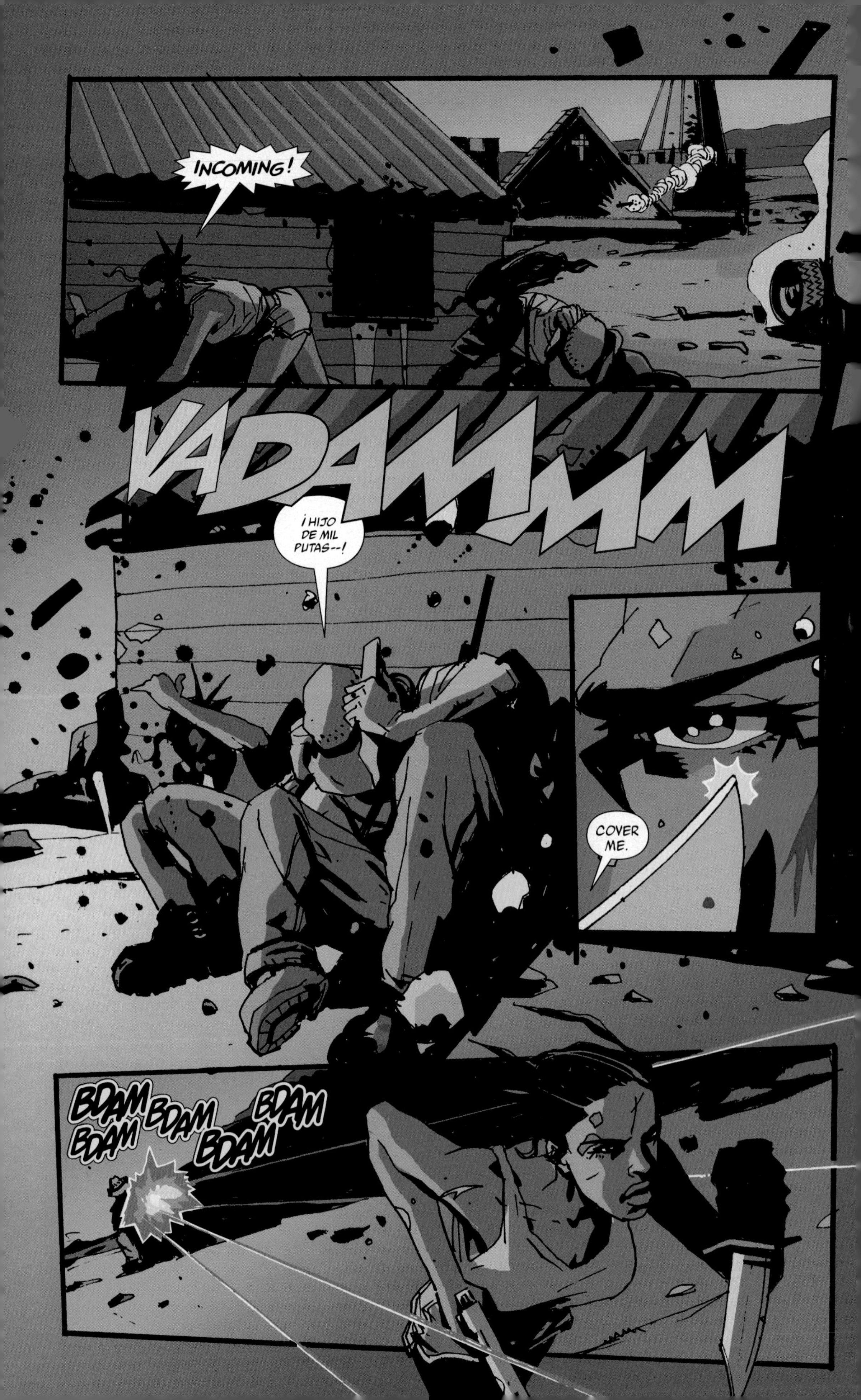
INCOMING!
VADAMMMM
¡HIJO DE MIL PUTAS--!
COVER ME.
BDAM BDAM BDAM BDAM BDAM

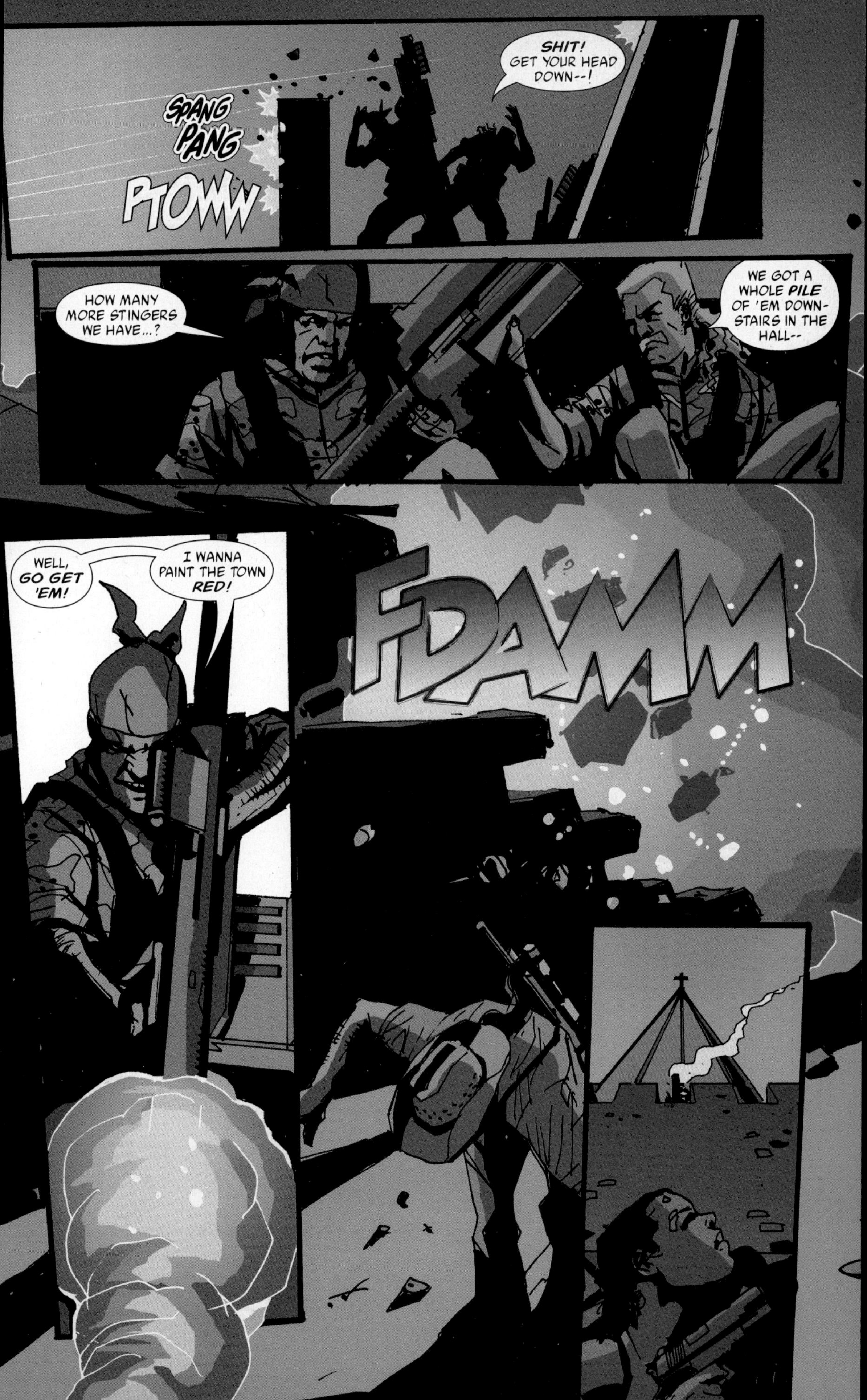
SPANG
PANG
PTOWW
SHIT! GET YOUR HEAD DOWN--!
HOW MANY MORE STINGERS WE HAVE...?
WE GOT A WHOLE PILE OF 'EM DOWN-STAIRS IN THE HALL--
WELL, GO GET 'EM!
I WANNA PAINT THE TOWN RED!
FDAMM

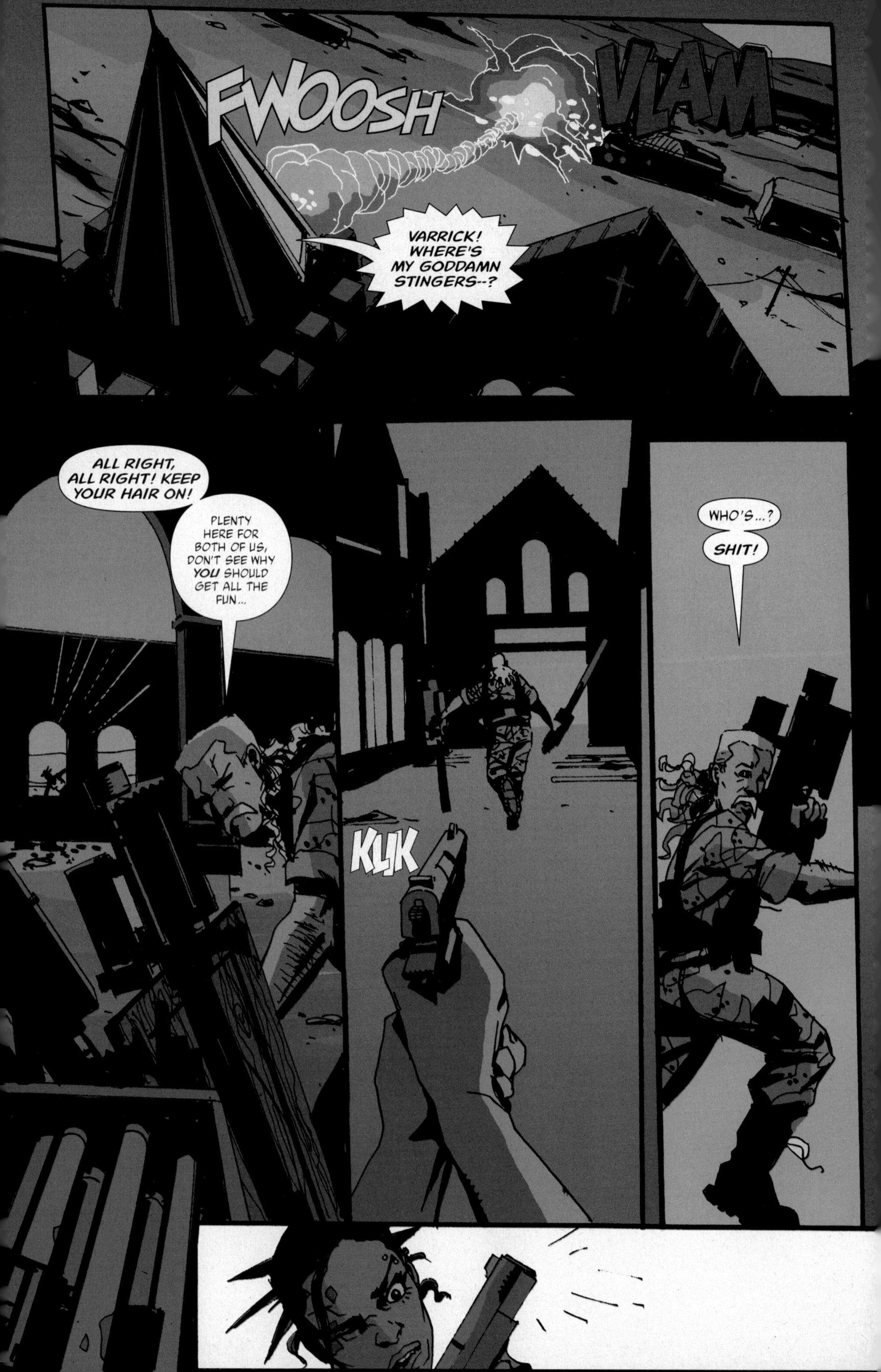
FWOOSH
VLAM
VARRICK! WHERE'S MY GODDAMN STINGERS--?
ALL RIGHT, ALL RIGHT! KEEP YOUR HAIR ON!
PLENTY HERE FOR BOTH OF US, DON'T SEE WHY YOU SHOULD GET ALL THE FUN...
KLIK
WHO'S...?
SHIT!

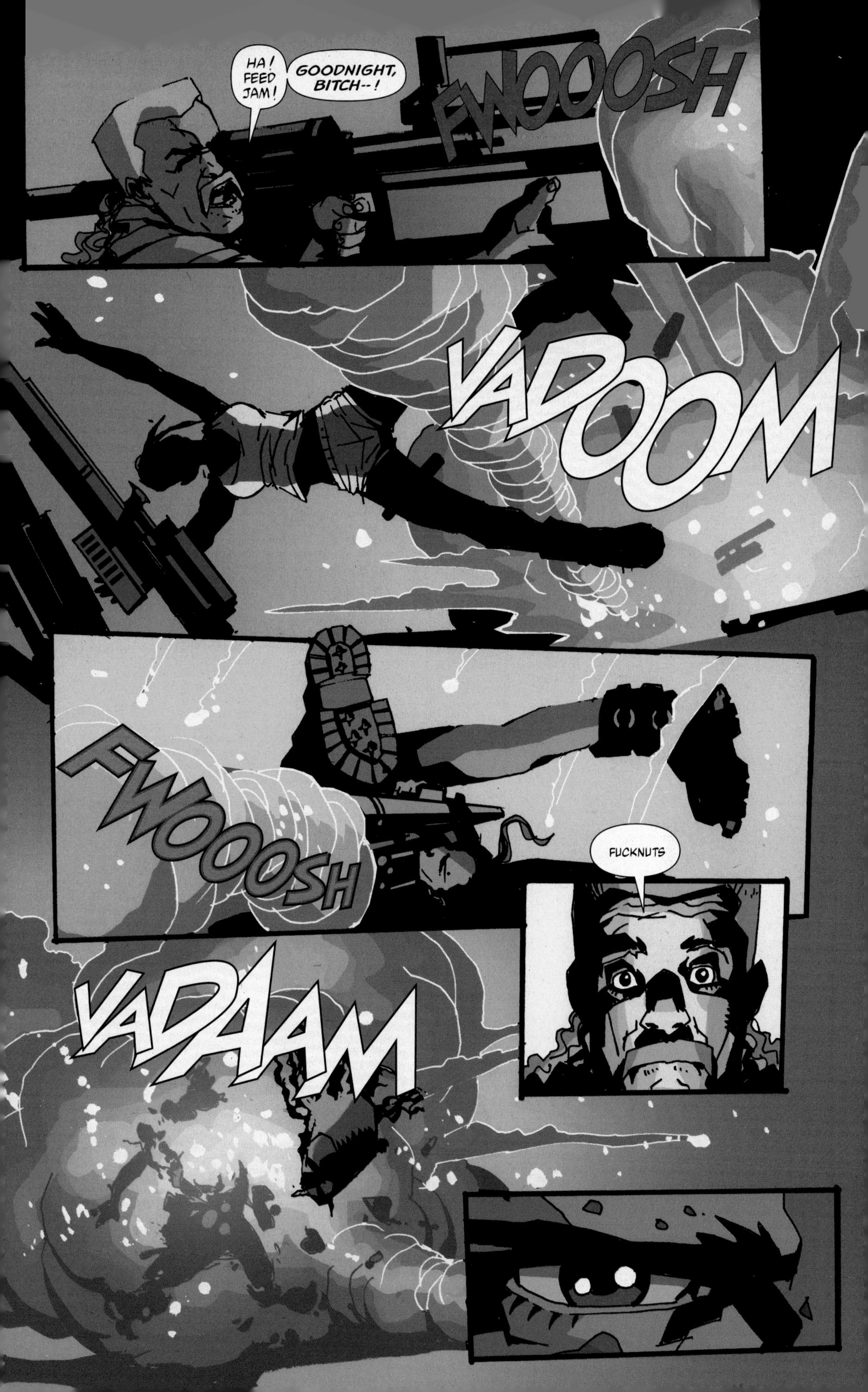
HA! FEED JAM!
GOODNIGHT, BITCH--!
FWOOOSH
VADOOM
FWOOOSH
FUCKNUTS
VADAAM

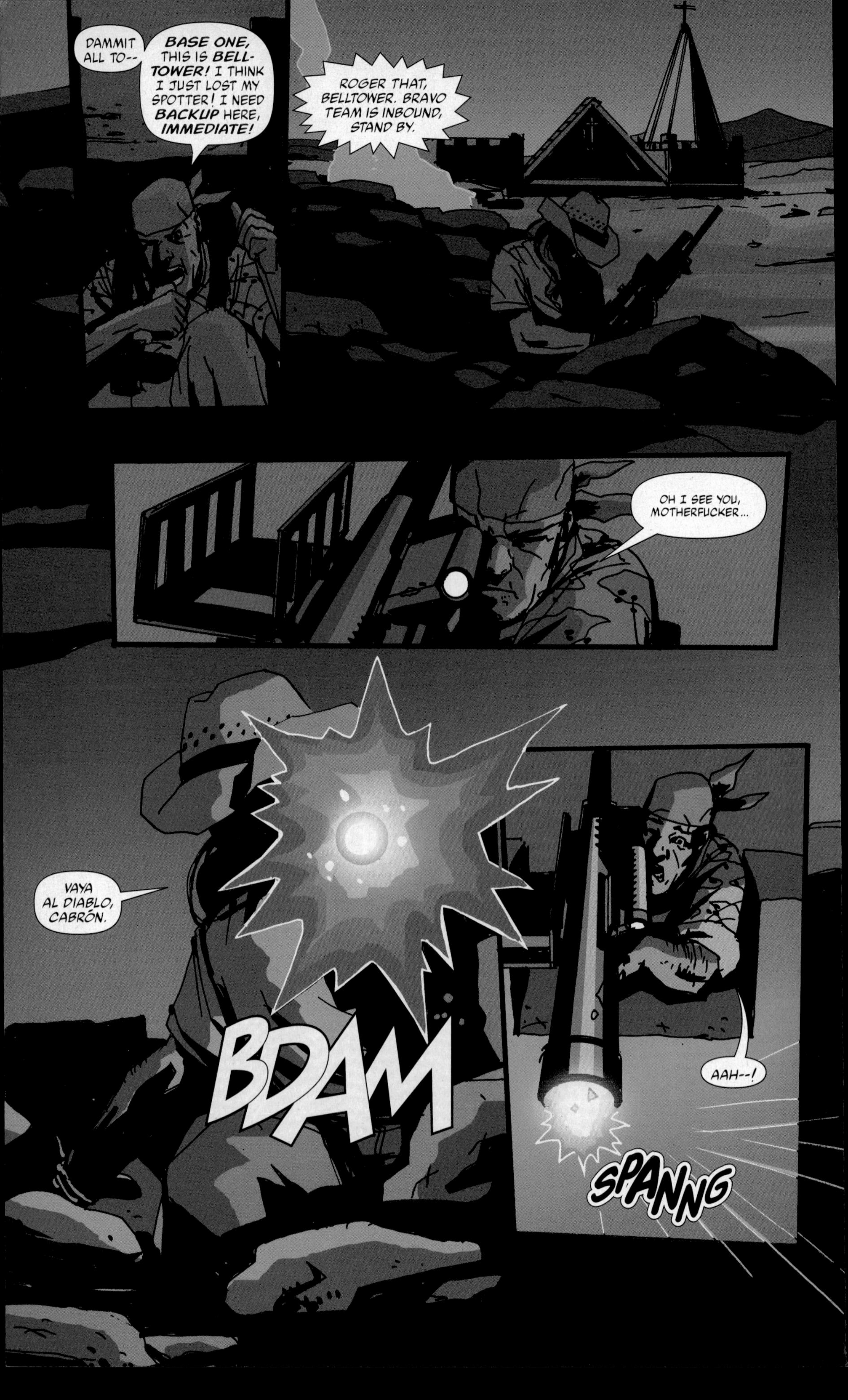
DAMMIT ALL TO--
BASE ONE, THIS IS BELL-TOWER! I THINK I JUST LOST MY SPOTTER! I NEED BACKUP HERE, IMMEDIATE!
ROGER THAT, BELLTOWER. BRAVO TEAM IS INBOUND, STAND BY.
OH I SEE YOU, MOTHERFUCKER...
VAYA AL DIABLO, CABRÓN.
BDAM
AAH--!
SPANNG

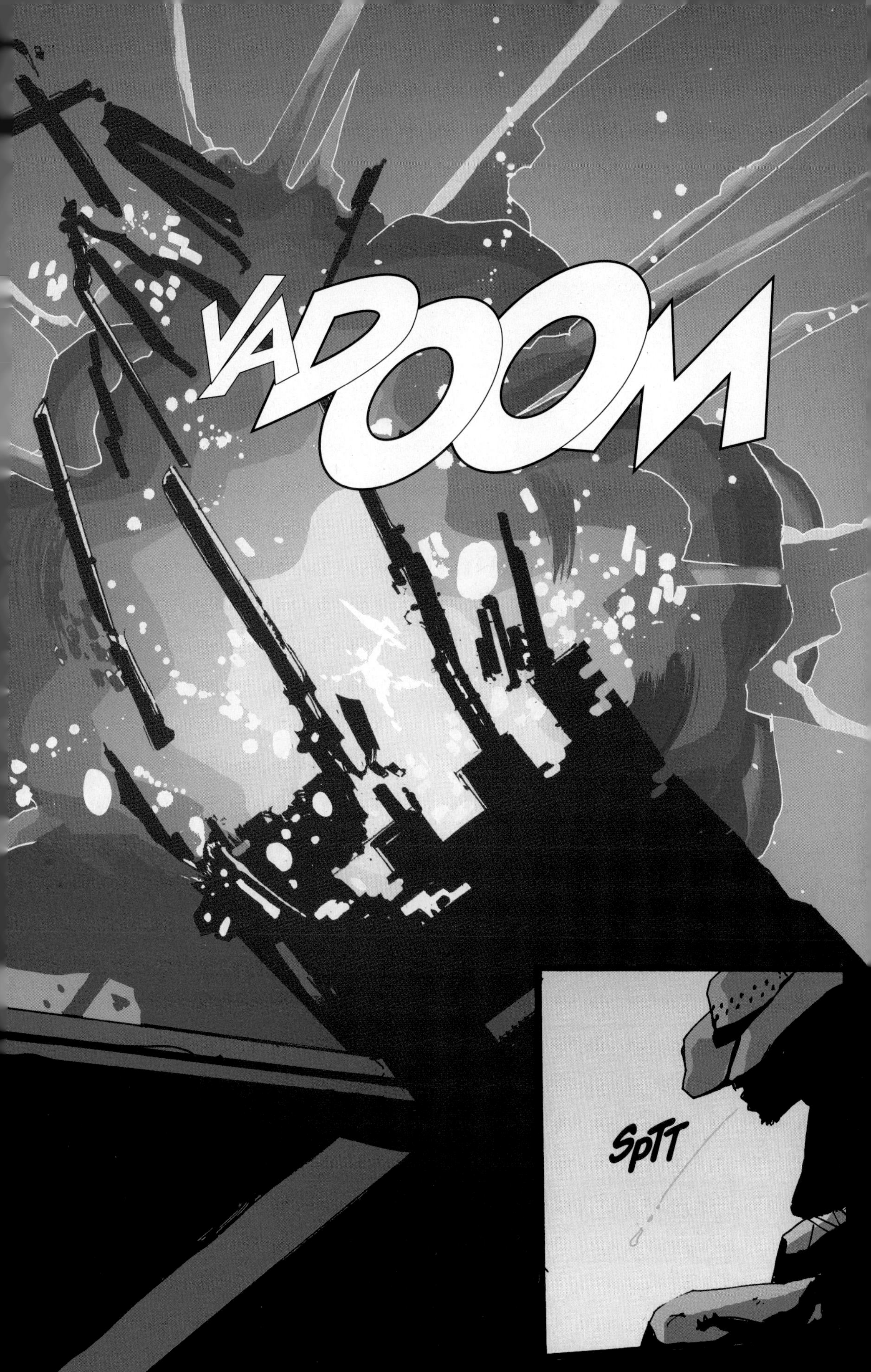
VADOOM
SPTT

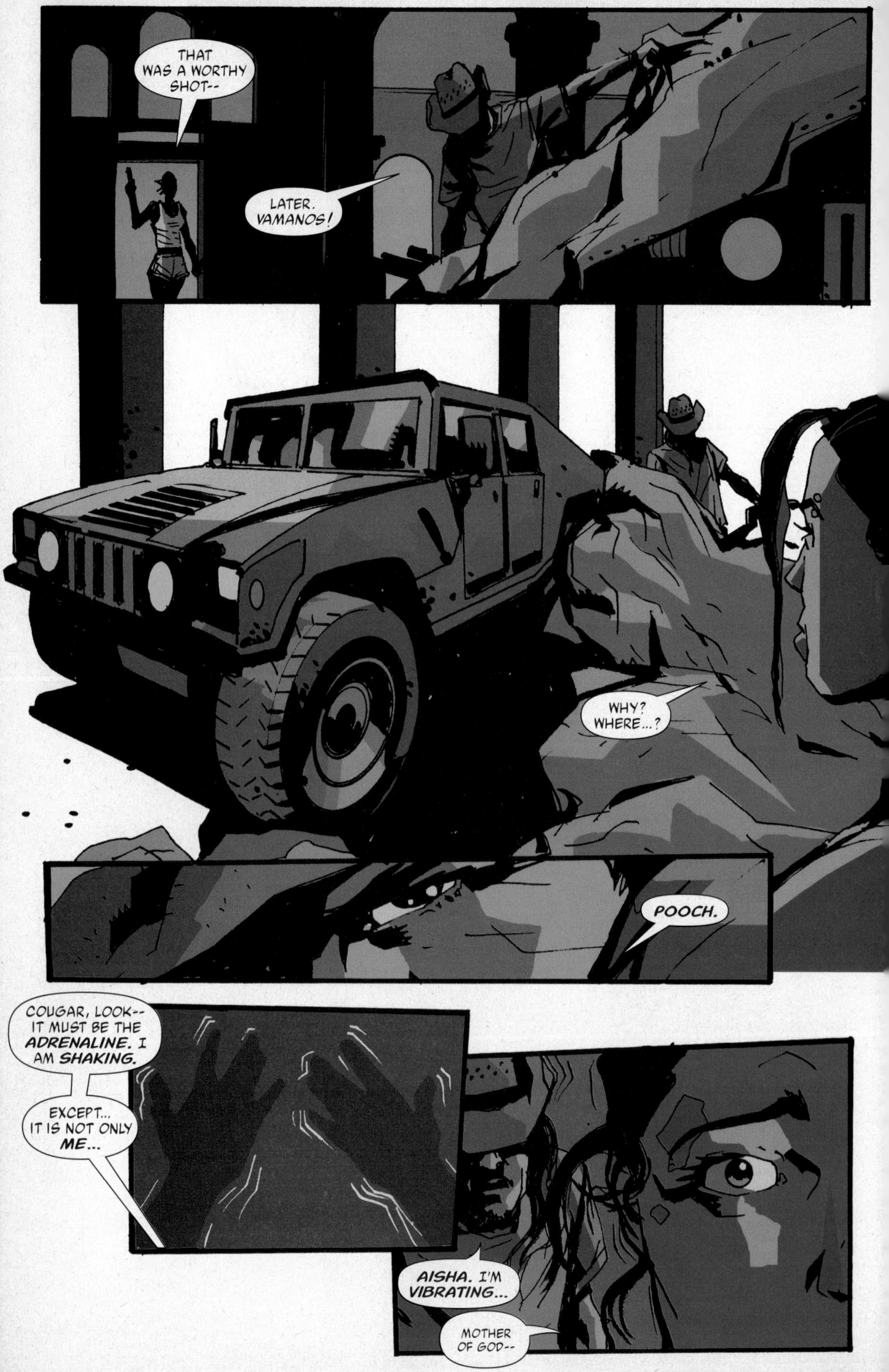
THAT WAS A WORTHY SHOT--
LATER. VAMANOS!
WHY? WHERE...?
POOCH.
COUGAR, LOOK-- IT MUST BE THE ADRENALINE. I AM SHAKING.
EXCEPT... IT IS NOT ONLY ME...
AISHA. I'M VIBRATING...
MOTHER OF GOD--

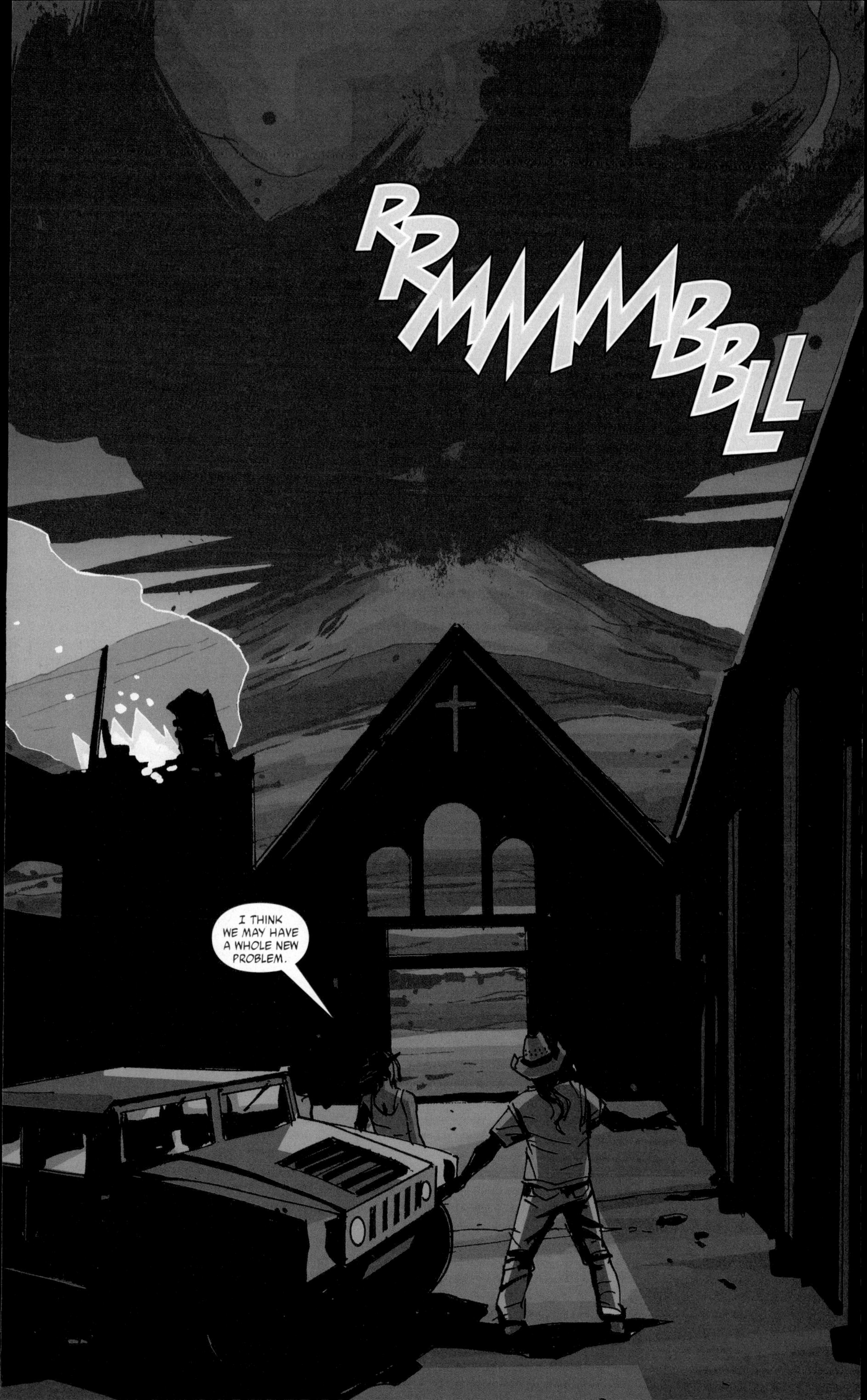
RRMMMMBBLL
I THINK WE MAY HAVE A WHOLE NEW PROBLEM.

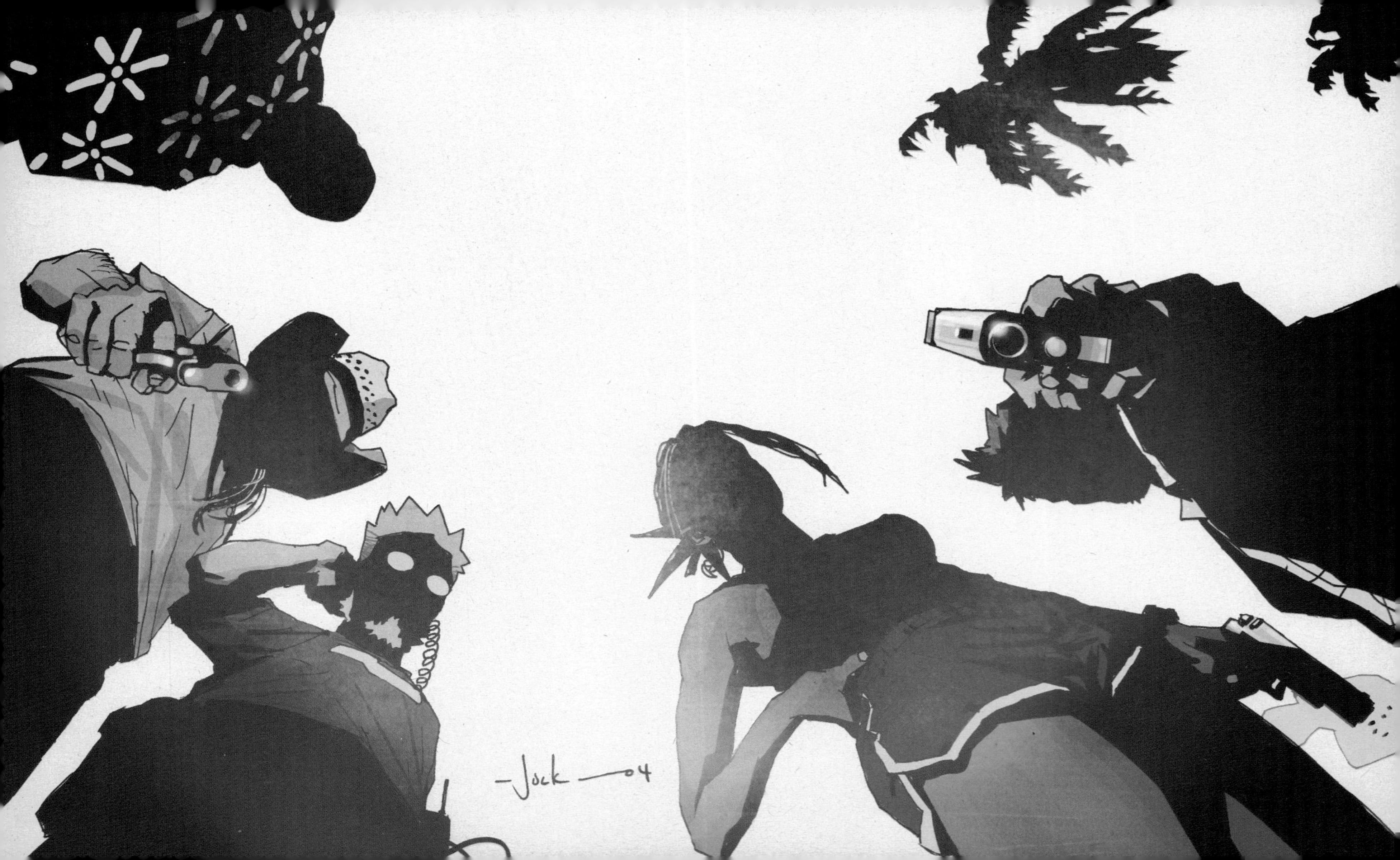
-Jock —04

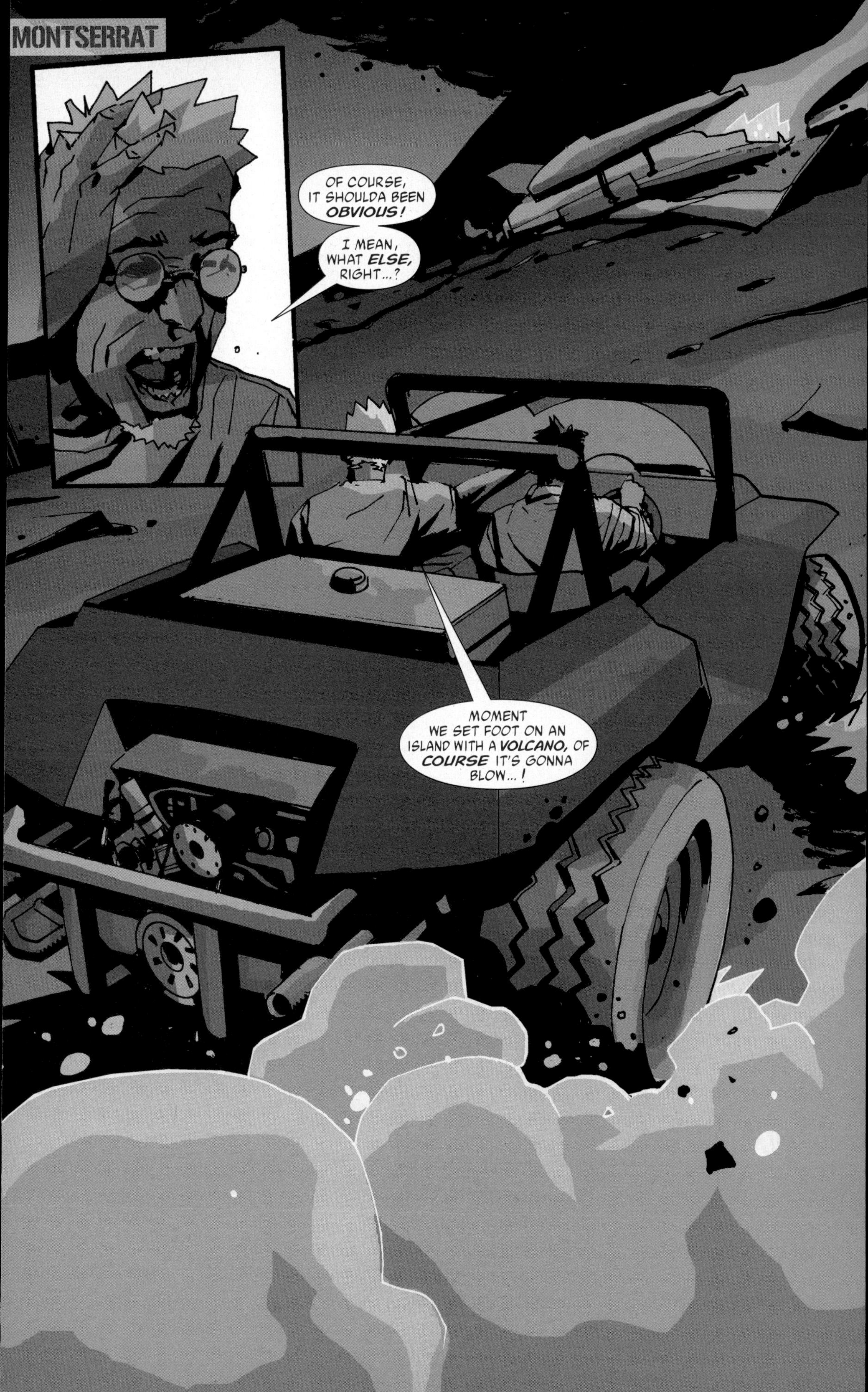
MONTSERRAT
OF COURSE, IT SHOULDA BEEN OBVIOUS!
I MEAN, WHAT ELSE, RIGHT...?
MOMENT WE SET FOOT ON AN ISLAND WITH A VOLCANO, OF COURSE IT'S GONNA BLOW...!

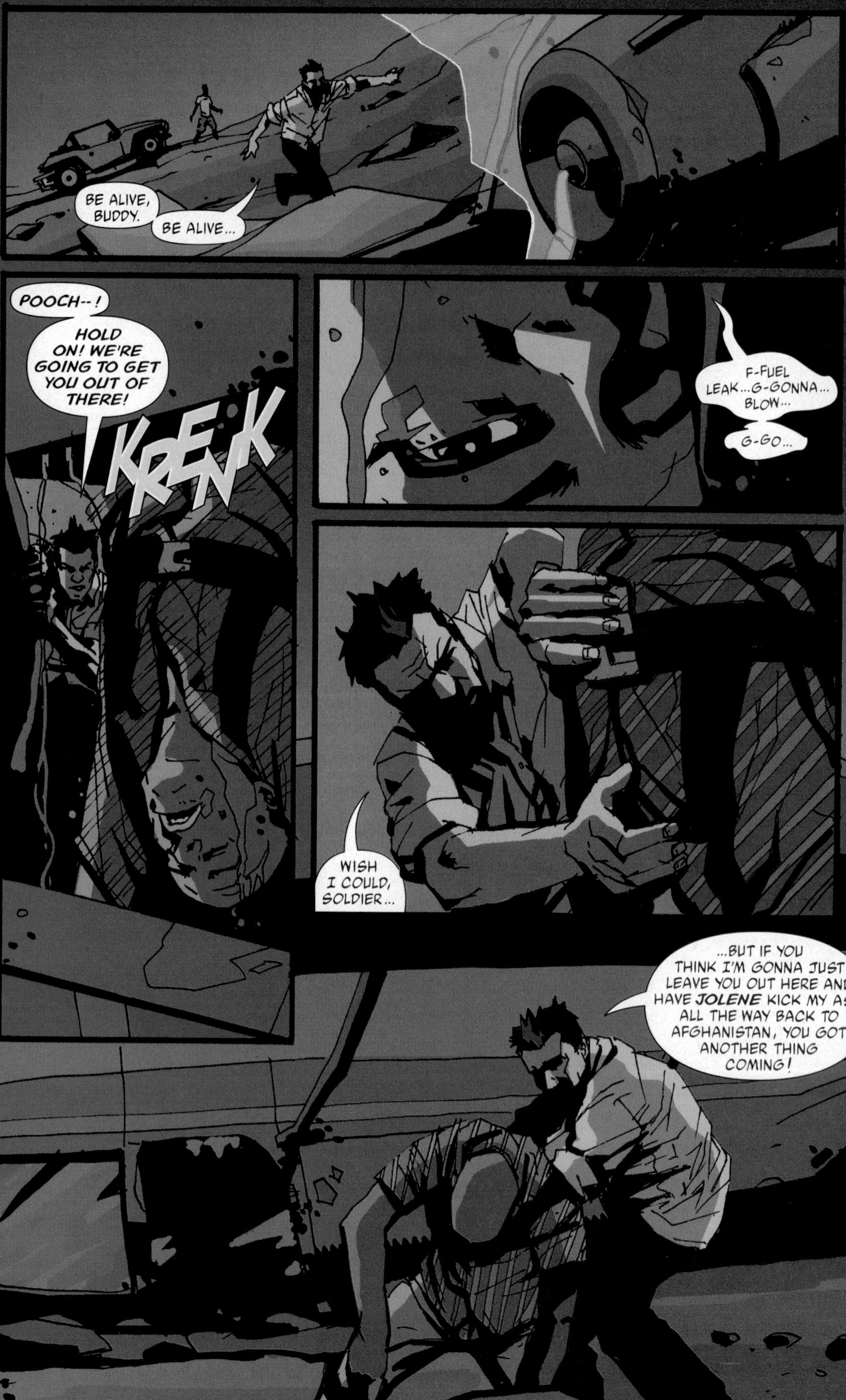
BE ALIVE, BUDDY.
BE ALIVE...
POOCH--!
HOLD ON! WE'RE GOING TO GET YOU OUT OF THERE!
KRENK
F-FUEL LEAK...G-GONNA... BLOW...
G-GO...
WISH I COULD, SOLDIER...
...BUT IF YOU THINK I'M GONNA JUST LEAVE YOU OUT HERE AND HAVE JOLENE KICK MY ASS ALL THE WAY BACK TO AFGHANISTAN, YOU GOT ANOTHER THING COMING!

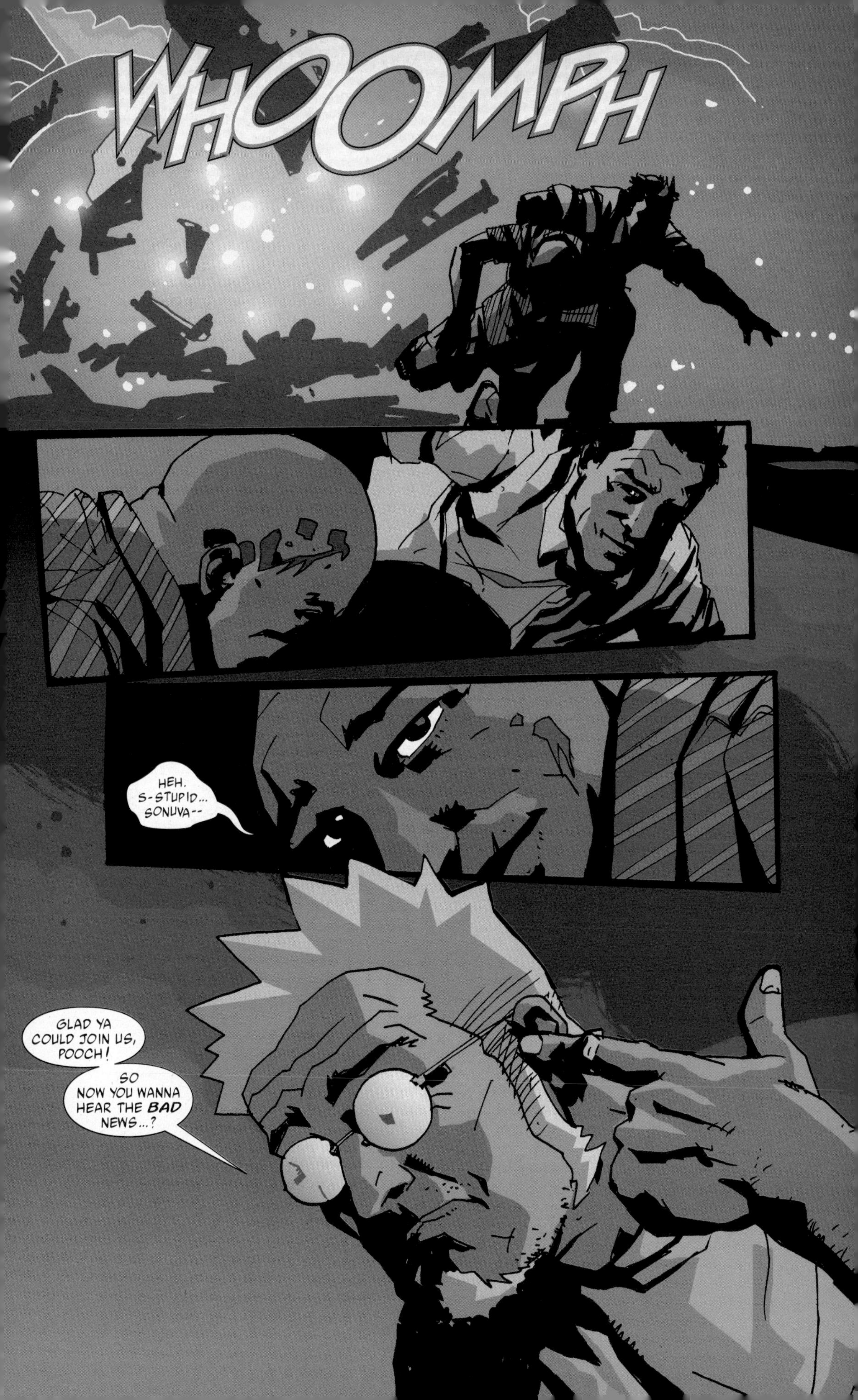
WHOOOMPH
HEH. S-STUPID... SONUVA--
GLAD YA COULD JOIN US, POOCH!
SO NOW YOU WANNA HEAR THE BAD NEWS...?

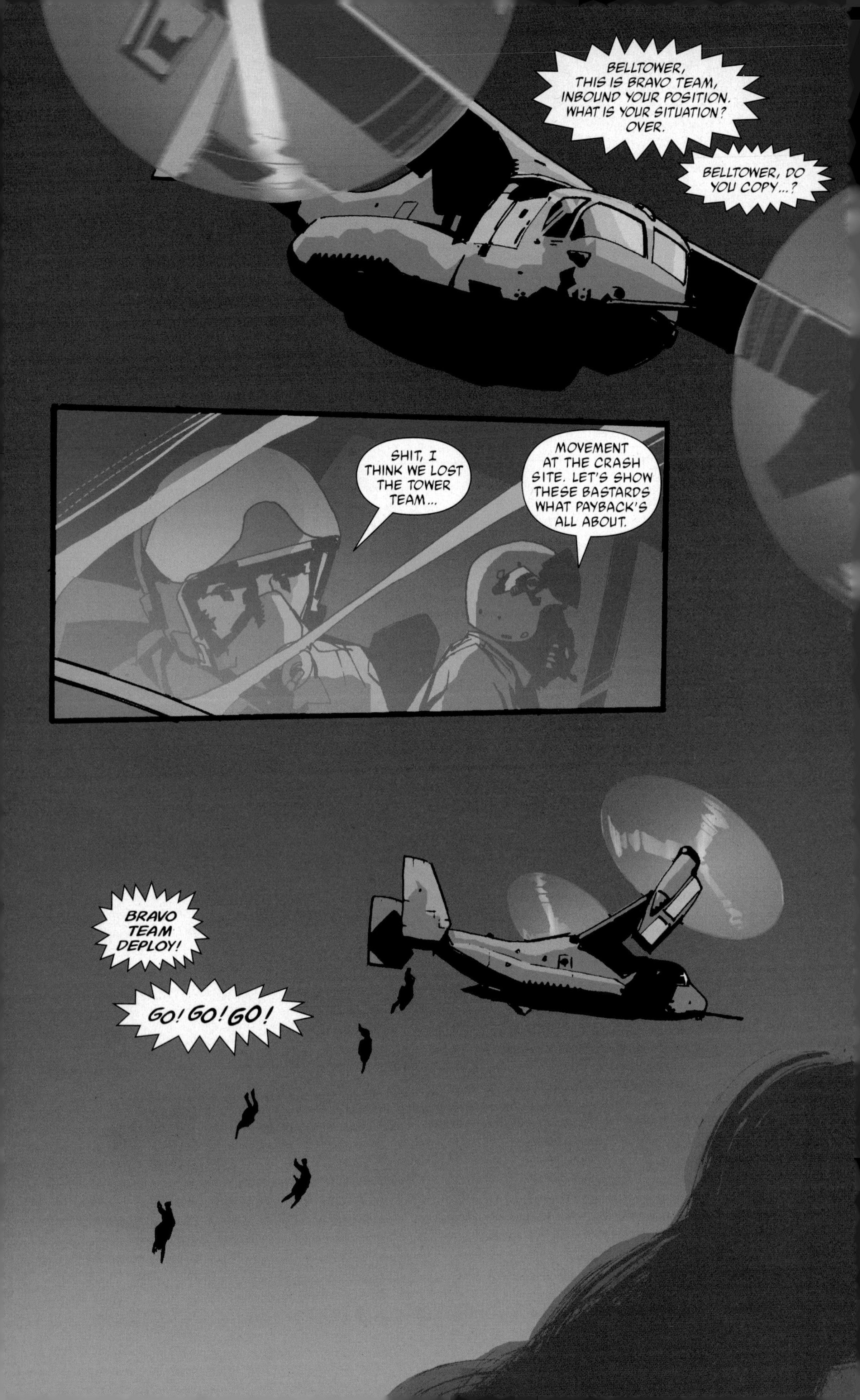
BELLTOWER,
THIS IS BRAVO TEAM,
INBOUND YOUR POSITION.
WHAT IS YOUR SITUATION?
OVER.
BELLTOWER, DO YOU COPY...?
SHIT, I THINK WE LOST THE TOWER TEAM...
MOVEMENT AT THE CRASH SITE. LET'S SHOW THESE BASTARDS WHAT PAYBACK'S ALL ABOUT.
BRAVO TEAM DEPLOY!
GO! GO! GO!

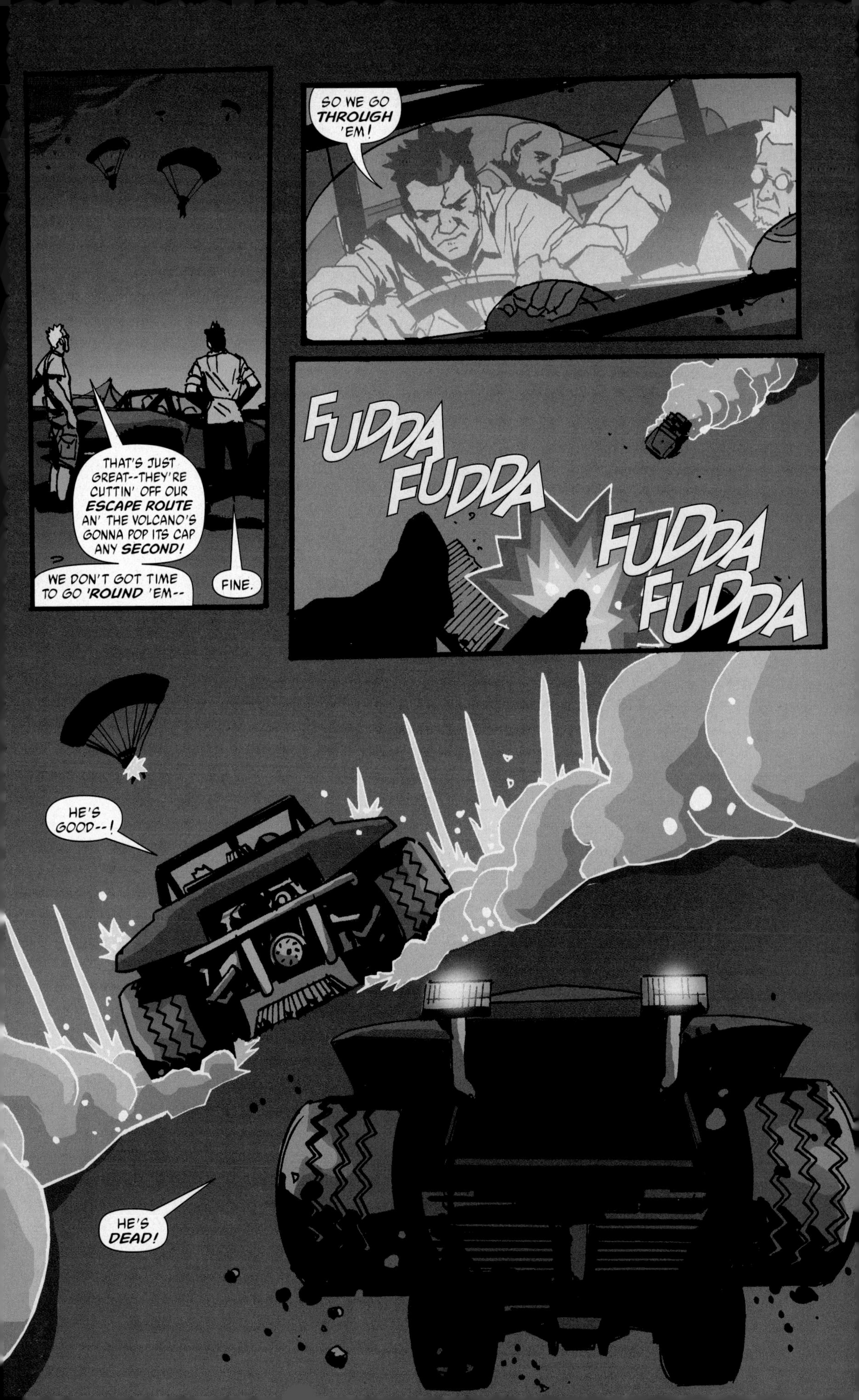
THAT'S JUST GREAT--THEY'RE CUTTIN' OFF OUR ESCAPE ROUTE AN' THE VOLCANO'S GONNA POP ITS CAP ANY SECOND!
WE DON'T GOT TIME TO GO 'ROUND 'EM--
FINE.
SO WE GO THROUGH 'EM!
FUDDA FUDDA FUDDA FUDDA
HE'S GOOD--!
HE'S DEAD!

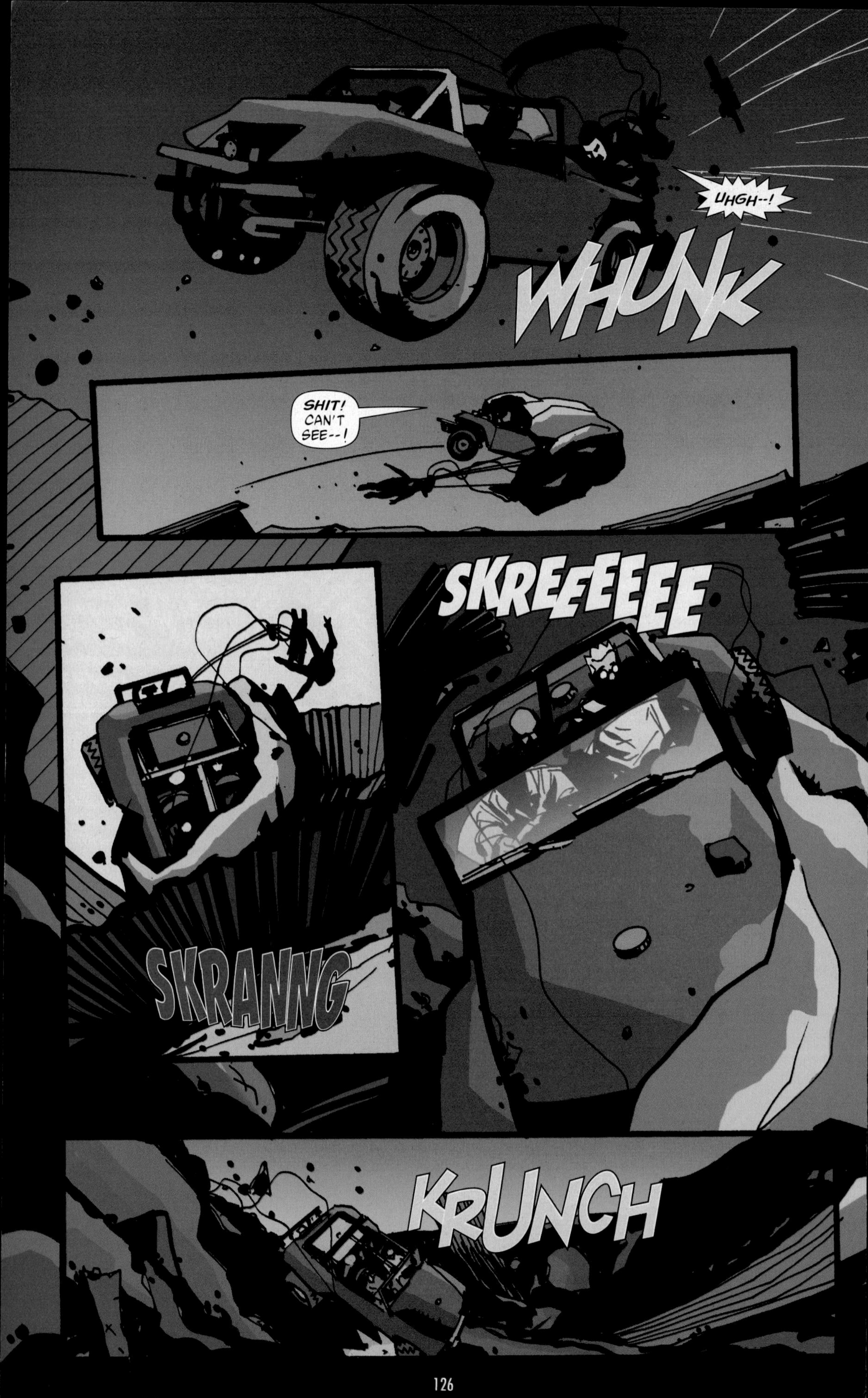
UHGH--!
WHUNK
SHIT! CAN'T SEE--!
SKRANNG
SKREEEEEE
KRUNCH

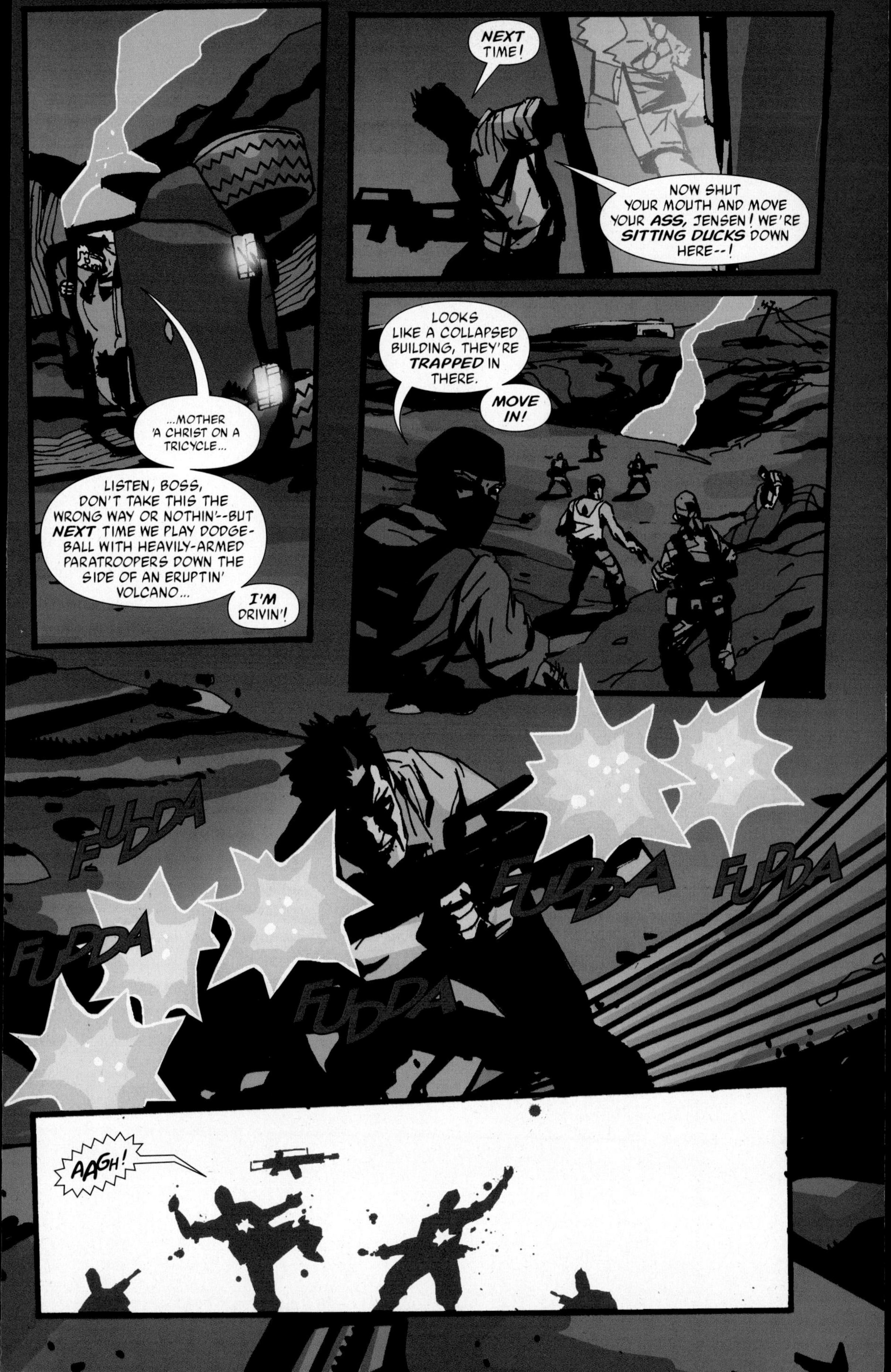

...MOTHER 'A CHRIST ON A TRICYCLE...
LISTEN, BOSS, DON'T TAKE THIS THE WRONG WAY OR NOTHIN'--BUT NEXT TIME WE PLAY DODGE-BALL WITH HEAVILY-ARMED PARATROOPERS DOWN THE SIDE OF AN ERUPTIN' VOLCANO...
I'M DRIVIN'!
NEXT TIME!
NOW SHUT YOUR MOUTH AND MOVE YOUR ASS, JENSEN! WE'RE SITTING DUCKS DOWN HERE--!
LOOKS LIKE A COLLAPSED BUILDING, THEY'RE TRAPPED IN THERE.
MOVE IN!
FUDDA
FUDDA
FUDDA
FUDDA
FUDDA
AAGH!

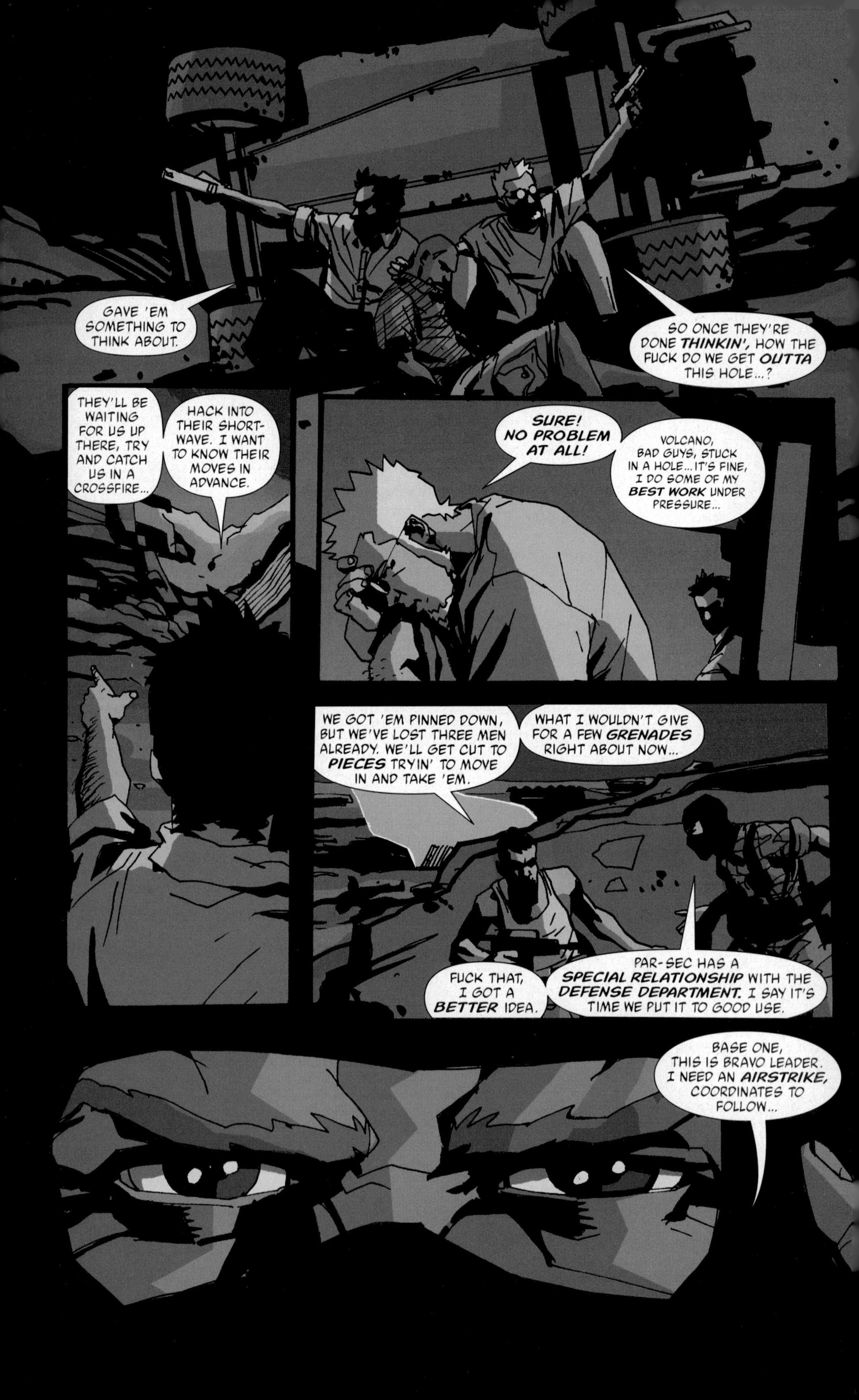
GAVE 'EM SOMETHING TO THINK ABOUT.
SO ONCE THEY'RE DONE THINKIN', HOW THE FUCK DO WE GET OUTTA THIS HOLE...?
THEY'LL BE WAITING FOR US UP THERE, TRY AND CATCH US IN A CROSSFIRE...
HACK INTO THEIR SHORT-WAVE. I WANT TO KNOW THEIR MOVES IN ADVANCE.
SURE! NO PROBLEM AT ALL!
VOLCANO, BAD GUYS, STUCK IN A HOLE...IT'S FINE, I DO SOME OF MY BEST WORK UNDER PRESSURE...
WE GOT 'EM PINNED DOWN, BUT WE'VE LOST THREE MEN ALREADY. WE'LL GET CUT TO PIECES TRYIN' TO MOVE IN AND TAKE 'EM.
WHAT I WOULDN'T GIVE FOR A FEW GRENADES RIGHT ABOUT NOW...
FUCK THAT, I GOT A BETTER IDEA.
PAR-SEC HAS A SPECIAL RELATIONSHIP WITH THE DEFENSE DEPARTMENT. I SAY IT'S TIME WE PUT IT TO GOOD USE.
BASE ONE, THIS IS BRAVO LEADER. I NEED AN AIRSTRIKE, COORDINATES TO FOLLOW...

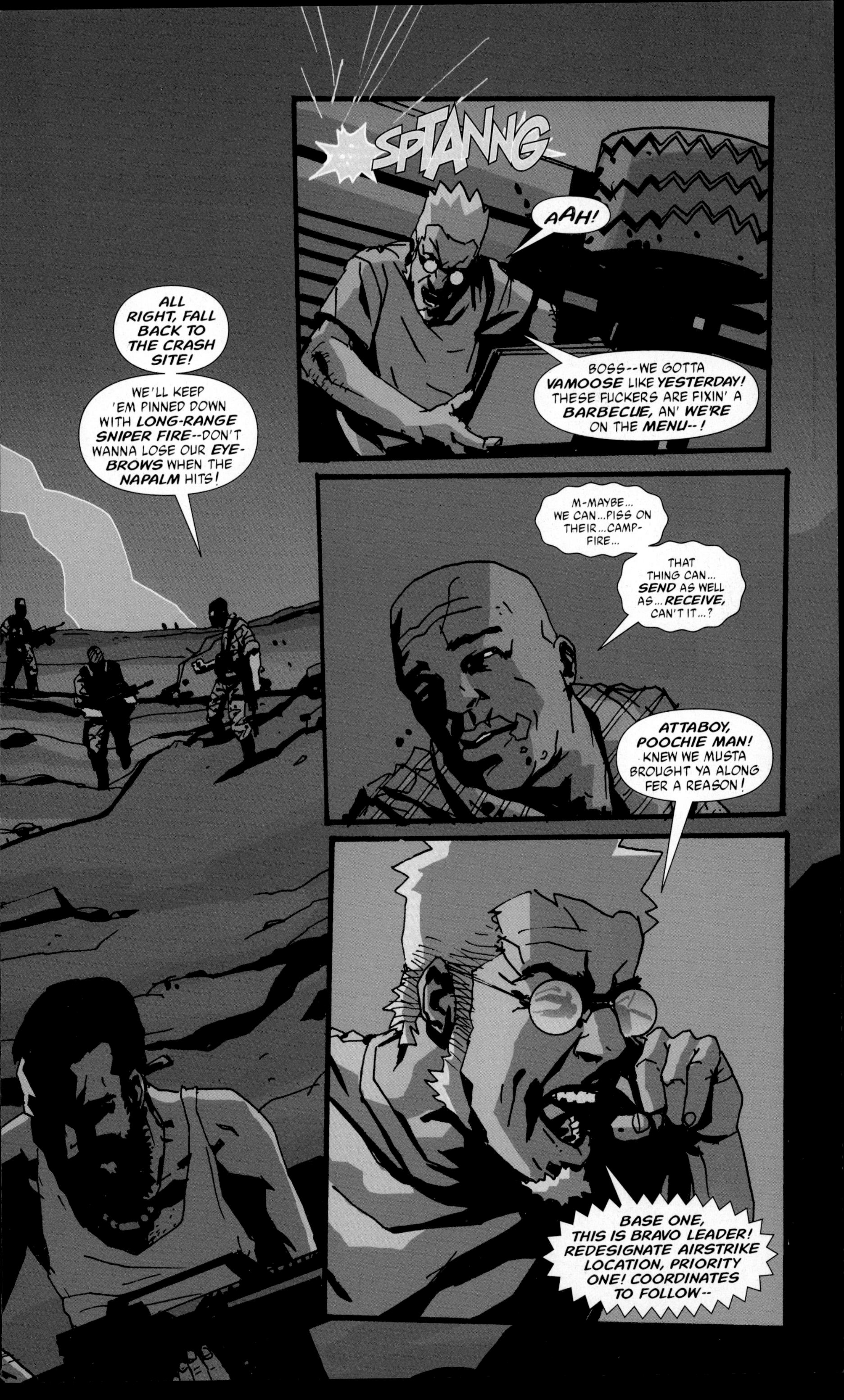
SPTANNG
AAH!
BOSS--WE GOTTA VAMOOSE LIKE YESTERDAY! THESE FUCKERS ARE FIXIN' A BARBECUE, AN' WE'RE ON THE MENU--!
ALL RIGHT, FALL BACK TO THE CRASH SITE!
WE'LL KEEP 'EM PINNED DOWN WITH LONG-RANGE SNIPER FIRE--DON'T WANNA LOSE OUR EYE-BROWS WHEN THE NAPALM HITS!
M-MAYBE... WE CAN...PISS ON THEIR...CAMP-FIRE...
THAT THING CAN... SEND AS WELL AS... RECEIVE, CAN'T IT...?
ATTABOY, POOCHIE MAN! KNEW WE MUSTA BROUGHT YA ALONG FER A REASON!
BASE ONE, THIS IS BRAVO LEADER! REDESIGNATE AIRSTRIKE LOCATION, PRIORITY ONE! COORDINATES TO FOLLOW--

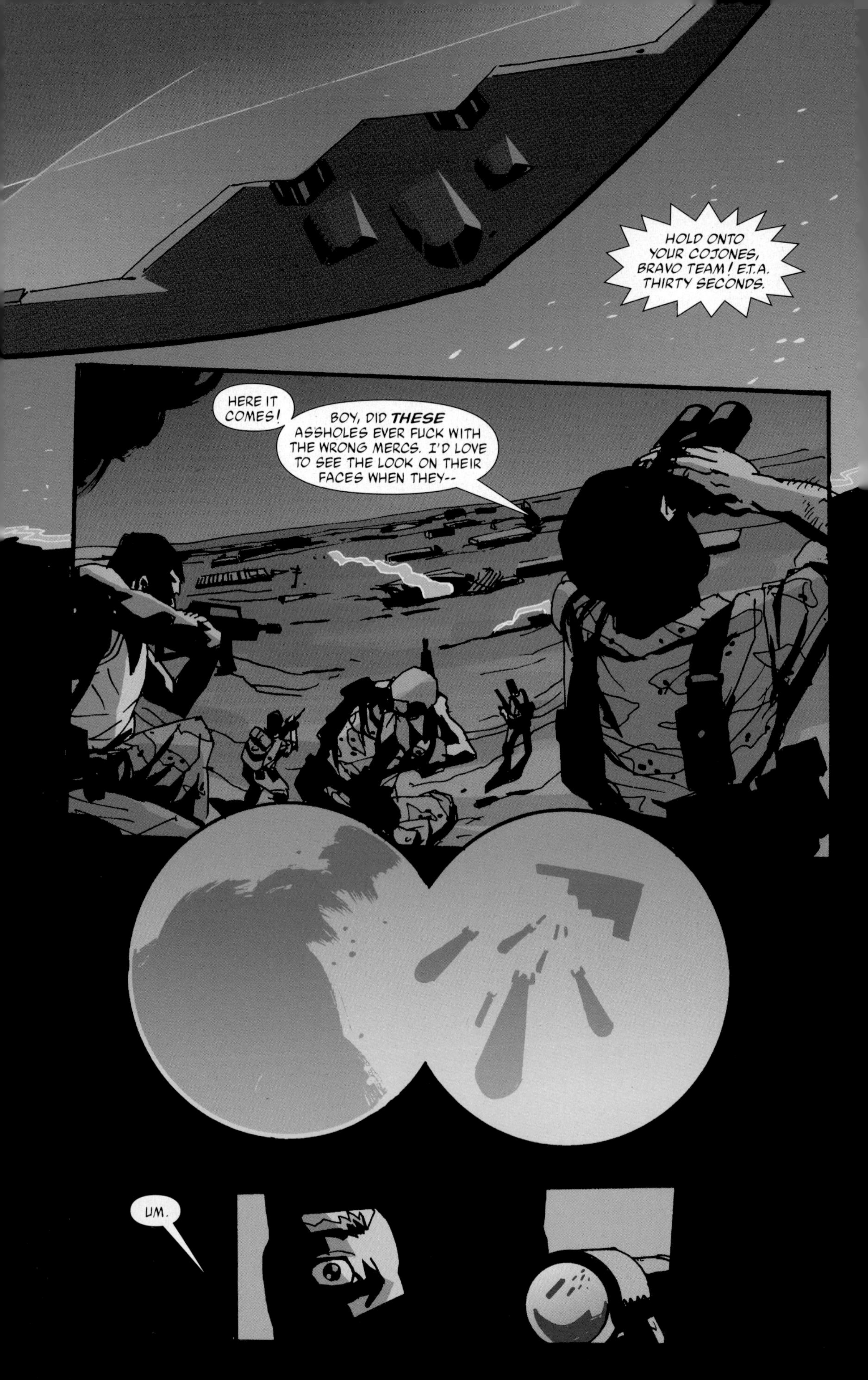
HOLD ONTO YOUR COJONES, BRAVO TEAM! E.T.A. THIRTY SECONDS.
HERE IT COMES!
BOY, DID **THESE** ASSHOLES EVER FUCK WITH THE WRONG MERCS. I'D LOVE TO SEE THE LOOK ON THEIR FACES WHEN THEY--
UM.

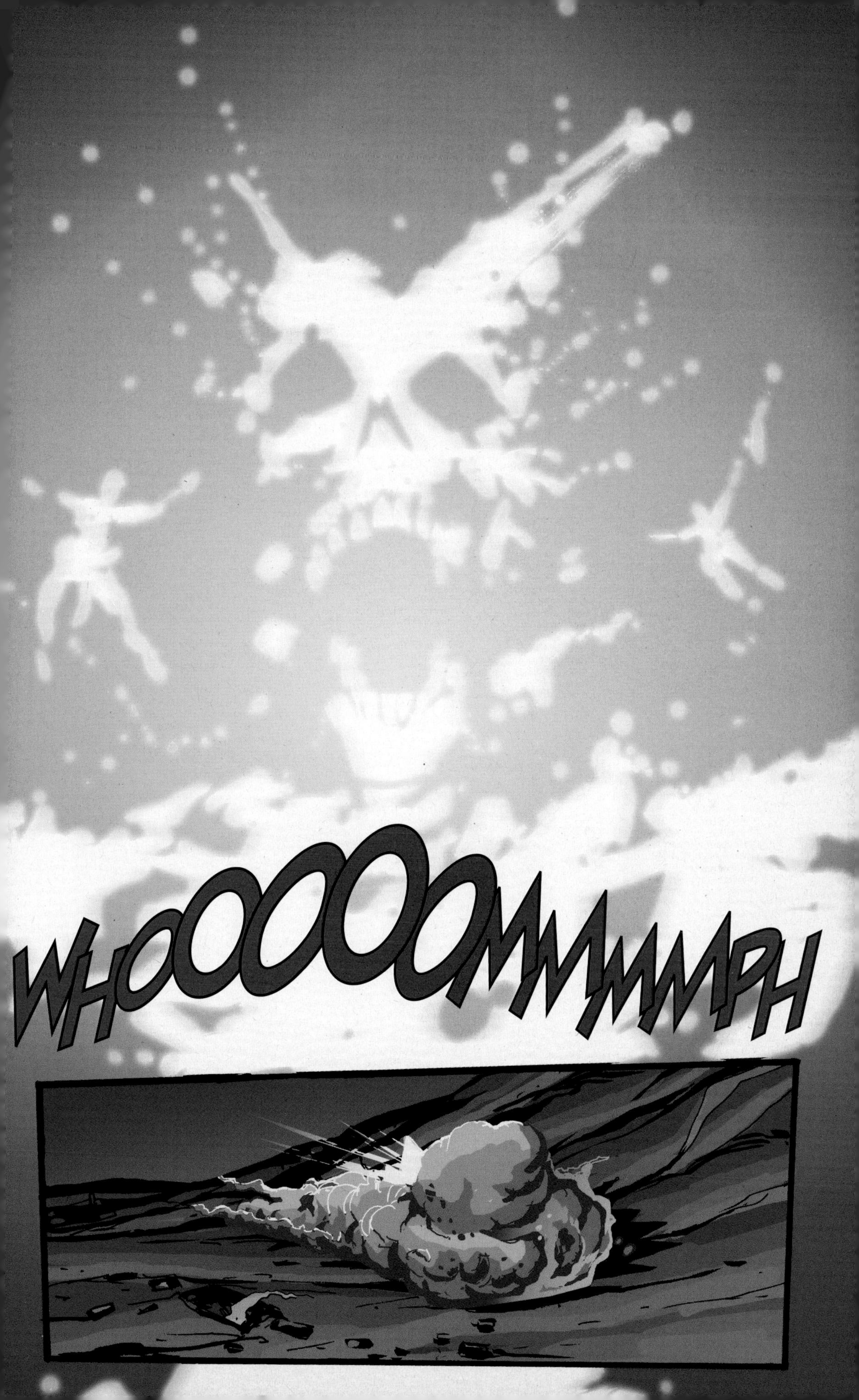
WHOOOOOOMMMMPH

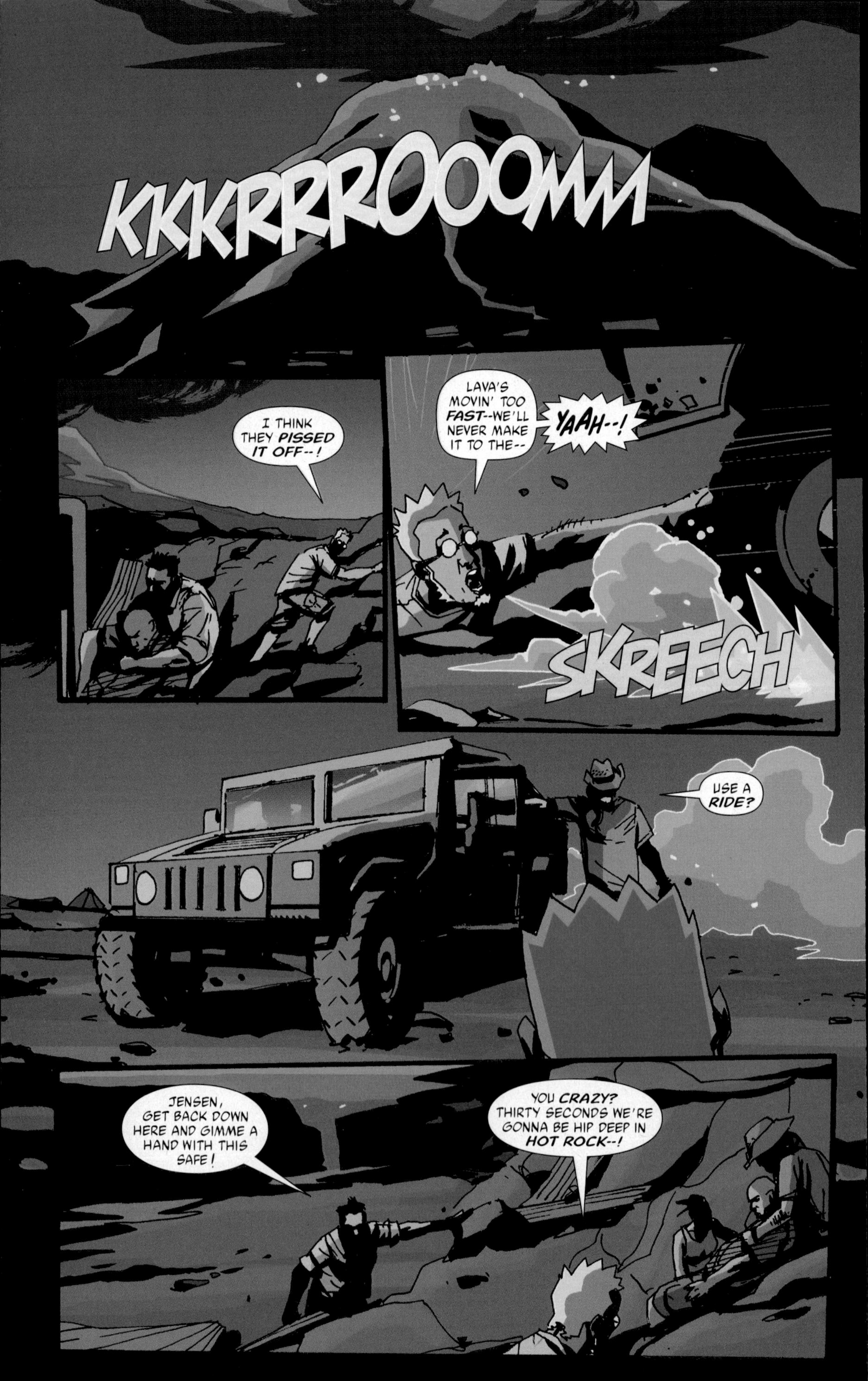

KKKRRROOOMM
I THINK THEY PISSED IT OFF--!
LAVA'S MOVIN' TOO FAST--WE'LL NEVER MAKE IT TO THE--
YAAH--!
SKREECH
USE A RIDE?
JENSEN, GET BACK DOWN HERE AND GIMME A HAND WITH THIS SAFE!
YOU CRAZY? THIRTY SECONDS WE'RE GONNA BE HIP DEEP IN HOT ROCK--!

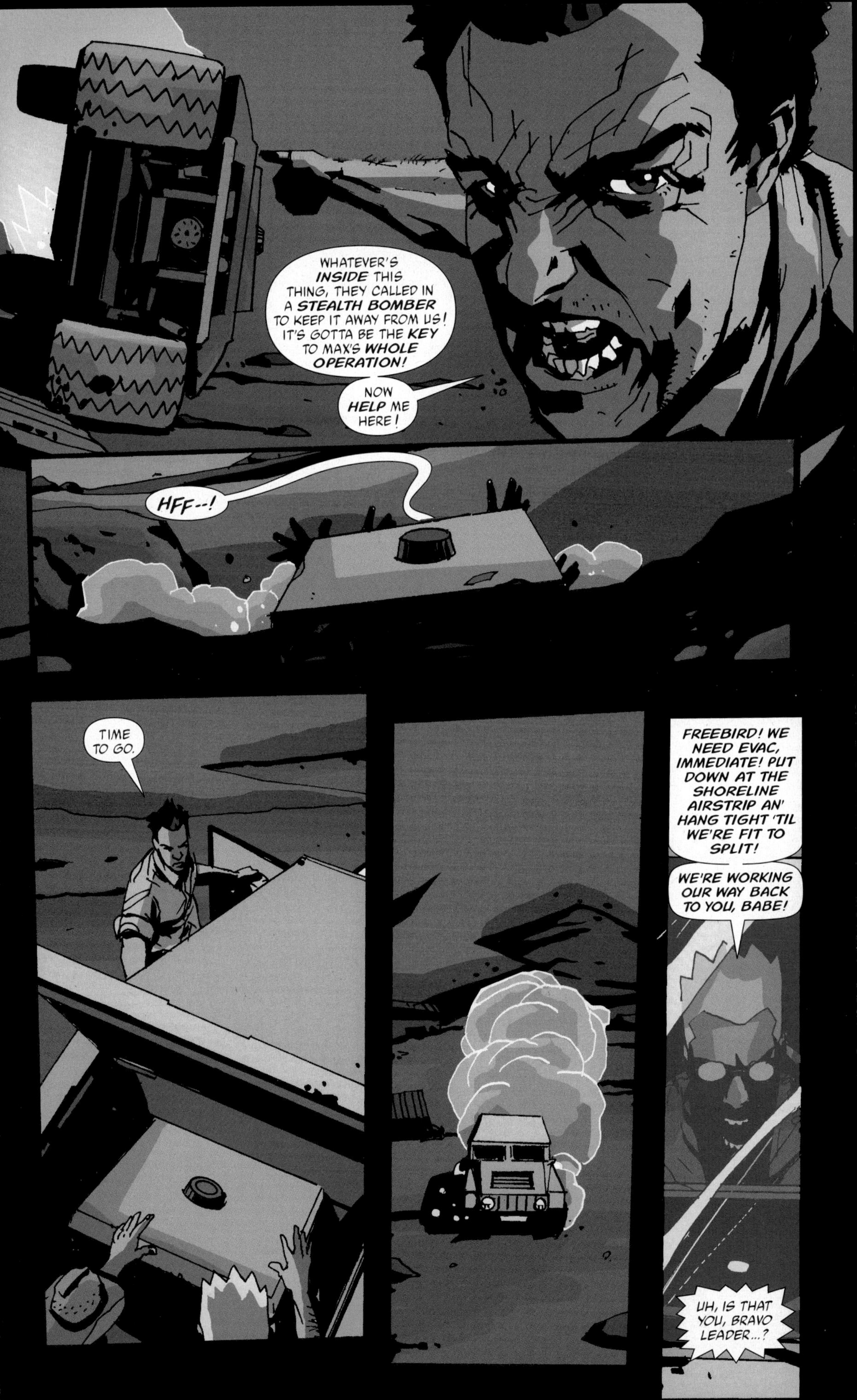
WHATEVER'S INSIDE THIS THING, THEY CALLED IN A STEALTH BOMBER TO KEEP IT AWAY FROM US! IT'S GOTTA BE THE KEY TO MAX'S WHOLE OPERATION!
NOW HELP ME HERE!
HFF--!
TIME TO GO.
FREEBIRD! WE NEED EVAC, IMMEDIATE! PUT DOWN AT THE SHORELINE AIRSTRIP AN' HANG TIGHT 'TIL WE'RE FIT TO SPLIT!
WE'RE WORKING OUR WAY BACK TO YOU, BABE!
UH, IS THAT YOU, BRAVO LEADER...?

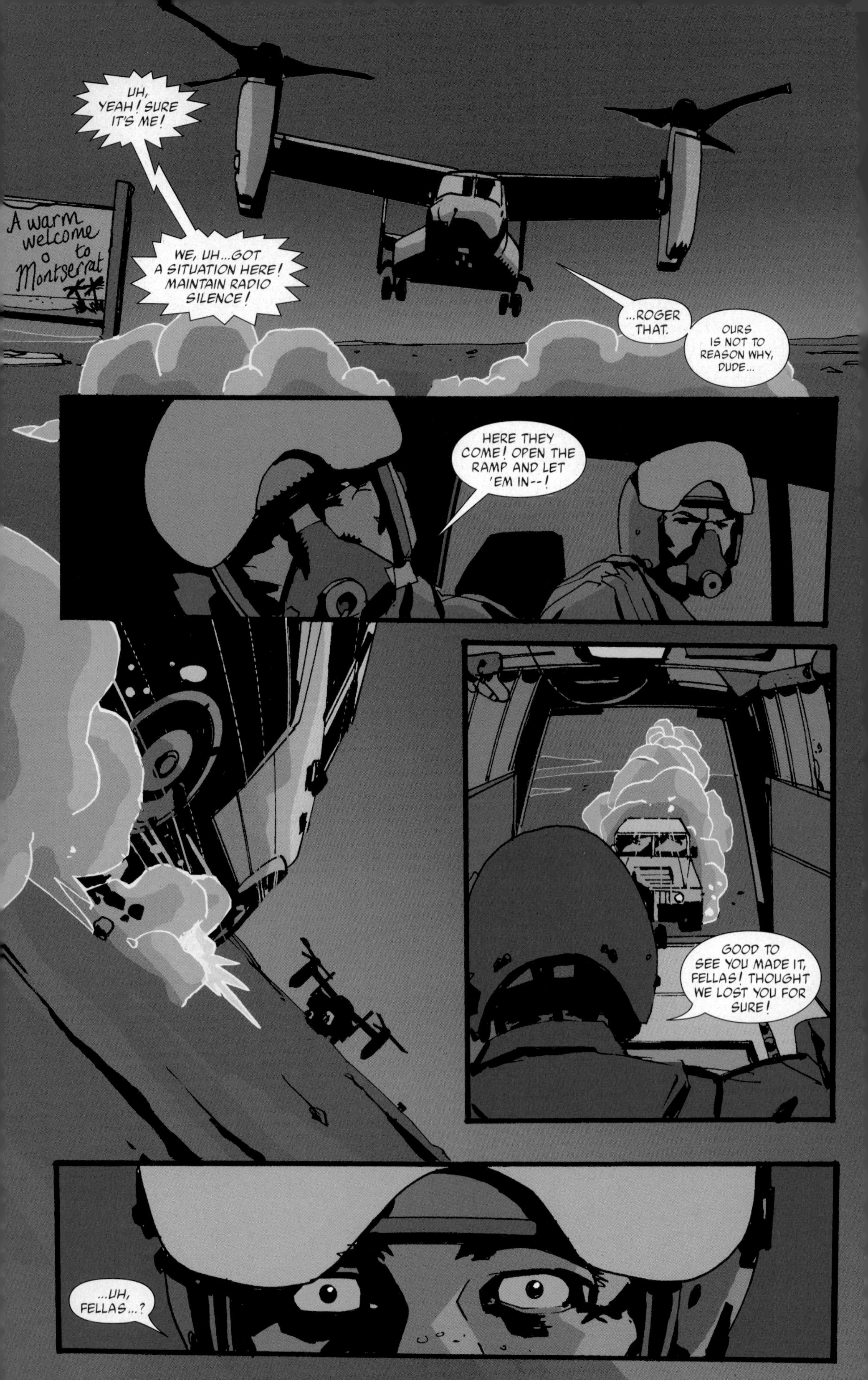
A warm welcome to Montserrat
UH, YEAH! SURE IT'S ME!
WE, UH...GOT A SITUATION HERE! MAINTAIN RADIO SILENCE!
...ROGER THAT.
OURS IS NOT TO REASON WHY, DUDE...
HERE THEY COME! OPEN THE RAMP AND LET 'EM IN--!
GOOD TO SEE YOU MADE IT, FELLAS! THOUGHT WE LOST YOU FOR SURE!
...UH, FELLAS...?

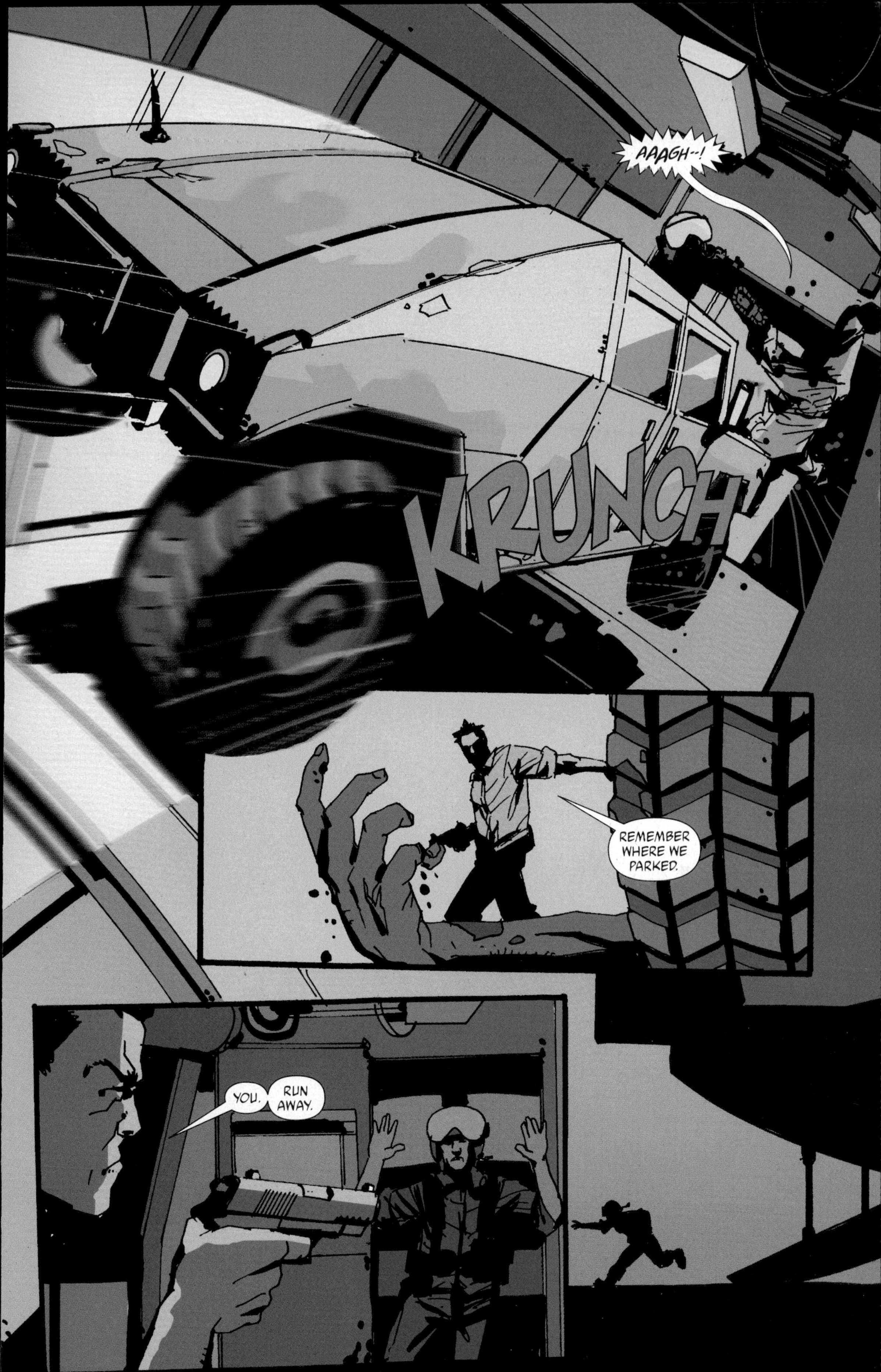
AAAGH--!
KRUNCH
REMEMBER WHERE WE PARKED.
YOU.
RUN AWAY.

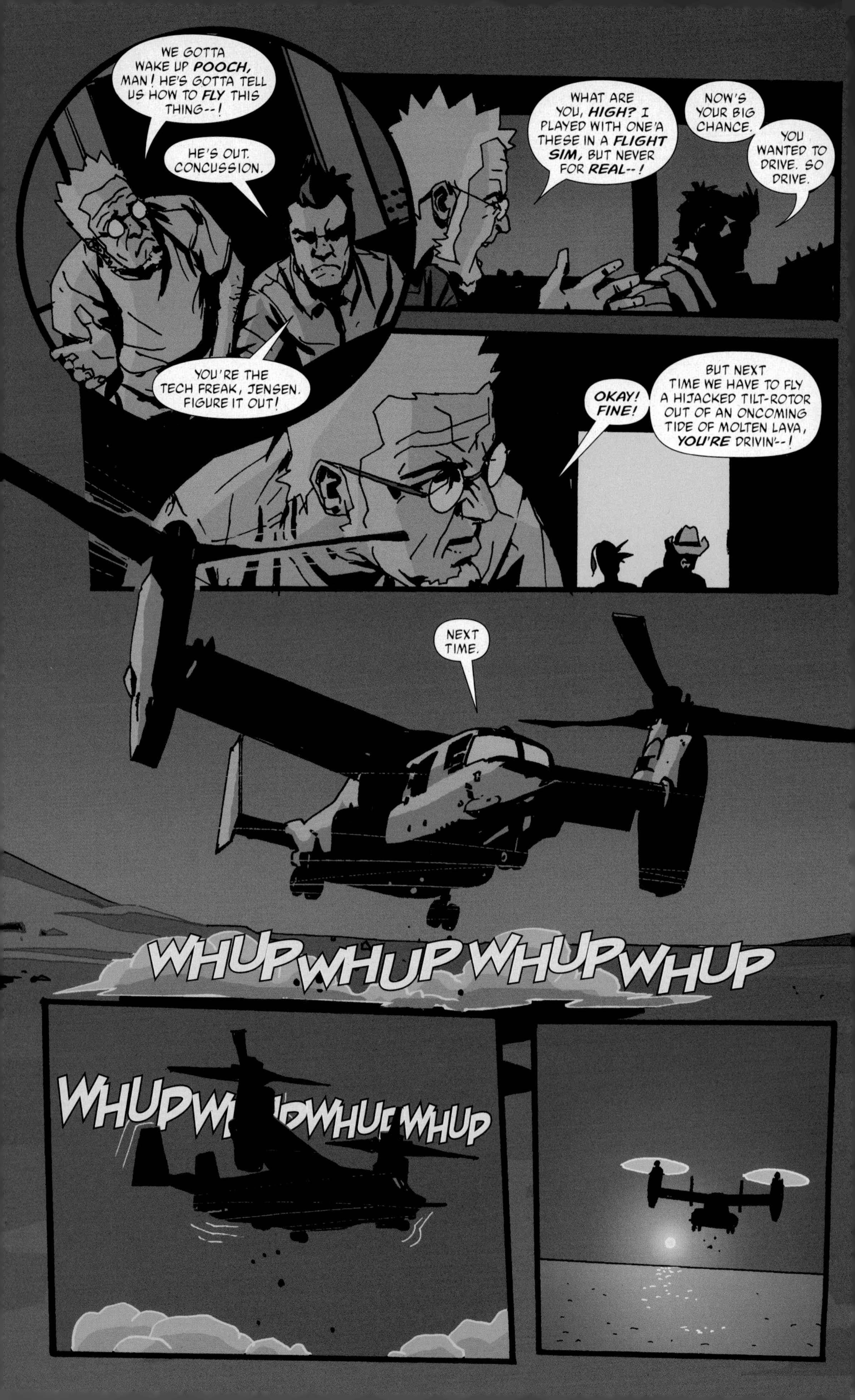
WE GOTTA WAKE UP POOCH, MAN! HE'S GOTTA TELL US HOW TO FLY THIS THING--!
HE'S OUT. CONCUSSION.
WHAT ARE YOU, HIGH? I PLAYED WITH ONE'A THESE IN A FLIGHT SIM, BUT NEVER FOR REAL--!
NOW'S YOUR BIG CHANCE.
YOU WANTED TO DRIVE. SO DRIVE.
YOU'RE THE TECH FREAK, JENSEN. FIGURE IT OUT!
OKAY! FINE!
BUT NEXT TIME WE HAVE TO FLY A HIJACKED TILT-ROTOR OUT OF AN ONCOMING TIDE OF MOLTEN LAVA, YOU'RE DRIVIN'--!
NEXT TIME.
WHUPWHUPWHUPWHUP
WHUPWHUPWHUPWHUP

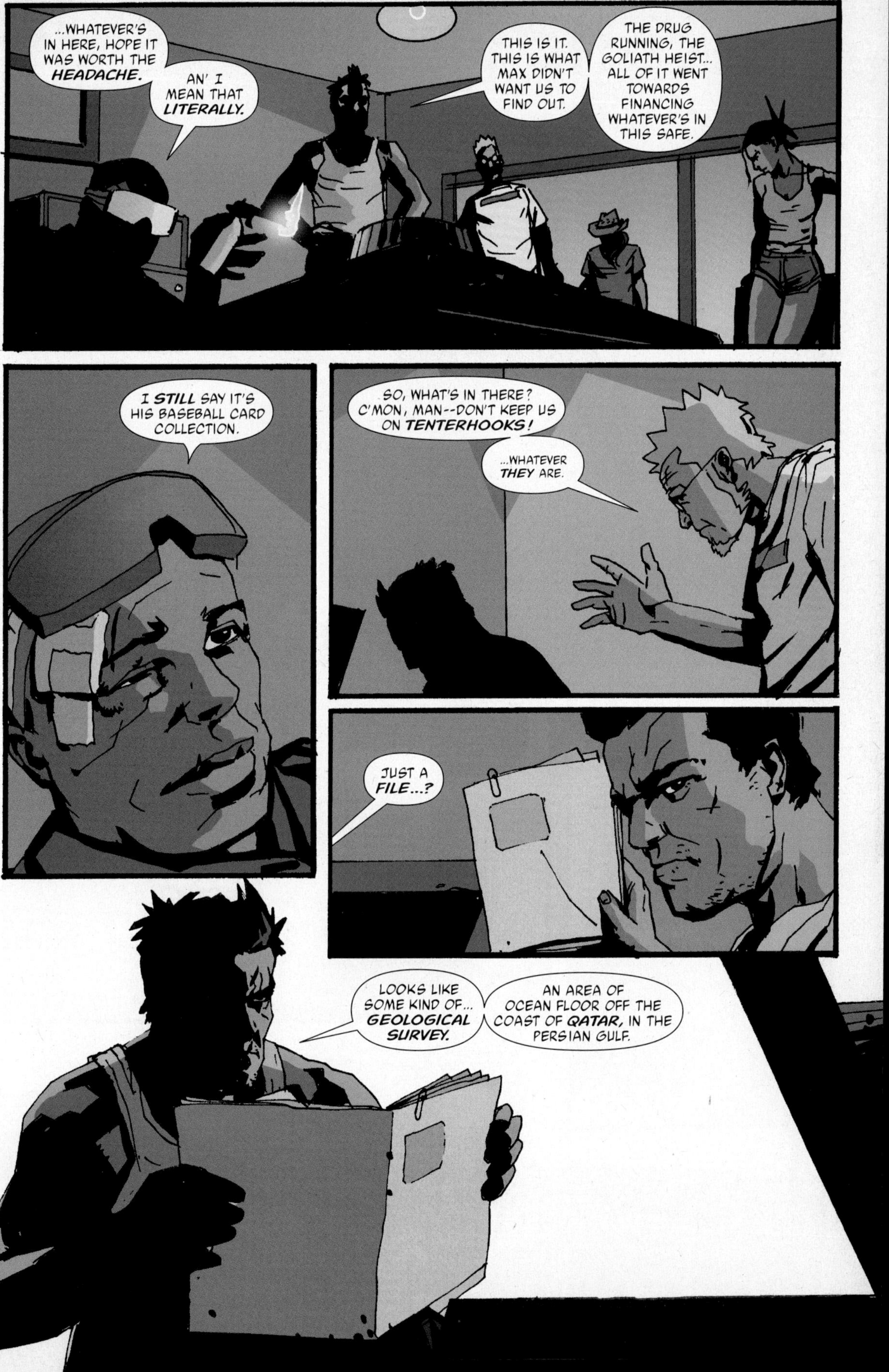
...WHATEVER'S IN HERE, HOPE IT WAS WORTH THE HEADACHE.
AN' I MEAN THAT LITERALLY.
THIS IS IT. THIS IS WHAT MAX DIDN'T WANT US TO FIND OUT.
THE DRUG RUNNING, THE GOLIATH HEIST... ALL OF IT WENT TOWARDS FINANCING WHATEVER'S IN THIS SAFE.
I STILL SAY IT'S HIS BASEBALL CARD COLLECTION.
SO, WHAT'S IN THERE? C'MON, MAN--DON'T KEEP US ON TENTERHOOKS!
...WHATEVER THEY ARE.
JUST A FILE...?
LOOKS LIKE SOME KIND OF... GEOLOGICAL SURVEY.
AN AREA OF OCEAN FLOOR OFF THE COAST OF QATAR, IN THE PERSIAN GULF.

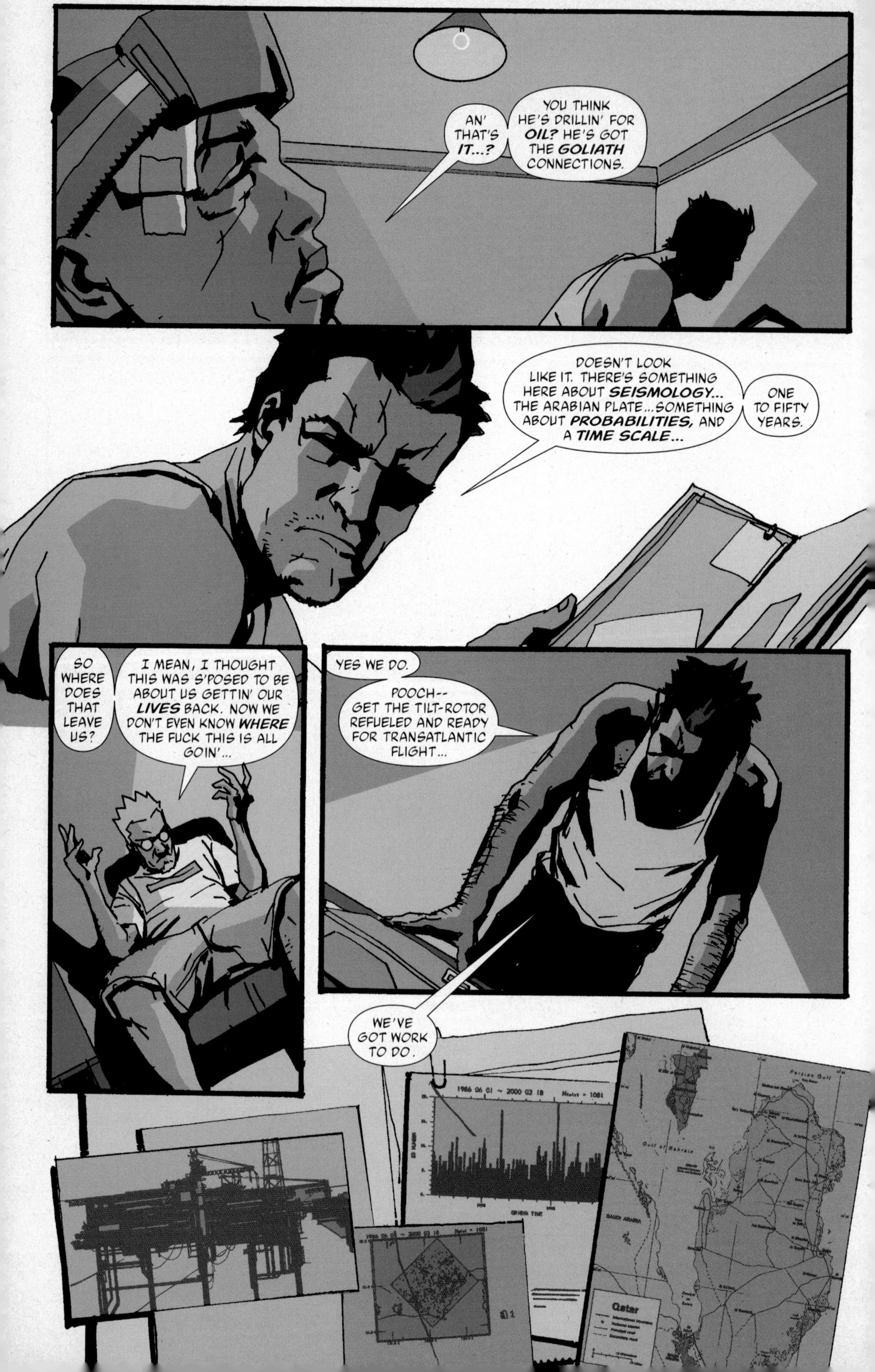
AN' THAT'S IT...?
YOU THINK HE'S DRILLIN' FOR OIL? HE'S GOT THE GOLIATH CONNECTIONS.
DOESN'T LOOK LIKE IT. THERE'S SOMETHING HERE ABOUT SEISMOLOGY... THE ARABIAN PLATE...SOMETHING ABOUT PROBABILITIES, AND A TIME SCALE...
ONE TO FIFTY YEARS.
SO WHERE DOES THAT LEAVE US?
I MEAN, I THOUGHT THIS WAS S'POSED TO BE ABOUT US GETTIN' OUR LIVES BACK. NOW WE DON'T EVEN KNOW WHERE THE FUCK THIS IS ALL GOIN'...
YES WE DO.
POOCH-- GET THE TILT-ROTOR REFUELED AND READY FOR TRANSATLANTIC FLIGHT...
WE'VE GOT WORK TO DO.

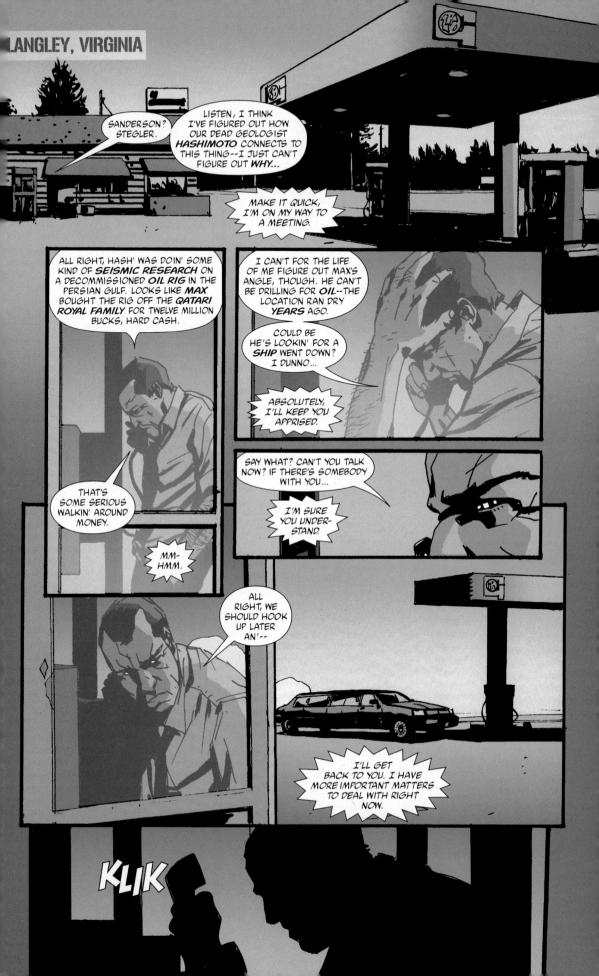

LANGLEY, VIRGINIA

SANDERSON? STEGLER.

LISTEN, I THINK I'VE FIGURED OUT HOW OUR DEAD GEOLOGIST *HASHIMOTO* CONNECTS TO THIS THING--I JUST CAN'T FIGURE OUT *WHY...*

MAKE IT QUICK, I'M ON MY WAY TO A MEETING.

ALL RIGHT, HASH' WAS DOIN' SOME KIND OF *SEISMIC RESEARCH* ON A DECOMMISSIONED *OIL RIG* IN THE PERSIAN GULF. LOOKS LIKE *MAX* BOUGHT THE RIG OFF THE *QATARI ROYAL FAMILY* FOR TWELVE MILLION BUCKS, HARD CASH.

I CAN'T FOR THE LIFE OF ME FIGURE OUT MAX'S ANGLE, THOUGH. HE CAN'T BE DRILLING FOR *OIL*--THE LOCATION RAN DRY *YEARS* AGO.

COULD BE HE'S LOOKIN' FOR A *SHIP* WENT DOWN? I DUNNO...

ABSOLUTELY, I'LL KEEP YOU APPRISED.

THAT'S SOME SERIOUS WALKIN' AROUND MONEY.

SAY WHAT? CAN'T YOU TALK NOW? IF THERE'S SOMEBODY WITH YOU...

I'M SURE YOU UNDER-STAND.

MM-HMM.

ALL RIGHT, WE SHOULD HOOK UP LATER AN'--

I'LL GET BACK TO YOU. I HAVE MORE IMPORTANT MATTERS TO DEAL WITH RIGHT NOW.

KLIK

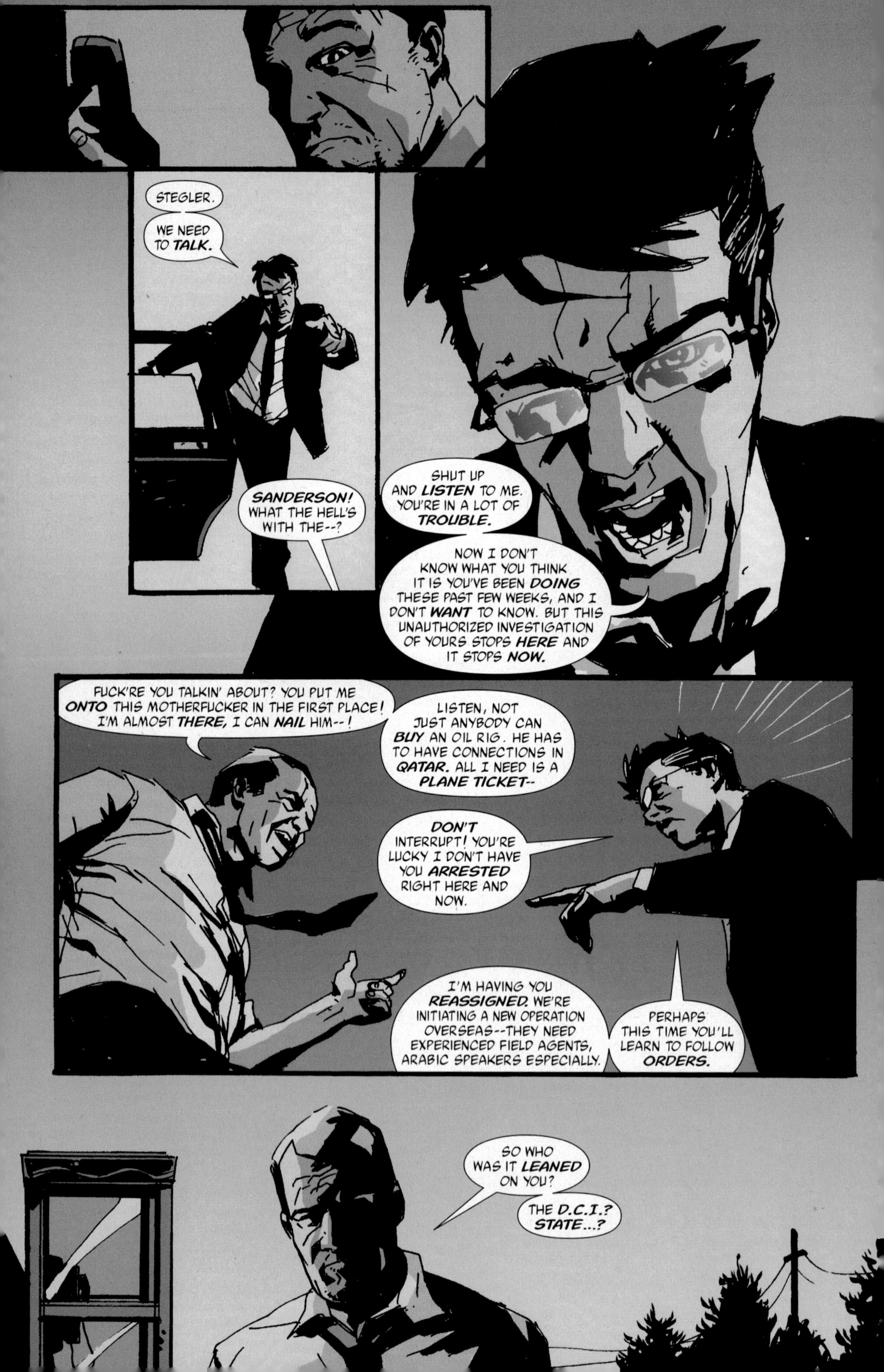
STEGLER.
WE NEED TO TALK.
SANDERSON! WHAT THE HELL'S WITH THE--?
SHUT UP AND LISTEN TO ME. YOU'RE IN A LOT OF TROUBLE.
NOW I DON'T KNOW WHAT YOU THINK IT IS YOU'VE BEEN DOING THESE PAST FEW WEEKS, AND I DON'T WANT TO KNOW. BUT THIS UNAUTHORIZED INVESTIGATION OF YOURS STOPS HERE AND IT STOPS NOW.
FUCK'RE YOU TALKIN' ABOUT? YOU PUT ME ONTO THIS MOTHERFUCKER IN THE FIRST PLACE! I'M ALMOST THERE, I CAN NAIL HIM--!
LISTEN, NOT JUST ANYBODY CAN BUY AN OIL RIG. HE HAS TO HAVE CONNECTIONS IN QATAR. ALL I NEED IS A PLANE TICKET--
DON'T INTERRUPT! YOU'RE LUCKY I DON'T HAVE YOU ARRESTED RIGHT HERE AND NOW.
I'M HAVING YOU REASSIGNED. WE'RE INITIATING A NEW OPERATION OVERSEAS--THEY NEED EXPERIENCED FIELD AGENTS, ARABIC SPEAKERS ESPECIALLY.
PERHAPS THIS TIME YOU'LL LEARN TO FOLLOW ORDERS.
SO WHO WAS IT LEANED ON YOU?
THE D.C.I.? STATE...?

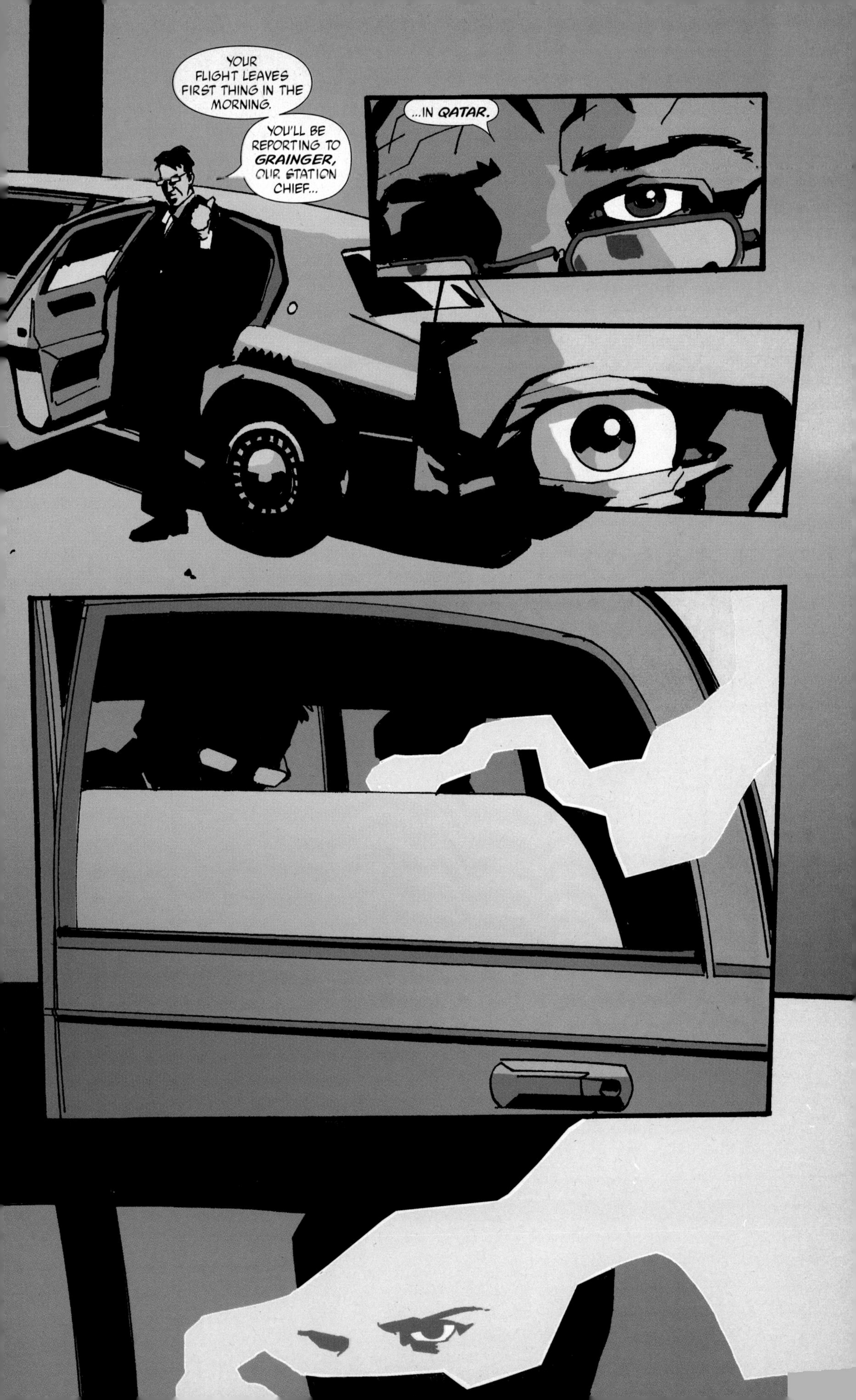
YOUR FLIGHT LEAVES FIRST THING IN THE MORNING.
YOU'LL BE REPORTING TO GRAINGER, OUR STATION CHIEF...
...IN QATAR.

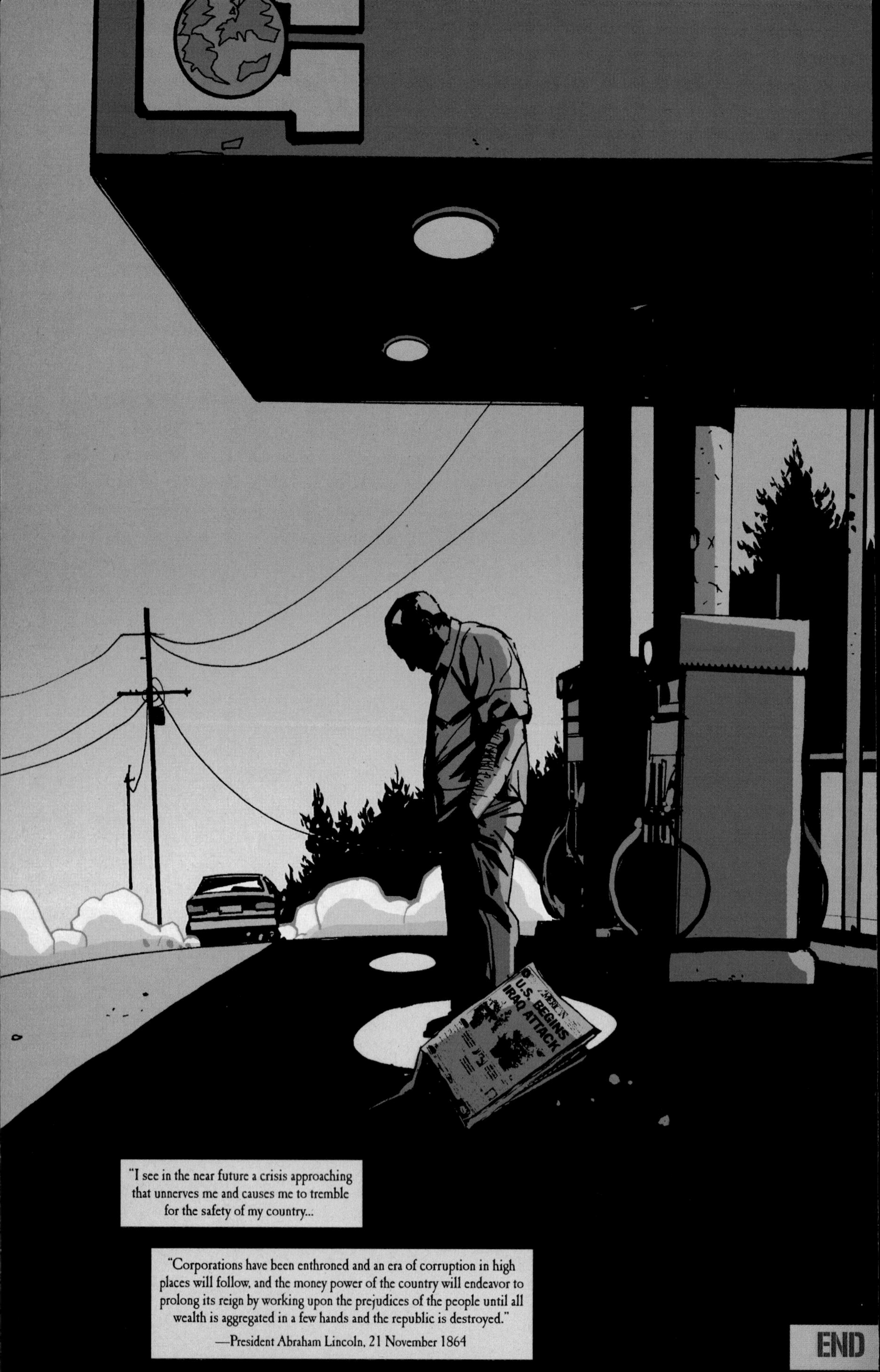
U.S. BEGINS IRAQ ATTACK
"I see in the near future a crisis approaching that unnerves me and causes me to tremble for the safety of my country...
"Corporations have been enthroned and an era of corruption in high places will follow, and the money power of the country will endeavor to prolong its reign by working upon the prejudices of the people until all wealth is aggregated in a few hands and the republic is destroyed."
—President Abraham Lincoln, 21 November 1864
END